AN INTRODUCTION
TO THE RUSSIAN NOVEL

By the same Author:

STUDIES IN EUROPEAN LITERATURE

GOGOL

TOLSTOY

NIETSZCHE AND MODERN CONSCIOUSNESS

IBSEN AND HIS CREATION

DOSTOEVSKY

An Introduction to the Russian Novel

by

JANKO LAVRIN

Whittlesey House

McGraw-Hill-Book-Company, Inc.

New York: London

AN INTRODUCTION TO THE RUSSIAN NOVEL

COPYRIGHT, 1947, BY THE MC GRAW-HILL BOOK COMPANY, INC.

The quality of the materials used in the manufacture of this book is governed by continued postwar shortages.

PUBLISHED BY WHITTLESEY HOUSE
A division of the McGraw-Hill Book Company, Inc.

PRINTED IN THE UNITED STATES OF AMERICA

Prefatory Note

THE MODERN Russian novel occupies one of the foremost places in world literature. There are three distinct types of novel in Europe: English, French, and Russian. And since they somewhat complete each other, it is essential to know at least the basic facts concerning the Russian novel and its importance.

The scope of the present book is to give the reader an orientation of this kind—as far as possible within so short a space. And since the growth of the Russian novel can hardly be understood without some knowledge of the society it represents, due consideration has been given to the historical and social-economic background.

Yet the word "novel" still remains rather vague. Where is the exact boundary between a long story and a novel? More-over, there is a wide margin where personal reminiscences, "documents," philosophic and sociological meditations may overlap the pattern of the novel itself. This can result in interesting hybrids of literature and pamphleteering jour-nalism, the elimination of which would, in some cases, be a mistake.

The substance of this work consists of my University lectures which have been modified and arranged so as to make them accessible to the general reader. My acknowl-edgments for quotations are due to several publishers and translators mentioned in the text.

J. L.

Contents

AN INTRODUCTION
TO THE RUSSIAN NOVEL

CHAPTER I

The Beginnings of Russian Fiction

RUSSIAN HISTORY started in the second half of the ninth century, when a band of Scandinavian vikings seized power in Novgorod. Warriors and merchants in one, they were anxious to safeguard the route to Constantinople. So they organized the Slav tribes, especially those in the Dnieper area, into a more or less ordered State with its capital in Kiev. Having merged with the natives in language and customs, they yet remained the ruling caste. By the end of the tenth century this "Kiev Russia" received Christianity from Byzantium and not from the West—a fact which largely determined the character of Russian civilization. Kiev's early cultural intercourse was almost exclusively with Byzantium and the Balkan Slavs—Bulgarians and Serbs. And as the Bulgarians had by that time a number of books translated into their own language for liturgical and edifying purposes, the Russian Church took these over. The old-Bulgarian or "Church-Slavonic" language—understood by the Russians but not identical with their own speech—became for centuries also the literary language of the country.

The early literary activities in Kiev, with their homilies, exhortations, moralizing parables, apocrypha, and legends, reflected the Byzantine spirit and were mainly in the service of the Church. It was predominantly a literature of translations and compilations. Yet before the twelfth century was out, Kiev gave at least two works of which Russian literature is justly proud. The so-called *Nestor's Chronicle*—a most

1

valuable specimen of its kind, sprinkled with delightful anecdotic material, and important for the early history of the Slavs—is one of them. The second is *The Lay of Igor's Raid,* now known all the world over, since Borodin's famous opera, *Prince Igor,* is based on it. Secular in character, this lay is written in fine rhythmic prose, which evidences its author's familiarity not only with Byzantine models, but also with the imagery of folk poetry.

Kiev could have developed into a flourishing cultural center had it not been sacked by the Tartars who, in the middle of the thirteenth century, conquered practically the whole of Russia. Their oppression lasted 240 years, and during that period Russia was in a state of compulsory stagnation. The country was cut off from the rest of the world, and particularly from Europe, at a time when the Western-European nations had left the Middle Ages behind and were working out a new era and a new consciousness: the Renaissance consciousness. It was the latter that gradually separated culture from the Church and made it secular—in the name of free individual thought, individual rights, and self-affirmation against any tyranny. But Tartar-ridden Russia was utterly remote from any movements of this kind. She might have been in a different world, on a different planet. Moreover, while in the West the Church was losing its grip on the advanced minds, in Russia it remained the only civilizing factor, the only symbol of national unity and stability.

Meanwhile the cunning Moscow princes obtained various privileges from the Tartars and finally shook off their yoke in 1480. This was the beginning of the autocratic and centralizing Moscow period of Russian history. Conservative and bigoted, the Moscow rulers were determined to "gather all the Russian lands" by fair means or foul. They found in the Church a willing supporter. The more so because, after the fall of Constantinople, Moscow regarded herself as the third Rome and the pivot of true Christianity. This gave her an additional pretext for keeping aloof from the "heretical" West. She preferred to indulge in her conservatism. Needless to say, literature, which was mainly in the hands of the priests, was bound to lag behind, devoid of any creative *élan* or originality.

Yet it was from the sixteenth century onwards that belated Western influences began to penetrate into Muscovite Russia. Italian, French, Breton, and German motives found their way even into the Russian folklore and merged with it. In other respects also the contact with the Western nations began to increase quite promisingly. The so-called troubled times, however, at the beginning of the seventeenth century, plunged the country into a dynastic, political, and social-economic chaos. With the election of the first Romanov to the throne, in 1613, peace was restored. But in the second half of the same century Russia was in the throes of religious polemics and persecutions. The head of the Russian Church, Patriarch Nikon, introduced some minor innovations into the Church books and ritual which were resented by the "old believers," i.e. by the adherents to tradition.

The Life or autobiography of their fanatical leader, the archpriest Avvakum, is now regarded as the best literary work of that period. It certainly is remarkable as both a personal document and a proof of heroic defiance—even if the cause itself was not worth the energy wasted on it. But we would look in vain for other masterpieces in those days. At a time when England had already left behind her Elizabethan age and when France was at the height of her *grand siècle*, Russian literature was fallow land. A different spirit set in however with the new Petersburg era, introduced by Peter the Great.

II

It was Peter the Great who finally secularized culture in Russia by separating it from the Church. In a way he undertook a task which on the Continent had been accomplished by the Renaissance and Humanism. But Peter the Great was concerned with practical matters only. Full of semi-barbaric vitality and constructive will power, he wanted to shake Russia out of her medieval slumber and annex her—politically and culturally—to Europe. And he did it, after a fashion. Through the foundation of the new capital, St. Petersburg (1702) in particular, he opened a "window on Europe" which marked a turning point in the destinies of his country. In order to undermine the power of the official Church, he abolished the Patriarchate and replaced it by a department of civil service—the so-called most holy Synod. In his haste to graft Europe upon Russia, he forced upon his country above all Western technique, science, social manners, commercial and administrative methods, without worrying as to whether Russia could or could not digest so much in such a short time.

But even apart from this, the fact that Peter's innovations had been imported from abroad instead of having grown organically out of the Russian soil and Russian past created certain dilemmas which raised, later on, the problem of relations between Europe and Russia in all its acuteness. Was Russia but a younger underdeveloped Europe, or did the two differ not only in quantity but also in quality? Was she to follow Europe passively or adopt a critical attitude, thus using the Western cultural achievements only as a means for her own self-realization, or perhaps even for a future synthesis between Russia and the West?

Modern Russia provided a battleground for all these

propensities. In two realms at least she even achieved a kind of synthesis: in music and literature. True enough, Russia needed the whole of the eighteenth century to adapt herself to Western standards—a process which was bound to be imitative rather than creative. In addition, the Russians had to work out their literary language. Their former literary medium had been, for the most part, the dead Church-Slavonic tongue. Since Peter the Great, however, the living spoken language began to prevail. Standardized by the savant and poet Michael Lomonosov (1711-1765), this language was soon to become one of the most powerful instruments for literary expression. Even before the eighteenth century came to an end, Russia had proved a talented pupil of the French pseudo-classic current and could boast of at least one great poet in this manner, Gavrila Derzhavin. Derzhavin's contemporaries, Fonvizin and Novikov, gave—the first in his comedies of manners, and the second in journalism, emulating the English *Tatler* and *Spectator*—brilliant examples of realistic character drawing and indictment. Realism, always dear to a Russian, was fostered also by a number of translated picaresque and didactic novels of manners. A translation of Le Sage's *Gil Blas* appeared in 1754 and passed through eight editions by the end of the century. Marivaux, too, was a favorite. So was the Abbé Prévost, whose novel *Le Philosophe Anglais* was translated in 1760.

Russian attempts of a similar type were to follow, but on a lower level. It should be borne in mind that Peter's reforms had civilized, more or less, only the landowning aristocracy and gentry, whereas the serfs remained in the same position as before. The gap between these and their masters, who could buy and sell them like cattle, was deepened by the fact that the education and even the language of the upper classes became French rather than Russian. The position was

somewhat different among the lesser gentry, who formed
something of a substitute for a middle class. Since the serfs
were illiterate, Russian prose was read principally by the
poorer country gentry and the lower middle class whose
tastes demanded adventurous, sentimental, and crudely
realistic narratives, verging on the chapbook. These were
supplied by the now forgotten Matvey Komarov. His novel,
*The Hapless Nikanor or the Adventures of a Russian Noble-
man,* was a great success with such readers. Another pur-
veyor of similar literature was M. Chulkov. More fastidious
tastes were catered for, however, by Dmitriev-Mamonov,
an emulator of Voltaire's didactic tales.

It sounds almost strange that in those days Russian literature was often encouraged by the Court. Such was particularly the case under Catherine II who, in spite of her German
extraction, wrote a number of Russian works (especially
comedies of manners) and did all she could for the literature
of her adopted country. But it was only with the passing
of pseudo-classic fashions that prose came into its own.
Moreover, it was the speech of the educated landed gentry
that was made, towards the end of the eighteenth century,
the literary language of Russia. The man responsible for this
reform was Nikolai Karamzin (1766-1826).

III

Karamzin marks the transition from the pseudo-classic to
the sentimental period. This applies to his poems and even
more to his prose. Emotionalism, mixed up with Rousseauesque nature worship, eighteenth-century deism, the ingredients of *Ossian,* Sterne, Richardson, Goethe's *Werther—*
such is Karamzin's literary make-up. And his *Letters of a
Russian Traveler* was the first prose work that took the
entire younger generation by storm. Modeled on Sterne's

Sentimental Journey, it was the fruit of the author's travels
—during 1789 and 1790—through Germany, Switzerland,
France, and England. It appeared partially in 1790 in *The
Moscow Journal*, but was published in four volumes seven
years later and supplemented by another two in 1801. What
appealed to its readers was above all Karamzin's polished
tone, his broad cosmopolitan spirit and his realism of everyday observations. Descriptive, lyrical, meditative and narrative in one, this work is remarkable also on account of
Karamzin's attempts at psychological analysis. Altogether, it
is an early landmark in the development of Russian prose.

A "hit," but for different reasons, was Karamzin's *Poor
Liza*—a rather pale and tearful story ("Ah, I love everything
that touches my heart and makes me shed tears of tender
sadness") about a peasant girl, jilted by her aristocratic
sweetheart. Although told for its own sake, the story obviously implies the naïvely humanitarian idea that even an
uneducated peasant girl is capable of true love. In another
story, *Flor Silin*, the author shows a prosperous simple
peasant who is such a philanthropist by nature as to give
away his wealth to the starving people during famine.

Karamzin wrote several other equally pale and equally
polished narratives, some of them in a pseudo-historical vein.
His imitation of Goethe's *Werther* remained unfinished. He
was also the founder of *The Moscow Journal*—the first purely
literary periodical in Russia. *The European Messenger*,
started by him later (1802), was, however, tainted by politics
and by that complacent patriotic tendency which came out
in his bulky *History of the Russian Empire* (1816). This one-
time disciple of Rousseau and admirer of the French revolution turned here into a reactionary conservative, praising
with glowing rhetoric the autocracy and pre-Petrine Russia.
But as his account of the Russian past was written for the

public at large, it had an enormous success and kindled, moreover, patriotic feelings.

Karamzin's sentimentalism had a number of followers, such as Prince P. Shalikov, P. Lvov, and others, who hardly contributed much to the quality of Russian fiction towards the end of the eighteenth century. There arose also difficulties of a political kind. Catherine II became so frightened by the blasts of the French revolution that she threw off her liberal and enlightened mask almost overnight. And the first literary victim of her change was a remarkable personality of that period, A. Radishchev.

About a year after the fall of the Bastille, Radishchev published his famous *Journey from Petersburg to Moscow*. This book, originally inspired by Sterne, is a daring blend of pathos and humor, of genre pictures and indictment, of meditation and protest. As a humanitarian and follower of the Encyclopaedists, Radishchev attacked with merciless realism the evils of Russian life—especially serfdom. Nor did he spare autocracy. Here is an example of his indirect attacks. In addressing Cromwell in his long *Ode to Freedom*, interpolated in the *Journey*, he says: "Ay, thou wert cruel and perfidious, a bigot and a hypocrite; thou hast profaned things sacred; thou wert the greatest villain in the world; for, possessed of the plenitude of power, thou hast abolished every manifestation of freedom in thy people. And yet thou art a great man, because thou wert the first to dare show a beneficent example to the peoples by executing, in accordance with the people's judgment, your King Charles; thou hast taught mankind how to avenge itself on its oppressors."

The book was at once seized and destroyed by the police, while its author was condemned to death by order of Catherine II. The death sentence was graciously commuted to exile in a remote part of Siberia. After Catherine's death Radishchev was set free by her son Paul.

IV

The humanitarian and sentimental trend in literature was fostered also by Freemasonry, which had spread in Russia during the second half of the eighteenth century and became rather strong towards its end. But the demand for the adventurous didactic-realistic narrative continued. A fusion of the two produced quite a remarkable novel, *Evgeny or Ruinous Consequences of Bad Education and Bad Company*, by A. E. Izmailov, which appeared in 1796. A partial follower of Karamzin, Izmailov excelled in realistic descriptions of village and manor life, of Petersburg, of the life of students and officers. These and similar aspects helped to enlarge the area of fiction, even when its technical side was not yet as it should be.

A belated echo of Le Sage was presented by V. I. Narezhny's (1780-1825) picaresque novel, *A Russian Gil Blas*, the first three parts of which came out in 1814. Its hero is an impoverished aristocrat, compelled to wander from place to place and to undertake one occupation after the other. In this way he meets all sorts of people and conditions. At the end of the third part there is a cruel satire on Masonic initiations which were regarded by the author (a Ukrainian by birth) as humbug. Democratic in its tendency and didactic in character, this novel, too, is highly realistic. Realism mixed with humor and satire is the note of Narezhny's *The Two Ivans or the Passion for Litigation*, describing two Ukrainian landowners who prefer total ruin rather than give up their senseless squabbles. His semihistorical romance, *The Divinity Student* (1824), takes us into the Ukrainian past. The hero of the novel is well drawn, in spite of the melodramatic denouement: he proves to be the son of the *hetman* at whose court he serves. (Both narratives had an influence on Gogol, the greatest prose writer of the next generation.) Narezhny's *Mountain Prince* is a fierce indictment of the plundering Russian administration in the Caucasus. His novel *Aristion* exposes the half-savage provincial gentry, while the unfinished *Garkusha* tackles the problem of social injustice and the iniquity of serfdom. Narezhny can tell a story vividly, but his realism and humor are often crude. Nor is his construction without flaws, although it represents a definite advance from the clumsily naïve eighteenth-century yarns.

A very popular didactic novel of manners, a "best seller" in fact, was *Ivan Vyzhigin* by the notorious *canaille littéraire* Faddei Bulgarin. It appeared as late as 1829, when Sir Walter Scott's influence was in the ascendant. Translations of Scott's historical novels were at that time in great demand. There were also successful Russian followers of Scott. M. N. Zagoskin's *Fury Miloslavsky* (a historical novel about the troubled period at the beginning of the seventeenth century) had a great reception, perhaps because of its idealization of the Russian past. Zagoskin wrote other historical novels, but of less account.

The interest in the past, fostered by Karamzin's *History*, was responsible for several other attempts in Scott's manner, but without Scott's merit. I. I. Lazhechnikov's novels, however, *The Last Novik* (1828-1833) about the times of Peter the Great, and *The Ice House* (1835) dealing with the Empress Anne and her favorite Biron, became deservedly popular. Well above the average was his *Basurman* (*The Heathen*), showing the fate of a Western enthusiast of enlightenment in fifteenth-century Moscow. Unfortunately, the author's sentimental and patriotic rhetoric has no longer any appeal. Pseudo-historic (with a touch of Mrs. Radcliffe) were several romances by Bestuzhev-Marlinsky, who was read by people with less tutored minds and tastes. Even Bulgarin was anxious to become a Russian Walter Scott, but without success. If we want to find a real classic of the historical narrative, we must go to Pushkin. And this brings us to a different and truly amazing period of Russian literature.

CHAPTER II

Pushkin and Lermontov

Alexander sergeyevitch pushkin (1799-1837) is the central figure of the entire Russian literature since Peter the Great. He is the national poet of Russia. But his work and personal tragedy can best be understood if we know something about the age he lived in.

After the autocratic madman Paul I had been strangled in a palace revolt, his son Alexander I aroused considerable expectations. These ran high during Napoleon's invasion of Russia in 1812, when the entire nation was united in its effort to resist the Corsican. The dawn of a new era seemed to be at hand. There were rumors of a forthcoming constitution, even of the abolition of serfdom. Subsequently, a number of young Russian officers went with their regiments as far as Paris, where they came into contact with the progressive Western nations and ideas. These officers returned to their homeland with the virus of discontent and criticism. The discontent kept growing after the formation of the Holy Alliance, whose reactionary tendencies were quite in keeping with the mystical moods of the Czar himself.

The guardianship of Russian letters, indeed of the entire Russian culture, was now in the hands of the progressive gentry which was in opposition to the Court and gradually turned literature itself into an effective satirical weapon. This became possible mainly because the number of readers was growing. It is enough to remember that Russia, which at the death of Peter the Great (in 1724) had some sixteen million inhabitants, could boast about a hundred years later of a population bordering on sixty millions. Such a rapid increase was accompanied by other changes. The growth of commercial relations with foreign countries, for example, had created new economic problems. Factories and the pioneers of a moneyed bourgeoisie came into evidence. As hired labor yielded better results than factories worked by serfs, serfdom began to look somewhat unprofitable, especially after the slump of the corn prices in 1820. This state of things coincided with the aspirations of those idealists who wanted to abolish serfdom also for moral and humanitarian reasons. Frustrated in their hopes, the liberal-minded officers and other representatives of the younger generation formed secret societies with a strong political coloring. Thus the "Northern Society," with its center in Petersburg, aimed at a constitutional monarchy. Its South Russian branch, the "Southern Society," dreamed of a republic and even of a vague federation of the liberated Slavs.

Since there was no freedom of the press, satirical writings (such as Griboyedov's biting comedy, *Woe from Wit*) spread in manuscripts all over Russia and contributed enormously to the fermentation which came to a head during the revolt in Petersburg on December 14, 1825. The leaders of that revolt were mainly officers in the guards (henceforth known as the Decembrists), that is, members of the gentry and of the higher aristocracy. Their attempt to force the new Czar Nicholas I to abdicate was brutally suppressed. With their failure the "gentry period" of Russian culture and literature was doomed also. The "leaden period" of Russian history set in. It ended only after the death of Nicholas I during the Crimean campaign.

Pushkin the boy witnessed not only the *élan* of the national consciousness in 1812, but also the disappointment that was to follow. No matter how serene his natural disposition may have been, he could hardly avoid the mood of general discontent. He reacted by a few scathing poems and epigrams for which he was duly banished to the South of Russia, soon after the publication of his sparkling mock-heroic epic *Ruslan and Ludmila* (1820). It was during his exile that he made acquaintance with Byron's works which, for a while, proved a stimulus to him.

It should be remembered that the witty brilliance of a generation fed on French literature still persisted. At the same time, tastes and fashions were rapidly switching over to romanticism with its prevalence of English and German influences. The poet Vasily Zhukovsky was the chief promoter of those influences. But with all his poetic elasticity, which made him one of the greatest translators, Zhukovsky was too much of a sentimental-romantic escapist. This made the gay mocking strains of the young Pushkin all the more welcome.

Brought up on eighteenth-century French literature (especially on Voltaire and Parny), he retained to the end the lucidity and discipline which no romantic influences could impair. Besides, his Byronic period was of short duration. So was his open opposition to the things he saw around him. After the December revolt, Nicholas I pardoned Pushkin's connections with the Decembrists and cunningly offered to be the only censor of his future works. Pushkin had to accept the Czar's "fatherly" interest in him in order to be left in peace. His contact with the Court became more and more involved, especially after he had married the brainless society beauty, Natalia Goncharova. There are reasons for believing that the Czar was perhaps more interested in Pushkin's wife than in Pushkin himself. The poet was soon plunged into a maze of gossip and the basest intrigues, manufactured by the Court sycophants. A duel followed in which Pushkin was mortally wounded. He died at the age of thirty-seven.

The surprising thing is that in spite of his short life and the conditions in which he worked, Pushkin yet became the national poet of Russia. Surrounded by a brilliant *pléiade* of talents, he headed that "golden age of poetry" which formed the climax of the gentry period of Russian culture. Pushkin was its synthesis, its highest peak. And no wonder, since he was a crystallized example of what was best in his own generation. Broad, liberal-minded, and unusually cultured, he remained to the end very Russian and at the same time very European. Hence he did not mind being stimulated by the creations of Western Europe, more particularly by British authors. It was under Shakespeare's influence that he wrote his historical drama *Boris Godunov*. Byron was responsible for some of his early narrative poems, and Sir Walter Scott's influence is noticeable in at least two of his prose works. Yet influences such as these were only stepping-stones towards the summits of Pushkin's own creative genius which, for all its adaptability, was highly original.

II

Pushkin's first attempt in prose, *The Negro of Peter the Great* (1828), was inspired by the *Waverley Novels*. It was the beginning of a fine historical narrative with the author's Abyssinian great-grandfather (on his maternal side) as the central figure. Pushkin never went beyond the first seven chapters, but they are enough to show his essentially realistic and visual—as distinct from pictorial—gift. This comes out in his naturalness, in his disciplined lucidity, as well as in his portraiture. Most successful is the portrait of Peter the Great. But his finished prose work, *A Captain's Daughter* (1836), which he also wrote under Scott's influence, is a greater achievement. Its tense yet flexible prose reminds one of the eighteenth-century French authors. As for the subject matter, Pushkin took it from the comparatively recent past: the rising of the Ural Cossacks under the leadership of the illiterate peasant Pugachov, in 1773. After a study of events in the area concerned, Pushkin first issued a masterly *History of Pugachov's Rebellion* (1834). In *A Captain's Daughter*, however, he made use of the same material for a literary classic, displaying a perfect balance between history, character drawing, and the manners of the period described.

Grinev, the youthful hero of the novel, is sent by his father (a squire in the Volga district) to a God-forsaken little fort round which the Cossack rising is already brewing. In a snowstorm he gives a lift to a half-frozen stranger who happens to be no less a person than the subsequent rebel chief. Through this chance meeting Grinev's fate becomes strangely involved with that of Pugachov. Grinev's arrival in the fort gives Pushkin a further opportunity for realistic portraiture. The simplehearted but dutiful Captain Mironov and his good-natured bossing wife are superbly drawn. The portrait of their daughter, who after gruesome adventures becomes Grinev's wife, is more conventional. But the author makes up for it by Pugachov: an unforgettable blend of fierceness, generosity, and elemental "Russianness" in everything he does. Finally, Grinev's servant Savelitch represents the very quintessence of the loyal old-world house serf whose shrewd common sense saves his master from many a calamity. Pushkin depicts here not only the rising, but all sorts of aspects of Russian life in the second half of the eighteenth century: the provincial manor, the distant fort, the army, the Cossacks, etc. And throughout the whole of the novel, even in the scene of Captain Mironov's and his wife's tragic death, he preserves the detachment of a great classical realist.

Like *The Negro of Peter the Great*, this work too is largely a novel of the family chronicle type, which became quite a tradition in Russian fiction. Its simplicity, naturalness, and rendering of character exercised an enormous influence. So did some of Pushkin's other writings in prose. These show the same perfection, however much they may differ otherwise. The five tales by a supposed obscure provincial, Belkin —a pathetic and comic figure in one—are intensified anecdotes, told in the style and with the accent of the presumed narrator. Even Pushkin's unfinished *Dubrovsky* is reduced to its anecdotic essentials. Its hero, a kind of conventional "noble brigand," is shown against a background of the uncouth manners prevailing on the country estates under Catherine II. *The Queen of Spades,* on the other hand, might have been invented by E. T. A. Hoffmann, but for its sobriety which actually makes the fantastic element of this Petersburg story all the more effective. Last but not least, Pushkin's mixture of fact and droll parody comes out in his *History of the Village Goryukhino,* narrated—once again—by Belkin, whose pathetically funny figure had several counterparts in subsequent Russian fiction. Yet however great the influence of Pushkin's prose may have been, his famous novel in verse (as he called it), *Evgeny Onegin,* proved even more important.

III

This masterpiece was written at intervals between 1823 and 1831, and was first published in a complete edition in 1833. As Pushkin worked upon it for several years, its eight chapters or cantos [1] reflect his development during the whole of that period. And those were precisely the years in which he overcame his early Byronic phase. Its traces are still noticeable in *Onegin* (reminiscences of *Childe Harold, Beppo,* and *Don Juan*), but in a sublimated manner. Moreover, while Byron grins and whips, Pushkin only banters with that

---

[1] Originally it was conceived in nine chapters, but one of them (the eighth) was dropped.

puckishly understated humor of his, which makes his verses sparkle like champagne. By his blend of humor, sentiment, and clarity he preserves a Mozartian lightness of touch throughout, even in his tragic passages.

Pushkin himself defined his hero as a "Muscovite in Harold's cloak." But Onegin is too superficial to fit entirely into the gallery of those uprooted characters who began to haunt European literature after Chateaubriand's *René* and Byron's self-assertive egotists. The actual social and psychological causes of most of those *déracinés* are to be sought in the breaking up of the old order after the French revolution. Impoverished yet unable to adapt themselves in time to the new bourgeois conditions, they were bound to feel superfluous and out of joint with the epoch in which they lived. The nostalgia for a Rousseauesque "back to nature," for exotic faraway countries, for glamorous adventures, accompanied by titanic self-dramatization, represents one aspect of that escapist thinking which turned Byronism into the most fashionable pose of the period. Its second aspect was, however, a sincere disappointment with the ideals of the French revolution. Behind an outward flippancy and cynicism there were hiding quite a number of wounded idealists, no longer able to believe in ideals. But having turned away from the political life of their time, they fell back upon their own superfluous selves, in which process they were often inclined to interpret their very isolation as a result of their misunderstood originality and uniqueness. Gradually, such a "pathos of the distance" helped to inflate (at least in theory) their personal appetites to Napoleonic ambitions. The discrepancy between their wishful ideas of themselves on the one hand, and their actual insignificance on the other, only made their words louder, their gestures more romantic.

In Russia, the Byronic "superfluous man" assumed a subtle and complicated shape in so far as he coincided with the privileged *déraciné*, brought up in the atmosphere of autocracy and serfdom. An educated Russian nobleman could not help feeling isolated, a stranger in his own country. The gap dividing him from the corrupt bureaucracy was of a moral nature. The one separating him from his illiterate serfs was both social and cultural. Pushkin gave the portrait of a Byronic *déraciné* in Aleko, the hero of his early narrative poem, *Gypsies*. But whereas Aleko still retains the air of romantic mystery and commits a double *crime passionnel*, Onegin is, with all his uprootedness, a product and a member of the actual Petersburg society of the 'twenties. His ennui, devoid of any titanic features, is all the more typical of a class whose existence had become empty and futile.

Onegin is introduced to us while hurrying to the deathbed of his uncle who bequeaths to him a country estate. This gives the poet an opportunity of describing with an inimitable accent Onegin's fashionable education and also his exploits in the Petersburg society. After the brilliant first chapter we are transferred to Onegin's inherited country mansion.

> *The country nook, that bored Evgeny,*
> *Was just a thing of pure delight*
> *We should thank heaven for, as any*
> *Lover of harmless pleasure might.*
> *A hill from all the winds excluded*
> *The master's house; it lay secluded*
> *Above a stream, and far away*
> *Stretched flower-besprinkled meadows gay*
> *With golden fields of harvest blended.*
> *A village twinkled here and there;*
> *Herds roamed the pastures everywhere;*
> *A huge wild garden, too, extended*
> *Its dense and canopying shades,*
> *A haunt for musing Dryad maids.*

And here a castle was erected
As castles should be: firmly based,
Quiet, a fabric much respected,
In the old, clever, charming taste.
The rooms were many and high; brocaded
Silks on the parlor walls paraded,
Ancestral portraits also, while
The stoves were shot with many a tile.
Now all had long been antiquated,
I know not rightly why, indeed;
My friend, however, had small need
Of this; nor cared he if he waited
In ancient, or in modish hall;
It mattered not—he yawned in all.[1]

It is in such surroundings that the bored young poseur comes into contact with the provincial gentry. Their life and manners provide the background for the novel. Onegin takes a vague interest in one of his neighbors, a certain Lensky, in whom he finds the opposite of his own skepticism and boredom. Lensky, a naïve idealist of the Göttingen[2] brand, introduces Onegin to the Larin family. Mme Larin is a countrified matron and a widow whose younger daughter, Olga, is Lensky's fiancée. In contrast to the lively, superficial Olga, her other daughter Tatyana is shy, but made of fine, solid material. Tatyana falls in love with Onegin and is honest enough to confess her feelings in a touching letter to the blasé young dandy. Onegin does not condescend to answer. But later, when taken by Lensky to a party at the Larins, he finds Tatyana alone for a moment and returns her the letter with a few trite remarks about his tiredness

---

[1] Translated by Oliver Elton (The Pushkin Press).
[2] Göttingen University was one of the centers of the Russian youths studying abroad. It played a considerable part in the idealistic thought of Russia.

with life and his inability to love anyone. Irritated on another occasion, he vents his annoyance on Lensky by deliberately flirting with Olga. A duel between the two friends follows, in which Lensky is killed. Onegin departs in haste. After years of travel he returns to St. Petersburg, where he again meets Tatyana—now a ravishing beauty, married to an elderly dignitary. This time the roles are reversed. It is Onegin who falls in love with Tatyana. He keeps on writing letters to her, but they remain unanswered. In despair he rushes one day into Tatyana's room and finds her alone, reading his letter. She confesses that she still loves him, but firmly declares her intention to remain faithful to her husband. Onegin leaves her, a sadder and a wiser man.

The pattern of this "novel in verse" is interwoven with excellent character drawing and pictures of Russian life. Behind its distilled realism the author's own attitude—a mixture of hidden sadness and amusement—can be felt. In spite of occasional echoes of Byron, *Evgeny Onegin* remains thoroughly Russian. No wonder it exercised such a strong influence upon the development of Russian fiction, especially of the novel. Tatyana became the prototype of the slightly idealized Russian woman (conspicuous in Turgenev's novels), whereas Onegin had a numerous progeny among those vacillating superfluous men whose variations we can follow—via Lermontov, Turgenev, Goncharov, Chekhov—until the recent revolution. The straightforward naturalness of Pushkin's pictures of Russian life also affected a number of realists. Even Onegin's elegiac denouement became a tradition —nay, almost a law in the Russian novel with its dislike of happy endings.

IV

However typical of his generation, Onegin was too much of a fashionable man-about-town to be really tragic. Even his

"Childe Harold's cloak" was an imported article. But a more indignant and tragic variety of the Russian *déraciné* (anticipated in Griboyedov's comedy, *Woe from Wit*) was bound to result from the atmosphere of the "leaden régime" which hung like an incubus over Russia after 1825. The autocratic rule of Nicholas I relied on a bureaucracy of opportunists and upstarts whose corruption was proverbial. Every sincere impulse was doomed in advance. The best younger representatives found no outlet for their energies or for their will to be useful in their own country. They were superfluous not only as members of a class thriving on serf-labor, but also as victims of a state machine with which they were in opposition. But energies, deprived of an outlet, grow destructive. An active character, unable to act, may easily be landed in mere negation, in rancorous nihilism. His strength may also turn against itself, in which case the individual runs the danger of disintegration. Such a process is rendered in *A Hero of Our Time,* a novel written by Pushkin's successor, the poet Mikhail Y. Lermontov (1814-1841).

This work is Lermontov's chief contribution to fiction. It is an analytical novel, written so skillfully that on its appearance (in 1840) Lermontov was hailed by the critics as a literary star of the first magnitude. Lermontov's prose is more temperamental, more spontaneous, than the overdisciplined prose of Pushkin. But here it serves its purpose magnificently, since *A Hero of Our Time* is an intensified personal document, reflecting the tragedy of the younger generation of the 'thirties—like de Musset's *Confession d'un enfant du siècle*. Petchorin, the chief character of the novel, is a new variety of Onegin, a sinister and tragic variety, the more so because he is endowed with intelligence, strength, and will power. Before 1825, he would probably have been a Decembrist. In the 'thirties, however, he was deprived even of such an outlet. So he became a rancorous *déclassé* from above, with all the elements of potential nihili.m. Sketched out in Lermontov's earlier unfinished narrative, *Princess Ligovskaya*, Petchorin is here presented as an ironically cold and aloof symbol of frustration; as a suppressed idealist, skeptical of all ideals. Superior to his surroundings by his gifts, his ambitions, his strength of will, he is yet devoid of any positive aim or channel. So his strength turns not only against himself, but also against the people who come in contact with him.

A Hero of Our Time consists of five narratives which can be read and enjoyed independently. They shed a light on Petchorin from several angles. The first two parts—*Bela, Maxim Maximytch*—depict him as he is seen by his acquaintances amidst the wild scenery of the Caucasian mountains (the Russian "romantic East"). It is a fine piece of indirect portraiture. But the people through whom we get to know him are also well drawn, especially the old Captain Maxim Maximytch: a literary offspring of Mironov in Pushkin's *A Captain's Daughter*. The remaining three parts—*Taman, Princess Mary, A Fatalist*—are records of Petchorin's own experiences, impressions, and reflections, showing him from within. Of these *Taman* is particularly good as a story. The chief hero thus stands out before us clearly as both a character and a representative of Lermontov's generation. The author may ridicule, in his preface to the second edition, the idea that Petchorin is a portrait of himself. A closer study makes us, however, suspect that Lermontov must have projected into Petchorin a number of his own defects, at least those for which he blamed the atmosphere of his hero's early upbringing. This is how he describes some of them:

"Yes, such was the fate allotted to me from my very early childhood. Everyone read on my face the signs of bad qualities which were not there; but they suspected them—

and so they were born in me. I was modest—so I was accused of cunning; I became secretive. I felt deeply good and evil; no one caressed me, but all offended me instead: I became resentful. I was sullen, while the other children were happy and chatty; I felt I was superior to them, but they put me lower than they: I became envious. I was ready to love the whole world but no one understood me, and I learned to hate. My colorless youth was wasted on a struggle with myself and the world; my best feelings, fearing ridicule, I buried in the depth of my heart and there they perished. I spoke the truth—I was not believed. I began to simulate. Having got to know well the world and the springs of society, I became experienced in the science of life and saw how the others were happy, making use without effort of those very advantages which I fought for so relentlessly. And then a despair was born in my breast; not that despair which is cured by the barrel of a pistol, but a cold, powerless despair, concealed by affability and a good-natured smile. I became a moral cripple. One half of my innermost self ceased to exist—it had dried up, evaporated, and died. I cut it off and threw it away."

In this novel Lermontov revealed certain inner springs of the superfluous man of his time. In fact, it was he who laid the foundations for the Russian psychological novel in general. Pushkin and Lermontov are, however, not the only authors responsible for the character of the modern Russian fiction. Another great and puzzling pioneer should be added. His name is Gogol.

CHAPTER III

Gogol and Realism

IF THE 'twenties of the last century were the great age of Russian poetry, the 'thirties and 'forties witnessed a sudden rise of prose. Here, too, Russia followed the Western currents and fashions which she gradually blended with a spirit and content of her own. The influence of Sir Walter Scott has already been mentioned. The rhetorical-romantic style in the French manner found an exponent in the former Decembrist A. Bestuzhev-Marlinsky, whose life was as agitated as the style of his prose. Although at present forgotten, his was such an influence towards the middle of the last century that even Lermontov's *A Hero of Our Time* did not escape from it entirely. A touch of Jean Paul Richter is noticeable in the work of A. Veltman, especially in his lengthy novel, *A Stranger* (1831). In his tendency to obliterate the line between reality and fantasy, Veltman anticipated, to some extent, Dostoevsky. There is a flavor of German romanticism in the writings of Prince Vladimir Odoevsky; in his *Russian Nights,* for example. The well-known publicist M. Pogodin, on the other hand, indulged in somewhat clumsy realistic experiments. He was drawn towards the types and the speech of the lower classes, the serfs included. Some realists combined a rhetorical style with veiled social criticism. Others preferred ethnographic themes, which are conspicuous in the writings of Vladimir I. Dal (1801-1872).

Dal's first stories appeared (under the pseudonym Kazak

Lugansky) in 1846 and had immediate success. Anecdotic and without pretensions, they too abound in lower class types. Yet Dal's literary output, considerable though it was, failed to justify the hopes aroused by his early works.[1] A different kind of realism was that of V. Druzhinin, whose *Polinka Saks* (1847) was a dissection of the problem of marriage, reminiscent of George Sand—the idol of the Russian intellectuals. Druzhinin, who was a connoisseur of English literature, became active (together with Annenkov) mainly as a theoretician of the aesthetic trend in criticism, but without much success.

All said and done, the Russian prose of the 'thirties and early 'forties would have lagged far behind the prose works of Pushkin and Lermontov but for the writings of Gogol, whose activities inaugurated the great era of Russian fiction.

II

Nikolai Vasilyevitch Gogol (1809-1852) was born into a family of petty gentry—a stratum which usually supplied minor officials or else social *déclassés*. Being of Little Russian Cossack stock, he spent his early years in the sunny Ukraine. Small of stature and unattractive—with a long ducklike nose —he became self-conscious and shy. It was probably in self-defense that he developed his inclination to look for what was ridiculous and ugly in other people. This propensity was combined in him with a highly neurotic temperament and with an imagination which often exaggerated his fancies and impressions into spooks of such intensity that he became literally haunted by them. As an incurable romantic, he saw both life and himself in a false perspective. Unable to come

---

[1] He is also the author of the monumental *Dictionary of the Living Russian Speech*.

to terms with either, he had to endure one shock after the other, until he discovered a temporary haven in art.

Gogol first came to grips with reality in Petersburg. He had arrived there hoping for a career, but found instead only one humiliation after the other. Anxious to escape from it all, he imagined himself in his native Ukraine with all its color, gaiety, and traditions. These he committed to paper with the vivacity of a southerner and with the skill of a born actor. The result was his *Evenings on a Farm near Dikanka* (1831-1832). The two volumes under this title were welcomed all the more eagerly on account of the folkloristic flavor which was then fashionable. But fashions or no fashions, Gogol's first stories still retain their liveliness and freshness—partly because of the style and partly because of the manner in which their romantic themes are blended with grotesquely realistic touches from the Ukrainian peasant and Cossack life. Yet hardly one of these stories was invented by Gogol himself. Many of them he must have heard as a child from his grandfather. Now he repeated them in his own way, intertwining them with folklore, personal impressions, lyrical outbursts, and occasionally also with literary influences—those of Tieck and Hoffmann, for example. The most re-markable thing is, however, Gogol's language. It is saturated with rhythm, ornament, and music as though the author had wanted to hypnotize himself by his own verbal flow. The very opening of his first story, *The Fair of Sorotchintsy*, is characteristic of Gogol's prose.

"How gorgeous, how intoxicating is a summer day in Little Russia! How languidly hot are the hours when the noon glitters in its sweat and silence, and when the immeasurable vault of heaven, bent over the world like a voluptuous cupola, seems to have fallen asleep, bathing in a sea of rap-ture—while holding and caressing the beautiful earth in its ethereal embraces. Not a cloud in the sky, not a sound in the fields. All is silent as if dead; only there, in the heavenly heights, a lark trembles, and silvery songs float on airy waves to the enchanted earth below; the call of a gull is heard, now and then, or the resonant voice of a quail echoes in the steppe. Lazily and lost in dreams like aimless wanderers stand the cloud-high oaks, and the blinding beats of sun rays light up masses of leaves, while on others they cast a shade dark as night, yet sprinkled with gold at every gush of the breeze. Emeralds, topazes, jacinths of ethereal insects are pouring over the gay-colored gardens, protected by stately sunflowers. Gray stacks of hay and golden sheaves of corn seem to be camping in the fields over all their boundless expanse. The verdant branches of cherry, apple, pear, and plum trees, bent by the weight of their fruits; the sky and its clear mirror; the river framed in the green, proudly elevated banks—how luxurious, how voluptuous is the Ukrainian summer!"

One step farther, and the author would be landed in a jungle of quasi-poetic effusions and clichés, but he always manages to stop at the right time. A perfect specimen of Gogol's prose is *A Cruel Vengeance,* which rolls on like a transposed folk ballad of the most gruesome type. While the classic-realistic manner reached its perfection in the prose of Pushkin, it was Gogol who developed the temperamental, ornate, and musical prose to its climax. Often he risked obliterating the distinction between prose and poetry, and mixing the two. His avoidance of such a mixture was due not to his literary culture (which was weak), but to his innate artistic instinct. With all its ornaments and rhythms, Gogol's prose still remains definitely prose.

A sharper external division between the romantic and the realistic elements comes out in Gogol's next collection of narratives, *Mirgorod,* published in 1835. The longest of them, *Taras Bulba,* is a would-be historical romance pure and simple: a kind of Cossack *Iliad* in prose. Partly inspired by Scott, it yet stands out as a fine original work. The Cossack fights with the Poles, the figures of Taras himself and of his two sons (the younger of whom becomes a traitor for the sake of a Polish belle, but is later caught and shot by his own father) recall folk ballads rather than the *Waverley Novels.* A contrast to this romantic rhapsody from the Ukrainian past is provided, however, by the two narratives from real life: *The Old-World Landowners,* and *The Quarrel between Ivan Ivanovitch and Ivan Nikiforovitch,* suggested by Narezhny's novel, *The Two Ivans.* Yet the realism of these two stories was itself due to a romantic impulse. The first of them embodies Gogol's idyllic yearning for a Rousseauesque return to nature—a return to that placid vegetable existence on the land where one's ambitions never go "beyond the fence of one's own orchard." The author depicts to us with relish all the charm of such an idyl, sheltered from the strain of civilization. In *The Quarrel,* on the other hand, Gogol's realism vibrates with rancor. From behind its humor there peers a romantic disgust with man and life, a special emphasis being laid on all that is laughable in human beings: "Agafya wore a cap on her head and a coffee-colored cloak with yellow flowers, and had three little warts on her nose. Her figure was like a cask, and it would be as hard to tell where to look for her waist, as for her to see her nose without a mirror. Her feet were small and shaped like two cushions. She talked scandal, ate boiled beet-soup in the morning, and swore desperately. Amongst all these various occupations her countenance never for an instant changed its expression, which phenomenon, as a rule, women alone are capable of displaying. . . ." And listen to the sudden transition from humor to melancholy at the end of the story: "The lean nags known in Mirgorod as post horses began to stamp their hoofs, which were buried in a gray mass of mud, with a sound very displeasing to the ear. The rain poured in torrents upon the Jew seated on the box, covered with a rug. The dampness penetrated me through and through. The gloomy barrier with a sentry-box, in which an old soldier was repairing his weapons, was passed by slowly. Again the same fields, in some places black where they had been dug up, in others of a greenish hue; wet daws and crows; monotonous rain, a tearful sky, without one gleam of light! . . . It is gloomy in this world, gentlemen!"

Gogol's grotesque twist of reality has often been compared with the manner of Dickens. The resemblance is only on the surface. Dickens's humor was prompted by a benevolent attitude towards life, and not by hatred and disgust as was the case with Gogol. In fact, Gogol hardly ever smiles—he only grins, or else "laughs through tears." This is why his portraits of repellent animal-like people are always intense and convincing, while his attempts to depict positive characters or beautiful women never go beyond commonplaces. The Polish belle in *Taras Bulba* is a collection of worn superlatives. His very humor weakens when there is nothing to ridicule and to attack. And so with the exception of *The Evenings* Gogol's humor is for the most part disguised parody and satire. In his "laughter through tears" there is too often a mixture of pity and inquisitive scorn. Some of Gogol's comic effects are due also to a deliberate incongruity between a solemn rhetorical tone and the triviality of the subject itself. But on the whole, it is the romantic exaltation of his mind on the one hand, and the rancorously "funny" and exaggerated realism of his vision on the other, that form the inner duality of his style and art. This comes out again in his Petersburg stories, most of which were written before his great novel, *Dead Souls*.

III

Gogol tackled city life only after his literary success had alleviated his initial bewilderment with Petersburg and with its dehumanizing effect. Stories such as *The Memoirs of a Madman, Nevsky Prospect* (1835), or *The Greatcoat* (published seven years later) probably sublimated some of his own painful experiences and observations. In *The Memoirs of a Madman*—a perfect thing of its kind—a downtrodden clerk falls in love with his chief's daughter and confides all his feelings to a diary. The exalted object of his love takes no notice of his existence. But this does not disturb him: he finds a compensation in his wishful thinking. Spurred on by his inferiority complex, he indulges in reveries of his imaginary grandeur. Finally he claims to be the fugitive king of Spain, and is taken to a lunatic asylum as a hopeless case.

Nevsky Prospect opens with a glowing description of the famous Petersburg thoroughfare, the name of which is used as the title of the story. The principal characters are two contrasted friends. One of them, an artist, meets a beautiful girl on the Nevsky, falls madly in love with her, and in the end discovers that she is a prostitute, bespattered with all the mud and vulgarity which cling to that profession. Unable to bear the shock, the artist commits suicide. His volatile friend—a lieutenant—is of a more practical turn of mind. He, too, meets a pretty dame on the Nevsky, follows her to her house, introduces himself, and starts an amorous intrigue. Caught by her husband, he gets a thrashing but quickly recovers and resumes his run of pleasures as lightheartedly as ever. Indifferent to the tragedy of the artist and to the farce of the lieutenant, the stream of life (symbolized by the Nevsky) goes on as before.

In *The Greatcoat* Gogol takes up, once again, the fate of an inferior clerk. Crushed by poverty, fear, and submission, the clerk Akaky is much too cowed to protest, or even to realize the depth of his own humiliation. His existence has been narrowed down to such an extent that the only ambition of his old age is to scrape enough money together to buy a fashionable greatcoat. After endless privations, he acquires the craved-for garment, puts it on, and beaming with delight feels for the first time that he, too, is of some importance. For the first time he is admired by his colleagues in the office and even by his superiors, one of whom actually gives a party in honor of Akaky's greatcoat. But returning late at night from the party, the slightly tipsy Akaky is suddenly knocked down by two gangsters. Before he fully realizes what has happened, the thieves are gone—together with his precious greatcoat. Akaky falls ill and dies from grief.

It was not Gogol who introduced the poor clerks into Russian literature. There had been plenty of stories about them before Gogol, but Gogol's art gave the final sanction. The ingredients of his *Greatcoat* became in fact the staple food of subsequent Russian realism. An insignificant plot, attention to apparent trifles, an "insulted and injured" character, the note of pity through fun—all this was incorporated in that "natural school" of Russian fiction whose champion was Gogol's ardent admirer, the critic Belinsky. "We have all come from under Gogol's Greatcoat," declared Dostoevsky a few decades later, when Russian realism was at its height.

As for Gogol's two remaining Petersburg stories, *The Portrait* is ultraromantic. Its theme—the interference of supernatural agencies with life (in this case with the life and fate of a painter who has sacrificed his genius to material success) —is reminiscent of Hoffmann. *The Nose*, on the other hand, is deliberately nonsensical and develops like a grotesque dream. An infatuated young fop is in search of his lost nose which has assumed an independent existence, and on this errand he meets with all sorts of fantastic and droll adventures. The story must have been prompted to Gogol by certain personal complexes, the definition of which is a matter of psychoanalysis rather than of literary criticism. The climax of his activities during that period was his satirical comedy, *The Inspector General* (1836)—an attack on corrupt officialdom. Such is a brief account of Gogol's works before the appearance of his masterpiece, *Dead Souls*, in 1842.

IV

This novel is one of the important achievements of European literature. Gogol wrote most of it during his long stay abroad (mainly in Rome), whence he could watch and judge his native country in relative quiet. Its theme was suggested to him by Pushkin, and Gogol took it up at first as an amusing anecdote. Gradually, however, he enlarged it so as to present through it a panorama and a criticism of Russian life, or at least of those aspects which were hateful to Gogol himself. The narrative is built upon so slender a plot that it is devoid even of a love intrigue. Its pattern, too, is simple: the pattern of the old picaresque novel. Its chapters are strung together, rather loosely, by the business trip of the main character, Chichikov. In spite of this, the novel is and remains a masterpiece: a tour de force of Gogol's art, as well as of his peculiar vision of life. Externally, Gogol is here more realistic than in any of his other works. And more than ever one is aware that his realism came from his romantic need to expose and to reject that actuality which he loathed.

Chichikov, the principal character of *Dead Souls*, is the very embodiment of the bourgeois golden mean; of smug, "gentlemanly" self-complacency, combined with great shrewdness in money matters. We are introduced to him when, after various reverses of fortune, he has decided to enrich himself again. For this purpose he sets out on his journey. In a county town, where he stops, he makes a favorable impression on all and sundry. For some reason, he is particularly interested in various landowners. Accompanied by his coachman and his servant, he starts visiting them one after the other. Gradually it transpires that the object of his errand is to buy a number of dead serfs or "souls" (as they were called in Russia) whose deaths have not yet been registered by the official census. He hopes to mortgage those fictitious "souls" for a substantial sum of money with which he would disappear—a rich man, once more. In his peregrinations, he comes across a variety of types: the infantile sentimentalist Manilov, the stolid animal Sobakevitch, the dried-up miser Plyushkin, the silly old widow Korobochka, the scandalmonger Nozdryov, all of whom have become nicknames in Russia. As Chichikov's intentions are not quite in harmony with the Code of Law, he approaches each of his potential clients warily, changing his tactics whenever required. Hence the subtlety and humor of the dialogue.

"Sobakevitch bent his head slightly, and prepared to hear what the business might be. Chichikov approached the subject indirectly, touched on the Russian Empire in general, and spoke with great appreciation of its vast extent, said that even the ancient Roman Empire was not so vast . . . (Sobakevitch still listened with his head bowed) and that in accordance with the existing ordinances of the government, whose fame had no equal, souls on the census list who had ended their earthly career were, until the next census was taken, reckoned as though they were alive, in order to avoid burdening the government departments with a multitude of petty and unimportant details and increasing the complexity of the administrative machinery, complicated as it is . . . (Sobakevitch still listened with his head bowed) and that justifiable as this arrangement was, it yet put a somewhat heavy burden on many landowners, compelling them to pay the tax as though for living serfs, and that through a sentiment of personal respect for him, he was prepared to some extent to relieve him of this burdensome obligation. In regard to the real subject of his remarks, Chichikov expressed himself very cautiously and never spoke of the souls as dead, but invariably as non-existent. Sobakevitch still listened as before with his head bent, and not a trace of anything approaching expression showed on his face. It seemed as though in that body there was no soul at all, or if there was that it was not in its proper place, but, as with the immortal Boney, somewhat far away and covered with so thick a shell that whatever was stirring at the bottom of it, produced not the faintest ripple on the surface.

" 'And so . . . ?' said Chichikov, waiting, not without some perturbation, for an answer.

" 'You want the dead souls?' inquired Sobakevitch very simply, with no sign of surprise, as though they had been talking of corn.

" 'Yes,' said Chichikov, and again softened the expression, adding, 'non-existing ones.'

" 'There are some, to be sure there are,' said Sobakevitch.

" 'Well, if you have any, you will doubtless be glad to get rid of them?'

" 'Certainly, I am willing to sell them,' said Sobakevitch, slightly raising his head and reflecting that doubtless the purchaser would make some profit of them.

" 'Deuce take it!' thought Chichikov to himself. 'He is ready to sell them before I drop a hint of it!' And aloud he said, 'And at what price, for instance? Though, indeed it is a queer sort of goods . . . it seems odd to speak of the price.' " [1]

In this manner Chichikov collects his "dead souls," always careful not to lose his dignity or to stumble over any paragraph of the Law. But in spite of his caution, his secret leaks out in the end.

Having sold her dead "souls" to Chichikov, the imbecile but thrifty Korobochka comes upon the idea that the queer buyer might have cheated her. Mad with fear, she hurries to the town in order to find out what prices are offered for dead serfs. A few hours later the most fantastic rumors about Chichikov begin to circulate. The town suddenly becomes so hostile that he prefers to clear out as quickly as he can.

When Gogol read the first draft of his novel to Pushkin, the great poet laughed. But his face was soon darkened with gloom: "How sad is our Russia!" Yet it is not Russia, but life in general—life with its greed, stupidity, and vulgarity—Gogol laughs at, while his Chichikov moves about like a Don Quixote of our acquisitive age. And Gogol's laughter is only a mask behind which he hides his own tedium. The meticulous realism of this "epic" (as Gogol calls it) is the subjective realism of disparagement. So much so that the novel is often at its gloomiest when it looks most comic on the surface. And as for Gogol's characters, one is struck above all by their uncanny static intensity. They are human beings intensified into spooks.

Such is the gist of the first volume, which can be regarded as a complete work in itself. Gogol intended to enlarge his epic into a kind of "Divine Comedy" of Russian life, the first part being only its "Inferno." The second and the third volumes were to show a gradual regeneration of Chichikov,

[1] From *Dead Souls*, translated by Constance Garnett (Chatto & Windus).

as well as of a few other characters. The picture of life presented there was to be on a higher level. Only five chapters of the second volume have been preserved. They contain some excellently drawn negative characters. Its positive or virtuous heroes are, however, stilted and lifeless.

v

In spite of its hidden subjectivity, *Dead Souls* showed up Russia in some of her most unpleasant aspects. As the politically dissatisfied 'forties were quite ready for such an indictment, this novel became a landmark in the social consciousness of the author's country. Mistaking Gogol's method for realism pure and simple, the critic Belinsky proclaimed it (together with *The Greatcoat*) as the cornerstone of the natural school of fiction which began to develop in the 'forties. We know, however, that Gogol's realism had grown out of his romantic urge to take revenge upon life which had failed to come up to his expectations. But while fighting with the existence he saw around him, he was fighting with himself; in so far at least as he was a self-centered moral hypochondriac, profoundly aware of his own defects and inhibitions. He needed his negative characters in order to project into them some of his own faults (whether actual or imaginary) which he thus exteriorized. Such a feature was, however, bound to foster his strong moralizing propensities. As long as these were able to find an outlet in his art and in his "laughter through tears," he remained a great author. But no sooner had the moralist in him become dissociated from the artist (in which he forestalled Tolstoy) than he succumbed to the temptation of didactic preaching and teaching. After Pushkin's death in particular, Gogol considered himself his heir and, consequently, a kind of mentor of his nation. This much can be gathered from his planned

continuation of *Dead Souls,* and even more from his correspondence. It is enough to read some of his letters in order
to realize how inveterate his moralizing vein really was.
Unable to resist its promptings, he published in 1847 his
Selected Passages from Correspondence with Friends—a book
which made an incredible stir in the ranks of the intelligentsia. This time it was the dilettantism with which Gogol
tackled important problems that irritated the progressive
minds of Russia. In spite of a few brilliant intuitive flashes,
he only proved his own incompetence outside the realm of
artistic creation. His pretentious commonplaces about religion, morality, politics, art, literature, and even husbandry
are written in the unpleasantly high-pitched tone of a man
who would like to be a new Messiah for the benefit of his
country but is not quite sure whether he is qualified for such
a role. Needless to say, the book was attacked from all
quarters. The fiercest onslaught came from the author's
former admirer, the critic Belinsky, who was exasperated by
Gogol's flirtation with reaction. "A preacher of the knout,
an apostle of ignorance, a defender of obscurantism and of
the darkest oppression, a eulogist of Tartar manners"—such
were some of the epithets hurled by him at Gogol.

The book marked the decline of Gogol's genius and even
of his sanity. Nor did he ever recover from the invectives
he had to endure from both friend and foe alike. Besides,
during the last few years of his life he became a prey to
depression and to superstitious fixed ideas, such as his ata-
vistic fear of hell and of the devil, which now played regular
havoc with him. The more so because his imagination was
incomparably stronger than his intelligence. In his effort to
atone for his sins and to work himself into a mood of sincere
religiosity, he even made a pilgrimage to Palestine. It was
all in vain. In spite of his will to be religious, his soul
remained cold and unmoved. Haunted by life at large and

by the dread within himself, he kept on roaming restlessly from place to place. In February, 1852, he had a fit of hypochondria during which he burned the manuscript of the second volume of *Dead Souls*. A few days later he died, probably from exhaustion caused by his ascetic practices.

This account of Gogol's personality and work was necessary in order to elucidate the part played by him, together with Pushkin and Lermontov, in the evolution of the Russian novel. But before proceeding farther, we must give a brief sketch of that intellectual background which accompanied and partly conditioned its rapid growth.

CHAPTER IV

Fermentation of Ideas

THE GENTRY period of Russian culture and literature reached its climax in Pushkin. Soon after Pushkin's death, however, the cultural life of Russia was profoundly affected by the formation of the so-called intelligentsia. The latter was a more or less successful union between the best representatives of the gentry on the one hand, and the educated commoners or *raznochintsy*[1] on the other. Such a process became almost inevitable after the Decembrist catastrophe. Starting in the 'thirties, it was completed only in the 'sixties, when the ranks of the commoners had grown rather strong, especially in journalism. The whole of that period was marked not only by a rapid growth of Russian literature, but also by a far-reaching fermentation of ideas.

After 1825 the focus of cultural life was transferred for a time to the Moscow University and its debating circles. Thus the circle of Stankevitch included, in the 'thirties, a number of young intellectuals whose names became famous before long. The philosophy of Hegel, Schelling, and Fichte, mixed up with naïve "Schilleresque" idealism, prevailed in that group. Hegel was the towering influence. But a section of more active youths began to study also Feuerbach, Comte, and the Utopian socialism of Fourier and Saint-Simon. These influences, together with the Hegelian left wing and the writings of George Sand, who was particularly popular in Russia during the 'forties, fostered all the more the dis-

---

[1] Singular *raznochinets*, a man of "other ranks."

content with Russian reality as it was. They also strengthened the Western or Europeanizing camp among the intellectuals. The adherents of this camp ranged from the balanced liberalism of Turgenev to the extreme radicalism of Bakunin. They looked upon Russia as a backward part of Europe and were anxious to follow in the latter's steps with regard to political, scientific, and social progress. Commoners and urbanized gentry *déclassés* seemed to be particularly drawn towards Westernism. Entirely different was the trend of the opposite Slavophil or patriotic camp. Its members consisted largely of landowners, living on their estates and surrounded by a patriarchal-feudal atmosphere. Unlike the Westerners, they distrusted the materialistic civilization of Europe and saw the salvation of Russia in a culture rooted in native traditions. Laying stress on the Russian type of Christianity, they would not and could not separate culture from religion, which they naturally identified with the official Church. But tendencies of this kind were not altogether new in Russia. Their distant precedents can be found in the idea of Moscow as the "Third Rome," in the conservative opponents of patriarch Nikon and, later, of Peter the Great. In 1833 they received a potential ally in the official nationalism, launched by the minister of education, Count S. S. Uvarov, in the name of autocracy, orthodoxy, and nationality—interpreted as the sum total of the specific qualities of the Russian people and civilization. Nor must we forget that Karamzin's *History of the Russian Empire* had been written in the same spirit. Uvarov's reactionary trinity was soon taken up by the servile section of the press, notably by the *Northern Bee*, under the wings of Bulgarin.

The early Slavophils had no contact with this or any reactionary nationalism. They worked for the progress of Russia with the same zeal as the Westerners, but they differed in their attitude towards it. The leading Slavophils—the brothers Kireyevsky, the brothers Aksakov, and the poet-theologian Khomyakov—adhered to a philosophy which was a mixture of Schelling, of Orthodox Christianity, and of romanticized Russian traditions. At the same time they were anxious to complete, as it were, Hegel's *Philosophy of History* by including the Slavs and especially the Russians (ignored by Hegel) in that historical process which had been proclaimed by the German philosopher as the self-revelation of Universal Spirit. Hence the Slavophil insistence on the inner spiritual factors of culture, culminating in their quest for a transcendental "Russian Idea," so enthusiastically taken up, later, by Dostoevsky.

II

The split between the Westerners and the Slavophils began in the 'forties and was fought out largely in the monthly periodicals, whose importance took on proportions almost unthinkable in the rest of Europe. Gradually, the antagonism widened to such an extent as to divide all intellectuals into two hostile factions. In the end the label "intelligentsia" became applied, as a rule, to the Western camp only. This may look one-sided, but we must not forget that the majority of intellectuals were, from the 'forties onwards, decidedly of a Western orientation and made no secret of it.

As for the ideological causes of the cleavage itself, the question as to whether Russia had a culture and a historical destiny of her own or whether she should follow Europe was provisionally answered by Peter Chaadayev (1793-1856) in the first of his *Philosophic Letters,* published in 1836. These had been written by him a few years earlier in French (under the influence of Schelling and of the French Catholic thinkers—Joseph de Maistre, Balanche, de Bonald) and can be regarded as the first Russian attempt at a philosophy of history from the standpoint of the dilemma: Russia and

Europe. Chaadayev did not mince words. Asserting that Russia had no culture of her own, no past and no achievements she could be proud of, he maintained that the very existence of his fatherland was something casual, and that the only outlet for the Russians as a nation was to cooperate or even to merge with the Catholic West.[1] These conclusions were startling enough to provoke general controversy and indignation. The Moscow *Telescope*, in which the essay had appeared, was suppressed. As an alternative to Siberia, Chaadayev was officially declared a lunatic and was even placed in the charge of a doctor. Yet nothing could silence the problems stirred up by his statements.

Many an intellectual with Western sympathies agreed with Chaadayev's views concerning Russian history and culture, while rejecting his religious bias: to a Russian liberal of those days progress meant above all the advance of scientific, liberal, and social-humanitarian ideas then prevalent in Europe. The budding Slavophils, on the other hand, were quite ready to accept Chaadayev's identification of culture and religion, but would have nothing to do with his Catholicism, since Russian Orthodoxy was, in their opinion, the only expression of true Christianity. As though in defiance of both Chaadayev and Hegel's *Philosophy of History*, they began to insist on the world-historical mission of Slavdom, and of Russia in particular. Eventually, some of them saw in the West nothing but growing materialism which should be counteracted by the "true" Christian culture of the Russian people. Far from seeking for any salvation in the West, Russia—they contended—was herself destined to save bourgeois Europe from complete spiritual decay. At

---

[1] In his subsequent *Letters* Chaadayev gives an apotheosis of Catholicism and develops the idea that both the Protestant and the Orthodox churches should return to it.

any rate there was not much to learn from a Europe enslaved by capitalism.

The feud between the Westerners and the Slavophils widened and soon found an echo in literature. One of the earliest skits on the Slavophils was Count V. A. Sollogub's *Tarantas* (1845)—a satirical journey, partly modeled on *Dead Souls,* but now rather dated. Other and more important references to the conflict were to follow, apart from the constant polemics between the two camps in the press. Because of its romantic character on the one hand, and its later philandering with official patriotism on the other, the Slavophil current was hardly likely to appeal to the radical-minded intellectuals, least of all to those from the lower classes. As it happened, Vissarion Belinsky (1810-1848), a commoner and the most prominent Westerner in the 'forties, was also the most influential literary critic of that generation.

III

Belinsky, who is often styled the "father of the Russian intelligentsia," was a *déclassé* from below. Having worked his way into the Moscow University, he was expelled from it but remained in close contact with the Stankevitch circle, where he was on friendly terms with the subsequent revolutionary and rival of Marx, Bakunin. Belinsky's development was on the whole erratic and not devoid of contradictions. As a thinker he was more enthusiastic than original. Yet whatever ideas and causes he embraced, he put into them the whole of his personality. He had all the virtues and quite a few defects of an able parvenu of culture, whose moral and intellectual integrity remained above suspicion. At first he was under the spell of Schelling and Fichte, especially of Schelling, who made him look upon art and literature as the means by which a nation expressed the "eternal absolute or divine Idea" in its own manner. Interested in such an idea, Belinsky did not bother at that stage about politics. Under Bakunin's influence he gradually turned from Schelling to Hegel. Hegel's dictum, "Everything that exists is reasonable," made him inclined to regard, for a while, even the existing Russian autocracy with all its evils as reasonable. But Feuerbach's materialism and the socialist-humanitarian theories of Saint-Simon helped him to work out a new attitude towards both literature and life. This change took place in him at the beginning of the 'forties. It was a switch over from the contemplative and philosophic 'thirties to the sociological interests, so typical of the new "fermenting" decade. Serfdom, socialism, the position of woman, and many other problems became not only questions of principle, but also of practical activities. The converted Belinsky gave up the "eternal absolute Idea" as the only reality that matters, and turned his attention to the grim realities of Russian life. He began to demand an objective description of those realities and, at the same time, a definite social significance, even social service, on the part of literature. This explains his enthusiasm over *Dead Souls*, in which he saw a true picture and an indictment of Russia. Truth to life and an attack on all negative forces of existence actually became the chief features of the natural school of fiction as formulated by Vissarion Belinsky.

The "furious Vissarion" first worked in Moscow and then settled in Petersburg, where he wrote (from 1839 on) for a mere pittance in *The Fatherland's Annals*. Finally, in 1846, he was appointed the leading critic of *The Contemporary*, which had just been bought by the poet Nekrasov and his friend Panayev.[1] It was in Petersburg that Belinsky's talent reached its full scope and maturity. Yet however acute some of his judgments may have been, his style remained voluble,

---

[1] *The Contemporary* (*Sovremennik*) had been founded by Pushkin.

frowsy, and far below the high level set up by Pushkin. Another feature, unpleasant to the modern ear, is his didactic and sermonizing tone. In spite of that, his personality was strong enough to make him authoritative both as a literary critic and as a leader of the radical thought.

Commoners of Belinsky's stamp were often more forceful than subtle, but they played a vital part in the Russian intelligentsia. For one thing, they were less hampered by traditions and class barriers than the uprooted Hamlet-like gentry intellectuals, among whom a new specimen began to crop up in the 'forties, the "repentant nobleman." Like his eighteenth-century predecessor Radishchev, the repentant nobleman, though himself a serf owner, disapproved of serfdom not so much for economic as for moral and humanitarian reasons. This was all the more laudable, because from 1839 corn prices were rapidly rising on the world market; which meant that, after a slump of twenty years, serf labor became profitable again (especially on the large estates) and made many a liberal landowner once more cling to serfdom. On the other hand, a number of noblemen joined those who were on the side of the oppressed and wanted to live up to their own ideals. Ashamed of being parasites of the masses, they championed the abolition of serfdom. They were also anxious to diminish the gap dividing them from the people, the interest in whom was now definitely on the increase.

Sentimental at first, this populist tendency gradually deepened and, after the abolition of serfdom, found an outlet in "going to the people." The movement became so strong in the 'seventies, for instance, as to make hundreds of well-to-do youths and girls give up their privileges and join the toiling masses they wished to help.[1] Needless to say, the

---

[1] Turgenev's well-known novel, *Virgin Soil*, deals with the underground activities of such a movement.

revolutionary populism on the one hand, and the conservative Slavophil idealization of the patriarchal peasantry on the other, were but two parallel tendencies on the part of the gentry intellectuals, who were anxious to find some bond with the masses in order to feel less isolated, less superfluous. The repentant nobleman thus represents a further variety of the superfluous man, now confronted not only by serfdom, but also by the problem of the intelligentsia and the people.

IV

The repentant nobleman became an active revolutionary in one of the most arresting figures of that period: Alexander Herzen, or Gertzen (1812-1870), as his name is pronounced in Russian. A pamphleteer of the highest order and an author of merit, Herzen was no less remarkable as a personality. He was a crystallized representative of the finest ethical elements in the Russian intelligentsia. Influenced by Hegel, Feuerbach, and the Utopian French socialists, he undertook a relentless feud against autocracy and serfdom, although he himself was a wealthy descendant of serf owners. The socialist ideas cherished by him and his group were even responsible for a certain cleavage between the moderate liberals (led by Professor Granovsky) and the radicals in the ranks of the intelligentsia. Yet Herzen's revolutionary enthusiasm was balanced by a skeptical and realistic sense which made him a good judge not only of theories, but also of people and conditions, of the entire *Zeitgeist* in fact. His very language, sparkling and homely, is expressive of a broad, generous mind.

Herzen was born in Moscow. Even in his undergraduate days he became the leader of a circle of students interested in social-political problems. As a result he was exiled to various provincial holes in northeastern Russia. When he returned to Moscow, he resumed his former activities, but in 1847 he left for abroad where he remained until his death. Like his friend, the poet Ogaryov, he joined those expatriated "Russian wanderers" to whom Dostoevsky refers so pathetically in one of his novels (*A Raw Youth*). The chief reason for Herzen's refusal to return was, however, his determination to fight to the bitter end from abroad, where he was beyond the reach of Russian police and censorship. For although an individualist at heart, Herzen had too strong a passion for justice to remain inert and silent. This passion was increased by his disgust with the February revolution which he witnessed in Paris. What appalled him most during his voluntary exile was the incurable Philistine and acquisitive spirit of Western Europe. In the end he settled down in London (1853) where he founded a free Russian press and issued his famous periodical, *The Bell* (*Kolokol*). Published between 1857 and 1861, *The Bell* was regularly smuggled into Russia, where it exercised an unheard-of influence upon the intelligentsia and became the nightmare of reactionary bureaucrats. After the liberation of the serfs in 1861, Herzen's influence declined. In 1864 he left London for Geneva. Six years later he died in Paris.

Herzen's contribution to literature consists of a problem novel, *Whose Fault* (1847), of a few stories, and above all of his voluminous masterpiece, *My Past and Thoughts* (*Byloe i Dumy*). Beltov, the hero of the novel (which, by the way, shows more intelligence and observation than creative power) is a well-portrayed superfluous man and a Russian Hamlet of the 'forties. He returns from his wanderings abroad to his native place where he soon finds himself amidst all the pettiness and vulgarity of a provincial existence, described by the author in a good-humored satirical vein. After an unhappy love affair with the wife of his former schoolfellow, Beltov again leaves for abroad—this time feeling more superfluous than ever. The problem of the love tangle is mainly psychological and reflects the influence of George Sand. Herzen's few stories, one of which (*The Stealing Magpie*) is a passionate indictment of serfdom, are of less importance. This cannot be said, however, of his *My Past and Thoughts*—a classic of memoir literature. The author begins with his childhood, after which he describes, most vividly, the intellectual life in Moscow during his undergraduate years. We follow him into the dreary northern places of his exile, witness his romantic elopement with his cousin Natalie, and get to know a whole gallery of people: Herzen's relatives, friends, various officials, and public figures. Later we are initiated into his exploits in France and England. Events and impressions keep on accumulating, all of them brimming with the author's wit, intelligence, and shrewd observation. The panorama ends with a few chapters from Switzerland and Italy, which make one regret that this long account of Herzen's life is not even longer. *My Past and Thoughts* is more than a free autobiography. It is a personal confession, as well as a cultural and social monograph of the entire epoch in which the author lived. And since he was in contact with such people as Garibaldi, Proudhon, Mazzini, Kossuth, Robert Owen, and Bakunin, his account of them is most valuable. He also presents them as vividly as he does the petty squabbles and jealousies of the political refugees in London.

Most of Herzen's other writings belong to the social-political thought, including his brilliant book of essays, *From the Other Shore* (1851), in which he gave vent to his loathing of Western Europe after 1848. "Social cannibalism"—this is how he defined the civilization he found in the bourgeois West. Aware of the dehumanizing tendency of capitalism, he now pinned his hopes for a better future to the working classes, and above all to the Russian people. It was in the

Russian village commune, with its collective tenure of land, that he believed he had found a peculiar institution and an element of true socialism. Because of his faith in the innate socialist instincts of the Russian peasant masses, Herzen was one of those early populists or *narodniki*, their founder, in fact, who were responsible for the cult of the peasant among the Russian intellectuals.

Morally sensitive and imbued with the French socialist Utopias, these *narodniki* hoped that socialism could be grafted upon the primitive conditions of Russia in such a way as to skip over the intermediate bourgeois-capitalist phase altogether. Their socialism had thus nothing to do with the Marxian doctrine (which began to penetrate into Russia only towards the end of the 'eighties). Aware of the gap between the agricultural and the proletarian types of mentality, the populists, whose influence reached its zenith in the 'seventies, sincerely endeavored to save Russia from the industrialized town proletariat. On account of its slogan, "Land and Freedom to the Peasants," their socialism was essentially agrarian, as well as highly ethical in character. It was through it that the repentant nobleman made his final step to atone for his own and his ancestor's guilt before the people. Parallel with this, literature itself took up, even as early as the middle of the 'forties, the fate of the serf not only as a social but also as a moral problem.

v

The final split between the Western and the Slavophil camps took place after the Crimean War, which, by the way, marked the end of the entire "barracks régime" of Nicholas I. Passions ran very high in the 'sixties, when the Westerners were in control of the influential press. Unwilling to yield their position, the Slavophils advocated more zealously than ever a culture on national and religious lines. They clung to the old patriarchal Moscow and worshiped the Russian people in a sentimental-romantic manner, indulging in all sorts of folklorist and ethnographic interests. A peculiar though less conspicuous variety of the Slavophil attitude emerged in the theories of the poet and critic, Apollon Grigoryev (1822-1864). Extremely gifted, but devoid of discipline, Grigoryev was a *déclassé*, wasting his energies on drink, on night life, and on gypsy choruses which he adored. In contrast to Hegel's idea of an abstract humanity, Grigoryev adhered to Schelling's and Herder's theory of nations as living organisms. He demanded from art and culture in general that they should be rooted in the collective national body, as well as in the soil of one's country. As the Russian word for the soil is *pochva,* the few adepts of this theory were called *pochvenniki.* Dostoevsky's Slavophilism and— more externally—the realism of the playwright Ostrovsky seem to have been affected by Grigoryev's views, summed up in his *Paradoxes of Organic Criticism.*

Actually, the beginning of this trend goes as far back as the early 'fifties when Grigoryev—an avowed opponent of Belinsky—took for a short period the leading part in Pogodin's [1] Slavophil journal, *The Muscovite* (*Moskvityanin*) and was joined by such talents as the young Ostrovsky, Melnikov-Pechersky, Pisemsky, and the ethnographer S. V. Maksimov. Quite a valuable document is Grigoryev's unfinished *My Literary and Moral Roamings.* Evidently inspired by Tolstoy's *Childhood* and *Boyhood,* Grigoryev intended to write his inner autobiography. He started with his boyhood in the 'thirties but passed, almost at once, to the description of the literary and cultural background of that period, as he himself had witnessed it in Moscow. Later he joined the staff

[1] Pogodin and his partner Shevyryov adhered, with all their Slavophil views, to official nationalism.

of *Vremya* (*Time*) and *Epokha* (*The Epoch*)—the two periodicals successively edited by Dostoevsky and his brother in the early 'sixties.

The radical intellectuals, on the other hand, provided some of the staunchest negators of Russian traditions. It was partly on this ground that a certain cleavage between the commoners and the nobles took place—in the 'sixties—even within the fold of the intelligentsia itself. The clash was fought out in their monthly, *The Contemporary*, which passed into the hands of the commoners. Those two layers of the intelligentsia thus remained subconsciously different even if their ideology was the same. The intellectuals of the gentry brand were steeped in various codes and traditions of their own class which they could not give up entirely. The commoners, on the other hand, had no reason to regret anything they had left behind: they were only too familiar with the backwardness of the social strata they had come from. So it was easier for them to carry certain radical slogans to their extremes, ignoring all that did not fit into those simplified, utilitarian formulae of progress, which were later ridiculed with such malice by Dostoevsky. Pushing their idea of freedom from the past to its farthest limits, the commoners of the 'sixties adopted the materialistic, anti-religious theories of Büchner and Vogt as a kind of new religion. They also had a blind respect for science, as we can see from the writings of such publicists and critics as Nikolai G. Chernyshevsky (1829-1889), Nikolai A. Dobrolyubov (1836-1861), and Dmitry I. Pisarev (1840-1868), who incidentally was a nobleman. All three continued in the direction indicated by Belinsky. Outspoken radicals, daring polemists and utilitarians with populist tendencies, they inherited Belinsky's sermonizing tone. But their aggressive sermons probably helped to clear certain issues more quickly than would have been achieved by milder methods.

Chernyshevsky joined the staff of *The Contemporary* in 1854. In the early 'sixties he was arrested and sent to Siberia, where he spent twenty years of his life. In spite of this, he remained active as a critic and one of the leading spirits of the younger generation. A born propagandist, versed in the writings of Belinsky, Feuerbach, Comte, Owen, Proudhon, Fourier, Louis Blanc, and John Stuart Mill, he took up the social-political thought of his time in some of its most advanced aspects. Yet, curiously enough, his greatest success was scored by his problem novel, or rather treatise in narrative form, *What Is to Be Done?* (1863). Badly constructed and deficient in psychology (its theme is the love tangle of a woman wavering between two men), it impressed the younger readers by its program of action from the standpoint of a dogmatic up-to-date radical. Chernyshevsky's follower, Dobrolyubov, was also a member of *The Contemporary* group and, in spite of his brief life, achieved fame as one of the most influential radical critics of his time. He contributed a great deal to our knowledge of the superfluous man in Russian literature. But he, too, indulged in preaching. So did the vehement individualist (even in Max Stirner's sense) Pisarev, whose brutal onslaught on art was perhaps due to his strong aesthetic leanings, of which he disapproved on principle. He is now remembered chiefly because of his attack on Pushkin (1865), the virulence of which was responsible for the decline of Pushkin's popularity in the 'sixties and 'seventies.

VI

The 'sixties were, to a large extent, under the sway of the commoners—practical and utilitarian to the point of rejecting all purely aesthetic valuations. Poetry, for example, was neglected in favor of realism in both literature and life. After the abolition of serfdom the intelligentsia was, moreover, strengthened by a number of economically ruined noblemen—now more or less *déclassés* and therefore favoring radical ideas. And since the relative freedom, granted by Czar Alexander II, once again led to disappointment (especially after the Polish rising of 1863-1864), secret revolutionary societies kept on springing up. Thus in 1862 the intensely populist "Land and Freedom" group was founded. The clandestine propaganda among the people assumed an almost missionary character in the 'seventies towards the end of which the terrorist society, "The People's Freedom," was formed as a continuation of the "Land and Freedom."

Yet in the 'seventies the gentry intellectuals emerged once more. For this was the decade of militant populism and of the repentant nobleman. The two leading social thinkers and leaders of that generation, Peter Lavrov and Nikolai K. Mikhailovsky, belonged to the nobility, and it was they who tried to work out the wider philosophic-ethical premises of what might be termed Russian populist socialism. Lavrov, the author of the once famous *Historical Letters,* was under the influence of Kant. Mikhailovsky, on the other hand, was indebted to the writings of Comte, John Stuart Mill, and Herbert Spencer. He was also a prolific literary critic during the last quarter of the nineteenth century. Having reached its climax in the 'seventies, the populist movement began to subside. The 'eighties were an age of reaction, of nostalgia, and of a Chekhovian sense of futility. But it was precisely during those years that the Marxian type of socialism began to spread in Russia.

The Russian social-democrat party was founded first abroad (under the leadership of Plekhanov) in 1883, and two years later in Petersburg. Its origin was partly due to the disintegration of the "Land and Freedom" group. There were other and more important causes as well. The great famine of 1891 in particular stirred up the ranks of the resigned intelligentsia to new activities. The influence of the social-democrat party with its economic and political program soon became popular not only with a section of the younger intellectuals, but also with factory workers, thus creating for the first time a *rapprochement* between the two. Parallel with that, a kind of resuscitated radical populism (with terrorist methods) emerged in 1892 and became prominent during the events of 1905 as the social-revolutionary party. The final conflict between the two rival socialisms took place in the recent revolution, when the Russian Marxians, led by Lenin, won the victory.

It was against the background of such currents and cross-currents that Russian prose, notably the Russian novel, gradually blossomed out in all its wealth and variety.

CHAPTER V

From Gogol to Turgenev

THE FERMENTATION of the 'forties was followed by the great wave of Russian realism which began with the natural school. The crest of this wave coincided with the 'sixties and 'seventies. After a temporary ebb during the next decade there arose, in the 'nineties, another wave—less powerful, but still impressive. The turn of the century was marked by the modernist current. And finally, the recent revolution has introduced certain trends and standards of its own. During all these phases Russian fiction remained an important medium, reflecting the consciousness of the nation with all its aims and struggles. Yet, however broad and many-sided Russian realism may have become, its primary sources can always be traced back to Pushkin, Gogol, and (to some extent) Lermontov. "The school of Pushkin and Gogol still continues, and we authors only keep on working out the material bequeathed to us by them," acknowledged one of Russia's principal novelists, Goncharov, while surveying his own work, many years later. Pushkin was responsible above all for the straightforward quiet and objectivity, as well as for certain basic characters in Russian fiction. Its anti-Philistine and satirical attitude towards life, its restless quest, and also its hidden subjectivity, were derived from Gogol. Its psychological analysis, so merciless in its frankness, had one of its pioneers in Lermontov. And the emphasis on character or characters rather than on plot is typical of all three.

The very fact that Russia was devoid of freedom of the

press helped her literature to become a first-rate social force. Since any direct discussion of "dangerous" problems and ideas was muzzled, those problems had to be smuggled into literature in such a way as to escape the vigilance of censors and of the police. A peculiar "Aesop's language" had to be invented for this purpose, and it is remarkable how quickly the Russian readers learned to read between the lines. The French humanitarian influences, and even more Belinsky's demands that art should be socially significant, enlarged the scope of the novel by including in it all the vital problems of Russia. Whereas minor authors were thus almost doomed to mix literature with didactic journalism, real creative talents had to find ways and means of expressing those problems not in terms of journalism but in terms of art. On the other hand, even when they succeeded in this, they were still preoccupied with the values of life rather than with those of art.

This attitude was partly responsible for their neglect of an elaborate plot, or for their scorn of mere escapist amusement. In its predilection for a rambling construction, the Russian novel often reminds one of the English novel; but in contrast to the latter, it is more outspoken about certain taboos. Imbued with a tragic rather than pessimistic view of life, the best Russian authors instinctively avoid also the sentimental romance with happy endings (wedding bells and all that). The aim of their art is not to provide a refuge, but to enlarge or rather to deepen our perception of both man and life. Merciless in their dissection of the human heart and mind, they often reach that region where psychology threatens to kill all respect for human beings. On the other hand, it is precisely here that a new kind of tolerance, even of tenderness, can be born—that resigned Chekhovian tenderness which seems to be beyond respect and disrespect. While at its height Russian realism prefers the intensified truth of life to any wishful thinking, its passion for debunking shows an unusual degree of inner earnestness and integrity. This is why it helped to shape not only the literature, but also the advanced consciousness of modern Russia, and partly even of Europe.

II

The first great novelist after Gogol was Ivan Turgenev. Before dealing with his work, we must mention, however, at least two other authors of that period: Grigorovitch and Aksakov. Vasily Grigorovitch (1822-1899) was both a repentant nobleman and a product of the natural school. Historically, he is important as a pioneer of the peasant story and of that humanitarian pity which had been insisted on by Belinsky. His manner reminds one at times of Dickens—minus Dickens's sense of humor. It was in his narrative, *The Village* (1846), and even more in *Anton Goremyka* ("Anton the Hapless," 1847), that Grigorovitch combined sentimental-humanitarian tendencies with some of the worst aspects of serfdom.[1] Both works contain social indictments. *The Village*, for example, depicts the fate of a peasant girl, Akulina, brought up among strangers and married to a man whose brutality brings her to an untimely death. Her little daughter, who is her only joy, has no other chance except to grow up in order to repeat the same experiences. Enthusiastically welcomed by Belinsky, this village story set a new fashion which was followed up by Grigorovitch's next narrative, *Anton Goremyka*, tackling the problem of the serf. The serf Anton is at the mercy of his squire's bailiff. Oppressed by him, he and his family fall into the depths

---

[1] The sinister side of serfdom is well illustrated by the fact that in spite of all the vigilance on the part of the authorities, there were 547 peasant disturbances between 1828 and 1854.

of misery. In addition, thieves rob him of his only horse. His mishaps accumulate, until he is compelled to join a band of robbers with whom he is caught and driven away to Siberia. The enormous success of this story was an indication that serfdom was not approved of generally, even by many serf owners. It was through Grigorovitch that the peasant made a triumphant entry into Russian realism.

A totally different author is Sergei I. Aksakov (1791-1859), the father of the two famous Slavophils, Ivan and Constantine. He discovered his talent rather late and mainly through his association with Gogol. Yet we look in vain in Aksakov for any traces of Gogol's ennui or morbid subjectivity. Even in literature he remains a landowner of the old patriarchal type—with the manor as the center of his world. And he describes his family estate near Ufa with such love and affection that he is often referred to as the Homer of the Russian manor. It was after his books about fishing and hunting in his native district—works in which he made animals delightfully alive—that he published, in 1852, his masterpiece, *A Family Chronicle*. Devoid of any plot, this work is a leisurely panorama of manor life under his grandfather's firm but just rule. Wavering between memoirs and fiction proper, the author not only turns the reconstructed facts into art, but presents all the characters and happenings with such refreshing homeliness as to make them memorable forever. Squires, officials, peasants, intriguing relatives, pass before our eyes as though they were our own acquaintances. The patriarchal grandfather himself, a mixture of gentlemanliness and autocratic pigheadedness, is particularly alive. Even the portrait of his insignificant son (the author's father) —a shy official, who after many adversities marries a town belle far superior to him—is convincing. The *Chronicle* ends with the birth of their first male descendant, that is, the

author himself, whose name is proudly added by the old
squire to the family tree.

Aksakov's *Recollections* and *The Childhood of Bagrov's
Grandson* are autobiographic. Devoid of affectation, they
are written, like the rest of his work, in that colloquial
Russian which tallies so well with the author's broad and
genial personality. Shunning any questions of the day, Aksakov transcends, as it were, the natural school by his very
naturalness. Even such a burning topic as serfdom is ignored
by him as a problem. There certainly was not much of a
repentant nobleman in him. Essentially honest and decent
in his patriarchal views, he did not worry about things which
he took for granted. But some of those things were viewed
by the younger generation from a different angle. And this
brings us to Turgenev.

III

It was in 1847 that Ivan S. Turgenev (1818-1883) published
in *The Contemporary* the first of those delightful jottings
which, five years later, came out in book form under the
title, *A Sportsman's Sketches.* The subject matter was mainly
the peasant, or rather the peasant and the squire in their
mutual contact. Yet unlike Grigorovitch, Turgenev refused
to sentimentalize the serf. He equally refused to flirt with
any direct purpose or propaganda. He just took up the
serf as a new human material with a mind and interests
of his own. This material he treated with such skill that his
intensified artistic truth to life perhaps contributed more
to the abolition of serfdom than any direct propaganda could
ever have done. Practically all the basic features of Turgenev
the artist (and he is one of the greatest artists in European
literature) come out in this early work. He preserves throughout a quiet tone the very strength of which is in its under-

statement. He does not analyze but only watches and always manages to catch the right touch, the right shade and tone, which he then organizes with an infallible tact. Here is a passage from his *A Hamlet of the Shchigry District*, showing his skillful arrangement of trifles:

"On parting from my host, I began walking through the rooms. Almost all the guests were utterly unknown to me: about twenty persons were already seated at the card-tables. Among these devotees of *préférence* were two warriors, with aristocratic but rather battered countenances, a few civilian officials, with tight cravats and drooping dyed mustaches, such as are only to be found in persons of resolute character and strict conservative opinions: these conservative persons picked up their cards with dignity, and, without turning their heads, glared sideways at everyone who approached; and five or six local petty officials, with fair round bellies, fat, moist little hands, and staid, immovable little legs. These worthies spoke in subdued voices, smiled benignly in all directions, held their cards close up to their very shirt fronts and when they trumped, did not flap their cards on the table, but, on the contrary, shed them with an undulatory motion on the green cloth, and packed their tricks together with a slight, unassuming, and decorous swish. The rest of the company were sitting on sofas, or hanging in groups about the doors or at the windows; one gentleman, no longer young, though of feminine appearance, stood in a corner, fidgeting, blushing, and twisting the seal of his watch over his stomach in his embarrassment, though no one was paying any attention to him; some others in swallow-tail coats and checked trousers were talking together with extraordinary ease and liveliness, turning their bald, greasy heads from side to side unconstrainedly as they talked; a young man of twenty, shortsighted and fair-haired, dressed from head to foot in black, obviously shy, smiled sarcastically." [1]

This gift of swift observation Turgenev blended with a melancholy lyrical vein, which found an outlet in his impressionist method of rendering the atmosphere. Before taking to prose, he had made his literary debut in poetry. But although his *Parasha* (1843) had been a success, he abandoned verse. On the other hand, his lyrical and musical talent made him write the most mellow prose in Russian fiction. An inveterate lover of beauty, he never indulges in poetic outbursts, nor does he take liberties with nature. Even in his most elaborate landscape pictures he remains discreet and too much of an artist to use glaring colors. He prefers the delicate method of the pastel. And instead of treating landscapes in the traditional manner, that is, as a mere background for his characters, he usually blends the two without forcing either of them. The same discretion is noticeable in his handling of the plot. An unrivaled storyteller, he yet avoids intricate and artificial entanglements. Even in his first sketches he acquitted himself as a realist in the best sense of this word. They are bits of life, taken at random and intensified by superb character drawing. Some of them—*The Singers*, for example—are among the best things he ever wrote. It was through its art, and art alone, that *A Sportsman's Sketches* helped to make the peasant and his fate all the more topical in Russian literature. This, however, served Turgenev's own purpose very well, since he himself was a bitter opponent of serfdom. He was a liberal Westerner, familiar with everything that was best in the Europe of his time. Turgenev spent a number of years abroad, partly perhaps for sentimental reasons. Having fallen in love (in 1845) with the French singer, Mme Viardot-Garcia, he followed

[1] Translated by Constance Garnett (Heinemann).

her all over Europe. The fact that she treated him only as a friend may have been one of the causes of his nostalgia, of his cult of frustration. The latter had, however, deeper reasons also. One of them was the dawning consciousness that the entire social layer he belonged to was already doomed by history, and therefore superfluous.

IV

Encouraged by the success of *A Sportsman's Sketches*, Turgenev wrote novels, stories, and even a few plays, most of which are now among the permanent treasures of European literature. The first of his novels, *Rudin*, appeared in 1855. It was followed by *A Nest of Gentlefolk* (1858), *On the Eve* (1859), *Fathers and Children* (1861), *Smoke* (1867), *The Torrents of Spring* (1871), and *Virgin Soil* (1876).

Rudin is above all an excellent portrait study. The title of one of Turgenev's previous stories was, significantly enough, *The Diary of a Superfluous Man*. In *Rudin* we meet a variation of the same type, shown from outside only, by a competent connoisseur of the gentry. Rudin, like most of Turgenev's superfluous men, is different, say, from Lermontov's Petchorin. Petchorin's destructiveness is in direct ratio to his frustrated energy. For this reason there is an element of tragedy in him. Rudin, on the other hand, is pathetic rather than tragic. If Petchorin is a blend of Childe Harold, Don Juan, and Hamlet, Turgenev's Rudin is only a Russian Hamlet whose will is undermined by reflection and by idleness to such an extent as to be too weak even for destruction. Out of joint with reality, he falls back upon his wishful thinking. He indulges in mental fireworks, in grandiose theories and projects, all of which are scattered at the very first contact with the actual tasks of life. In portraying Rudin, Turgenev reveals him to the reader bit by bit. His most contradictory features follow each other so unexpectedly that each time we meet him he seems a different person who has nothing in common with his previous characteristics. Yet gradually these contradictions blend, and there emerges a confused rather than complicated human being, whom we seem to have known for years. An inspiring talker and a sponger, an idealist in theory and a parasite in practice, a breaker of ladies' hearts and a coward when tested by the trust of a loving woman—such is Rudin. His good intentions are always undermined by his lack of will power, as they were with so many Russian intellectuals from among the gentry. Rudin himself is supposed to be a somewhat distorted portrait of Bakunin. Another character—Pokorsky— is often identified with Belinsky, while Natasha bears certain features of Pushkin's Tatyana. The background is that of the landed gentry of the 'thirties. Another broader and more intimate picture of the country gentry was given by Turgenev in *A Nest of Gentlefolk*.

The only defect of this novel is that it is almost too perfect in its neatness and composition. In contrast to the bulk of Russian authors, Turgenev was meticulous about the artistic finish of his writings. Here, at any rate, the balance between antithetic characters is worked out with mathematical precision, while the narrative itself is all the more impressive because of its quiet, even static, manner. The plot is simple enough. Lavretsky, whose dissolute wife lives abroad, falls in love with Liza—another literary descendant of Tatyana. The growth of their mutual love is rendered by Turgenev's usual method of suggestive understatement. Their reticence is broken only on Lavretsky's reading the news of his wife's death on the Riviera. Happy and as if reborn, they both prepare for their wedding, when one day Lavretsky's wife suddenly turns up—her death having been a false rumor. After such frustration, the two lovers submit to their fate.

Years later they see each other again in Liza's convent, but only for a moment and without speaking to each other: a scene which is saved from melodrama only by Turgenev's consummate art. The gentry atmosphere of the 'forties, the manor and some of its habitués—whether superfluous seekers like Lavretsky, or brilliantly shallow dilettantes like Panshin—are presented to us with a skill which often makes them more concrete, more real than the people we meet in life. And the elegiac atmosphere, so typical of Turgenev, hovers over the novel with all its elusive moods and shades.

V

A "nest of gentlefolk" is evoked once more by Turgenev in his best novel, *Fathers and Children*. This time the action takes place about two decades later. Its theme is the clash between the overgentlemanly generation of the 'forties and the turbulent youths of the 'sixties. The 'sixties were a decade of the commoners who began to assert themselves not only in culture, but in public life as a whole. Bazarov, the chief character of *Fathers and Children*, is such a type. And as though with his tongue in his cheek, Turgenev suddenly plunges him into the daily routine of a manor, full of genteel but soporific respectability, where he is likely to play the part of a bull in a china shop. Thus we witness not only two different generations, but also two different social worlds, facing each other with all their conscious and subconscious hostility. Bazarov is moreover a nihilist,[1] a negator of all traditions and values; or at least of those values which were so dear to the Russian gentry class. But as Pisarev pointed out, the word "nihilist" was inaccurate in this case. For Bazarov wanted to debunk and to destroy

[1] This word was not coined by Turgenev as some people think, but it was he who introduced it into literature.

not for the sake of mere destruction, but in order to clear the ground for a new order of things; for a new and better society than the one he saw in the Russia of his days.

At a closer glance one can detect, however, even in Bazarov a kind of inverted Rudin. He, too, is uprooted, but like a man without any traditions. The very arrogance and the studied lack of manners he assumes before his social betters is a proof of his rankling inferiority complex. Similarly, Bazarov's rude frankness and cynical pose are a proof of his own suppressed sentiment. Hence his insistence on mere logic and reason, on practical work, and on natural science.[1] Quite a remarkable feature of this novel is also the subtlety with which Turgenev points out the instinctive difference between Bazarov and his genteel friend Arkady Kirsanov, who is doomed to remain a tame product of the gentry no matter how hard he tries to be as much up-to-date as Bazarov himself. And Turgenev's impartiality is amazing. Rather puzzled by this new type or new force, he himself seems to waver all the time between dislike and hidden admiration. Yet the fact that the novel was published in Katkov's antiradical monthly, *The Russian Messenger* (*Russky Vestnik*), proves that Turgenev's personal sympathies were hardly on the side of Bazarov. The author was too much a descendant of the 'forties with all their abstract idealism to be able to sponsor wholeheartedly the materialistic gospel of the younger generation. At the same time he could not help watching it as an artist, anxious to depict also that phase of Russian life as objectively as possible. And in this he succeeded.

Turgenev the portrait painter is here at his best. Particularly impressive are some of his minor characters: Bazarov's

---

[1] This was why Pisarev welcomed Bazarov and defended him (against an attack in *The Contemporary*) with such verve as to cause the first conspicuous cleavage among the radical intellectuals.

old parents, for example. And Bazarov himself is the only strong man Turgenev ever depicted convincingly. This plebeian devotee of science, of Büchner's *Kraft und Stoff*, is with all his utilitarian dogmatism a simplified rather than simple character. He is full of hidden contradictions and does not hesitate to commit violence upon his real nature for the sake of his reasoned out principles. Yet he has at least two advantages over his gentlemanly antagonists: his vitality and his lack of mental, social, or any other taboos. Like Turgenev himself, we are both fascinated and repelled by him. But admiration takes the upper hand towards the end, when we watch Bazarov's agony in one of the most powerfully understated death scenes in literature.

VI

The social-political note of *Fathers and Children* is organically blended with its artistic side. This cannot be said, however, to the same extent of Turgenev's last two novels, *Smoke* and *Virgin Soil*. In both of them he scrutinizes contemporary life with the eyes of a balanced liberal of the 'forties. In *Smoke* he even passes judgment (with plenty of caustic remarks) upon the new trends and factions. His reference to the fashionable Russians abroad is spiteful: they all seem to him unreal as smoke. The novel is crammed with topical allusions and discussions which do not merge sufficiently with the delicate love intrigue between the two chief characters, Irene and Litvinov. The end is, once more, inconclusive and elegiac. On the other hand, Turgenev has reached here the high-water mark as a painter of the feminine mind, of the intricate and elusive nuances of love.

A certain discrepancy between the artistic and the social-political elements is noticeable also in *Virgin Soil*, which deals with the populist movement of the 'seventies. In spite of the reproaches hurled at him that, being out of touch with the younger generation, he was hardly entitled to judge it, Turgenev saw clearly what was amiss with the "going to the people" on the part of the revolutionaries. This novel reflects the tragedy of misunderstanding between the radical intelligentsia and the people: in so far as the masses, whom the intellectuals wanted to help, were either apathetic or diffident. The gap between the two strata had made them alien to each other. What Turgenev wanted to point out was not only the frustration of the movement, but also its causes. And once again he tried to give us the portrait of a strong character (a kind of Bazarov of the 'seventies) in Solomin. This time he failed. As hard-working and devoted to his task as Bazarov, Solomin is yet too wooden to be really alive. The equally active but warmhearted Marianna is, however, alive and convincing. So is the superfluous revolutionary Hamlet, Nezhdanov, whose tragedy was probably typical of many a young populist. Several episodic characters are also well drawn.

Of the remaining two novels *The Torrents of Spring* is a long short story rather than a novel. Its pace is quick and vivid. Turgenev's usual dilemma—love between a vacillating weakling and a generous, self-reliant woman—is worked out without a flaw. The hero is enticed away from the girl he loves by her opposite: the rapacious but fascinating female whom Turgenev also delights in portraying—as though taking revenge upon someone. Both women are very alive, especially if compared with Elena, the heroine of his earlier novel, *On the Eve*. Elena—another Tatyana type—is frankly overdone, whereas the strong man Insarov is as wooden as Solomin in *Virgin Soil*. Yet even with occasional defects such as these, Turgenev remains a superb narrator.

How superb he really was can be gathered from his

shorter and longer stories, which are among the finest in the world literature. As most of them are retrospective and therefore told rather than "written," he raised the colloquial style and language into high art. His *First Love*, *Andrey Kolosov*, *Asya*, *The Backwater*, *A King Lear of the Steppes*, and many others are familiar to all lovers of fine reading. And here, too, he is at his best when dealing with pathetic weaklings, with love, or else with wistful elegiac moods and themes. He becomes less convincing, however, as soon as he tackles subjects which are beyond his emotional and visual range. His few stories on occult and mysterious themes, such as *Clara Militch*, *A Dream*, leave one cold.

VII

As for Turgenev's ventures in playwriting, his comedy, *A Month in the Country*, should be mentioned, partly on account of its recent popularity abroad, and partly because its essential features hardly differ from those we find in his novels and stories. Here, too, we see a "nest of gentlefolk": this time disturbed not by a nihilist, but by a young student whose spontaneity acts like a tonic. The atmosphere is skillfully suggested, and the frustration at the end of the play is amusing enough to make even the author smile. Turgenev's few shorter plays and scenes are dramatized anecdotes or else amusing pictures of manners. All said and done, the distinctive characteristics of his work as a whole are unusual aesthetic sensibility and unrivaled observation—especially of human character; a discreet impressionist method; a carefully worked out structure; a sense of measure; and a musical flow of language, full of minor notes, which imbue his prose with an autumnal charm and magic. In the art of evoking atmosphere he is equaled only by Chekhov.

Although a champion of progress and Westernism, Turgenev the artist lived essentially in the past of his own gentry class. He was so steeped in the old nests of gentlefolk as to be unable to adapt himself wholeheartedly to any other form of life, even when he approved of it in theory. With his mind on the present and with his instincts in the past, he belonged neither to one nor the other. Hence his nostalgia of a superfluous man, complicated by his love for Mme Viardot-Garcia. Disappointed with love and with life, grieved also by the unfriendly reception of some of his works, Turgenev was glad to spend his later years outside Russia. The pessimism of his old age is reflected in his *Senilia*—a collection of short poems in prose, written before his death. Yet while staying abroad, especially in France, he became a vital link between Russia and the West. In addition to counting among his frends such men as Flaubert, Daudet, Renan, and the brothers Goncourt, he was the first Russian author to be translated and admired all over Europe. He paved the way for the triumph of Russian literature as a European power.

CHAPTER VI

Goncharov

ALMOST SIMULTANEOUSLY with Turgenev's first *Sportsman's Sketches*, Ivan A. Goncharov made a hit with his *A Common Story*. This novel appeared in *The Contemporary* in 1847 and took the public by storm. Belinsky was so impressed by its realistic technique that he prophesied a great future for its author. But it took more than ten years before Goncharov published, in *The Fatherland's Annals*, his masterpiece *Oblomov* (1859), which some eleven years later was followed by his third and last novel, *The Precipice* (*Obryv*). His writings include also a substantial volume under the title, *The Frigate Pallas*—a record of his journey round the world on a Russian warship.

Goncharov is perhaps the most pedestrian author in Russian literature. Yet he raised his very pedestrianism to the level of genius. By his origin, he belonged to both the gentry and the well-to-do merchant class, and his life was (but for his journey round the world) one of uneventful civil service. There is a good deal of the cold and shrewd official even in his writings, which are devoid of wings, of dizzy ideas and visions. On the other hand, this very defect made him a remarkable observer of ordinary existence.

Following Gogol the "realist," and emulating the quiet naturalness of Pushkin, Goncharov became one of the masters of *Kleinmalerei*, of small external details. His method is accumulation rather than elimination: accumulation of trifles, which he organizes in such a manner as to make them significant. Another fact which emerges from his three novels is that they reflect the early stages of transition from the old system of landowners and serfs to the new bourgeois Russia of capitalists and businessmen. At the same time they are, with all their surface objectivity, personal documents—in so far as they indicate Goncharov's own attitude to such a transition. Thematically, these novels, too, deal with the conflict between fathers and children; between the inert, idyllically drowsy gentry period on the one hand, and the encroaching capitalist era with its spirit of enterprise on the other. Thus Alexander Aduyev, the hero of *An Ordinary Story*, is a typical product of the romantic gentry mentality of the early 'forties. He decides, however, to leave his soporific nest of gentlefolk and start a new life in Petersburg. On arriving in the capital, he is taken in hand by his experienced uncle Peter Aduyev, who belongs entirely to the new era. Cold, even callous, he keeps an eye on success (both commercial and social) and sacrifices his life to mere opportunism. His soft-hearted nephew from the provinces finds it difficult to adapt himself to such a mode of existence. After years of vain struggle, he returns to his manor, where he finds a haven of peace. But having tasted of life in the capital, he soon feels bored and superfluous in the provinces. So he leaves for Petersburg once more, this time determined to succeed. With the help of his uncle he actually makes good. The naïve idealist becomes transformed into a wealthy pillar of society, outstripping in opportunism even his own uncle.

The quiet narrative is poor in incident but rich in character drawing. It is also charged with unobtrusive, almost unconscious irony between the lines. Goncharov himself seems to be quite willing to admire a successful businessman, so different from the futile Russian dreamers. Yet, as though against his own intentions, he shows how such a man becomes dehumanized by success. No wonder that Peter Aduyev's sensitive wife pines away under the weight of her husband's prosperity. And the height of irony: the uncle begins to see the truth behind his practical philosophy of life at the very moment when his converted nephew is thrilled by his own success of the same Philistine brand. The novel depicts a blind alley of which Goncharov himself was perhaps only half aware. However much his own will may have been turned towards the new bourgeois era, his subconscious sympathies were still with the gentry period; or at least with what he regarded as worthy and beautiful in it.

II

This duality came out, rather unexpectedly, even in his greatest work, *Oblomov*. Here Goncharov took up the same dilemma as in *An Old Story*, but from a different angle. He deepened the contrast between Tentetnikov and Kostanzhoglo (the second half of *Dead Souls*) into a unique realistic symbol. The vegetative existence of Gogol's *Old-world Landowners* becomes in this novel a pleasant dope, undermining the will power of the new Rudins. How sympathetically Goncharov describes the hero's native place in *Oblomov's Dream*—a section which was printed about ten years before the novel itself!

"The sky there seems to come nearer to the earth, not in order to fling sharper arrows at it, but to hug it more warmly and lovingly; it hangs as low overhead as the trusty roof of the parental home, to preserve, as it were, the chosen place from all calamities. The sun there shines warmly and brightly for about six months in the year and then withdraws gradually, as though reluctantly turning back, as it were, to have another look or two at the place it loves and to give it a warm, clear day amidst the autumn rain.

"The hills seem to be mere models of those terrible mountains far away that frighten one's imagination. They rise in gentle slopes, pleasant to slide down on one's back in play, or to sit on, dreamily watching the sunset.

"The river runs cheerfully, sporting and playing; now it spreads into a wide pond, now flows on in a vapid stream, and hardly moves along the pebbles, sending out to all sides lively brooks, the ripple of which makes one delightfully drowsy.

"The whole place, for ten or fifteen miles around, is a series of picturesque, bright, and smiling landscapes. The sandy, sloping banks of the clear river, the small bushes that come down from the hill to the water, the curving ravine with a brook running through it, the birch copse— all seem to have been fitted together on purpose and drawn with a masterly hand.

"A heart worn out by troubles or wholly unfamiliar with them longs to hide in this secluded spot and live there happily, unnoticed by all. Everything there promises a calm, long life till the hair turns from white to yellow, and death comes unnoticed like sleep." [1]

It is a landowner's Arcadia. The more so, because under the system of serfdom all the work is done by slaves. The owner's part is only pleasure, demanding no effort of thought or will, "until death comes unnoticed like sleep." But somebody has to pay in the end for generations of such drowsy parasitic existence. Ilya Ilyitch Oblomov is precisely that victim, whose inherited indolence becomes his fate, his undoing. Not that he is a bad fellow. Far from it! The author

[1] All passages are quoted from Natalie Duddington's translation in *Everyman's Library*.

introduces him as "a man of thirty-two or three, of medium height and pleasant appearance, whose complexion was neither rosy nor dark, nor pale, but indefinite, or perhaps it seemed so because there was a certain slackness about the muscles of his face, unusual at his age; this may have been due to lack of fresh air or exercise, or to some other reason. The smooth and excessively white skin of his neck, his small soft hands and plump shoulders, suggested a certain physical effeminacy. His movements were restrained and gentle; there was a certain lazy gracefulness about them even if he were alarmed. If his mind was troubled, his eyes were clouded, his forehead wrinkled, and an interplay of hesitation, sadness, and fear was reflected in his face; but the disturbance seldom took the form of a definite idea and still more seldom reached the point of a decision. It merely found expression in a sigh and died down in apathy and drowsiness."

Let us now see how discreetly Goncharov proceeds from this physical portraiture to the inner characteristics of his hero, especially to one of them—his indecision. The novel starts with a most unusual occurrence: Oblomov woke up early—about eight o'clock, and was rather perturbed.

"He was obviously suffering from an inward conflict and his intellect had not yet come to his aid. The fact was that the evening before Oblomov had received a disagreeable letter from the bailiff of his estate. It was no joke! One had to think of taking some measures. In justice to Ilya Ilyitch it must be said that, after receiving the bailiff's first unpleasant letter several years before, he had begun to think of various changes and improvements in the management of his estate. He proposed introducing fresh economic, administrative, and other measures. But the plan was not yet thoroughly thought out, and the bailiff's unpleasant letters came every year inciting him to action and disturbing his peace of mind. Oblomov knew it was necessary to do something decisive.

"As soon as he woke, he made up his mind to get up and wash, and, after drinking tea, to think matters over, taking various things into consideration and writing them down, and altogether to go into the subject thoroughly. He lay for half an hour tormented by his decision; but afterwards he reflected that he would have time to think after breakfast, which he could have in bed as usual, especially since one can think just as well lying down.

"This was what he did. After his morning tea he sat up and very nearly got out of bed; looking at his slippers, he began lowering one foot down towards them, but at once drew it back again.

"It struck half-past nine."

III

A few more touches of this kind, and before our eyes emerges an incurable Russian Hamlet—incurable in spite of his good will and resolutions. Herein lies the cause of his doom. The primary cause goes, of course, farther back: to his native Oblomovka and its lotus-land existence which had cast a spell over its owners. True enough, there was a time when young Oblomov had actually done all he could to rid himself of that spell. He, too, had left the old-world idyl behind and exchanged Oblomovka for Petersburg. Yet unlike the young Aduyev in the previous novel, he had no energy left to turn such a step to his advantage. After an attempt at a career in Petersburg, he relapsed into his sloth and refused to move on with life. Blind to any tasks and opportunities, he became a victim of stagnation, bequeathed by the old Russia. Oblomov is thus a symbol not only of the superfluous man, but also of the doomed gentry class as a whole.

The novel, which is a great character study, moves on

at a slow pace and is crammed with trifles—all of them to the point. It would be difficult to find a more static work. But there is a charm, an atmosphere about it which is likely to impress a reader more than any artificial plots for their own sake. Besides, all the small happenings and trifles seem to evolve out of Oblomov's human weakness so obviously, so naturally, even so humorously at times, that a plot becomes unnecessary. Another striking feature is the author's carefully disguised self-observation. Goncharov's realism, like the realism of Gogol, is considerably more subjective than would appear on the surface. Most ingenious, however, is the manner in which Oblomov becomes part and parcel of his own surroundings, of the accessories of his daily life—such as his dressing gown, his bed, his slippers. Entirely at the mercy of circumstances, he no longer lives but only vegetates. And even when realizing his own position, he never goes beyond theoretical resolutions, dreams, daydreams, and arguments with his inseparable old servant Zakhar, who is sunk knee-deep in the same morass as his master. Neither the love of the generous and strong Olga (a cross of Turgenev's heroines and Pushkin's Tatyana), nor the admonitions of his efficient half-German friend, Stolz, are of any avail. Moreover, he shrinks from Olga as soon as he discovers that he cannot live up to her expectations. He prefers to forfeit her love rather than free himself from his own sloth. Unable to ward off the blows of life, Oblomov finds at last a substitute for the parasitic manor life in the flat of his kind-hearted suburban landlady, whose lover he becomes. In her motherly care he goes on drifting, until death saves him from impending troubles.

This novel is an indirect indictment of that system of serfdom which made such products possible. The atmosphere of doom, achieved by the accumulation of *petits faits,* reaches in the last chapters an almost unbearable tragic intensity, although Oblomov himself is much too passive to be really tragic. He is pathetic instead. The more so because we feel that in spite of all his failings, he is made of essentially fine and noble material. This comes out rather subtly, even if we compare him with his own antithesis: his active, honest, and always reliable friend Stolz. Like Aduyev senior in *An Ordinary Story*, Stolz represents the new capitalist era —the era of the enterprising bourgeoisie, which began to thrive at the expense of the gentry. Stolz is shown to us in a more favorable light than Aduyev. Yet in spite of his civic and private virtues, we get much fonder of the weakling Oblomov. Oblomov is dearer also to Olga—even after she has become Stolz's wife, as the author points out with great psychological tact. It is true that Stolz is not quite convincing. On the other hand, we must bear in mind that with all his conscious rejection of Oblomov, Goncharov's real sympathies still remain with the latter. And how well he points out the moral gulf between Oblomov and the lower middle-class schemers, anxious to exploit and bleed him white!

Goncharov's prose is not on the same high level as the prose of Turgenev or Tolstoy. But in this novel he makes up for it by his tone and his peculiar sense of humor. This consists not so much in what he says about people and things as in his manner of approaching and seeing them. Unique, too, is the way he turns Oblomov into a symbol not only of a doomed class, but of all that is (or was) slothful yet childlike and sometimes charmingly helpless in the Russian character as a whole. Oblomov and "oblomovism" became nicknames which alas, had to be frequently used in the prerevolutionary Russia![1]

---

[1] The critic who contributed most to the popularity of Goncharov's masterpiece was Dobrolyubov—by his essay, "What is Oblomovism?"

IV

Goncharov's third novel, *The Precipice*, was conceived as early as 1849 during the author's stay in his native Simbirsk, on the Volga, but was completed only in 1869, when it appeared in *The European Messenger*. Here, too, we see the conflict between two generations, between fathers and children. So the novel is full of open or hidden controversy which arose mainly out of Goncharov's fears of the radical Russia of the 'sixties. And the author (a man of the 'forties) asserted himself, this time, with vehemence against practically everything the new generation stood for. In fact, he was at pains to show in glowing colors the passing Russia of the old-world landowners—that very Russia which he had deliberately set out to discredit in his two previous novels. His polemical animosity, on the other hand, often developed at the expense of his artistic sense—a defect which makes *The Precipice* the most uneven of his works.

Raisky, the chief hero of the novel, is another variety of the superfluous man. This talented and vacillating dilettante returns, as did Goncharov himself, after many years in Petersburg, to his native "nest of gentlefolk" on the Volga. He is fascinated by the good patriarchal aspects of manor life, and even more by its living symbol: his old-fashioned great aunt or "granny," as everybody calls her. He falls in love consecutively with his pretty cousins Marfinka and Vera. The first is a harmonious product of the old order, whereas Vera represents the new woman. Proud, reticent, and exasperatingly capricious, she falls under the influence of the nihilist Volokhov—probably a deliberate caricature of Turgenev's Bazarov. The mysteriousness of Vera, the jealousies of Raisky, the hollowness of Volokhov's revolutionary ideas come to a head after Vera's surrender to him.

But after her fall, Vera collapses and—quite unexpectedly—refuses to have anything more to do with her seducer, or even to see him. Her agony, pain, and tedium nearly finish her. She begins to regain inner peace only through a return to the old-world views of the granny and Marfinka. The superfluous Raisky leaves for Petersburg. Vera's shattered life finds a hope in the love of her suitor Tushin—another Stolz, but this time thoroughly Russian both in his simplicity and in the modesty of his strength.

Artistically, *The Precipice* is below Goncharov's previous novels. It is bulky, rambling, and deficient in construction. Certain facts are psychologically too little motivated: Vera's love for Volokhov, for instance, or her behavior after her surrender. But Goncharov compensates us by his portraits of women. The granny in particular is magnificent. She dominates the scene as a lovable figure of the same "dear old Russia" or Oblomovka which Goncharov had previously condemned. Another well-drawn character is Marfinka, who is truly happy because she never deviates from her granny's views and values of life. Raisky, on the other hand, lacks the clearness of Oblomov or Aduyev, especially towards the end, when his figure becomes rather blurred. The least satisfactory character, however, is the nihilist Volokhov. Apart from being a parody of Bazarov, he obviously served as a scapegoat for everything Goncharov himself feared and disliked in the younger up-to-date radicals. According to him, Volokhov "degraded man to a mere physical organism and rejected all that was not animal-like in him. The mere process of life was proclaimed by him as the goal of life. But while denying humanity in human beings who have a mind and are entitled to immortality, he yet preached a kind of new truth, new frankness, and a new will to a better life, without being in the least aware that all this becomes superfluous if our life is something casual and if human beings are degraded to a swarm of midgets in hot weather: mixing, fidgeting about, procreating, basking in the sun, and vanishing in a senseless process of existence only in order to make room for another swarm of the same kind."

Goncharov was more than biased when insisting that this new force (the radicals of the 'sixties) in Russian life was merely destructive without being able to bring forth any compensation for ideas and things destroyed. Nor was he profound enough to probe into the metaphysical depths of nihilism at its worst—a task which was done with frightening insight by Dostoevsky in *The Possessed*. Little wonder, then, that *The Precipice* was fiercely attacked also on account of its ideological weakness. Goncharov's reputation survived the onslaughts because of his other two novels, or rather because of *Oblomov*, which is among the masterpieces of world literature.

v

Goncharov's pedestrian nature comes out best in his *The Frigate Pallas* (1856)—a description of his journey to Japan and the Far East. It is pleasantly uneventful, packed with small observations and descriptions, but its most valuable passages are those about himself and his life. One can almost say that Goncharov excites one's mind precisely by being so utterly unexciting. Competent at describing things seen and experienced, he remained, however, a mediocre thinker.

This brings us incidentally once more to the problem of the objectivity of his writings. For a long time Goncharov was regarded as one of the most detached and objective of Russian realists. But his aloofness from the reader should not be mistaken for detachment. There are autobiographic elements in the young Aduyev, in Raisky, and even more in Oblomov. Besides, he himself has written an author's confession to this effect. Like Gogol, he felt the need to exteriorize some of his own defects in order to see them better and perhaps to resist them. The fact that most of Goncharov's writings were mainly a process of sublimation was proved by his inability to write to order. Disregarding the publishers and the public, he only suited himself. He created when inwardly impelled to do so. Hence the authenticity of his style, so remarkably fitting his pedestrian vision of life. Whatever faults may be found with the latter, Goncharov the portraitist and the painter in words will always occupy one of the foremost places in Russian fiction.

CHAPTER VII

Critical Realism

(PISEMSKY AND SALTYKOV-SHCHEDRINE)

THE FIRST landmark of modern Russia was the war of 1812; the second, the Crimean campaign. The five years preceding it (1848-1853) were perhaps the worst period of the political "barracks régime." The more so because the revolutionary outburst on the Continent, in 1848, had ended in failure. The death of Nicholas I during the Crimean campaign and the defeat of the Russian army made a profound impression on public opinion. The latter was quick to realize that the fiasco in the Crimea was due to the Russian régime rather than to the nation as a whole. The years between the fall of Sebastopol in 1855 and the abolition of serfdom in 1861 were tense with expectation. And those were the years during which Herzen's periodical, *The Bell*, printed in London, had an enormous circulation. Finally, the abolition of serfdom, carried out by Alexander II, marked a new chapter not only in the economic, but also in the social-political life of Russia. For the first time there was a relaxation of censorship. The battle of various trends and ideas assumed a lively, even a fierce character. As far as the intelligentsia was concerned, the class barriers between the gentry and the commoners were now removed within its ranks. On the other hand, numerous impoverished noblemen were compelled by the new economic conditions to mix with the moneyed bourgeoisie in business and industry, or even to merge with it. All sorts of latent energies awoke. The younger generation looked forward to a better future.

These hopes were soon shattered. But the energies, once awakened, could no longer be stemmed. The pressure from above was answered by the formation of secret societies among the radical youths, beginning with the already mentioned "Land and Freedom" group, founded in 1862. A proclamation "To the Young Russia," issued by one such group in the early 'sixties, even predicted that Russia would be the first country to go socialist, and its program was curiously similar to the one carried out by the recent revolution. The amount of practical achievements during that decade was imposing. Naturally, it was taken almost for granted that literature, too, should assume a practical character. There was a decline in poetry whose very language was "de-poetized" by Nekrasov. There was a tendency, especially on the part of the commoners, to make prose as direct and straightforward as possible. And while rejecting any art-for-art's-sake attitude, the younger readers expected, or even demanded, from the authors some guidance in that bewildering maze of views, ideas, and polemics. Hence literature not only reflected life, but did its best to be its mentor, or at least its critic. This explains why even such a mediocre novel as Chernyshevsky's *What Is to Be Done?* became one of the most widely read books of the period.

Gogol's and Belinsky's attitude towards literature as a judge and critic of life thus persisted and kept on growing. There were the evil consequences of the serfdom era which had to be exposed. There were corrupt officials, land speculators, industrial exploiters, ruined landlords, whose doings called for a realism saturated with gall and venom—for a critical realism, in short. The differentiation in economic life demanded a differentiation in literature. There was a rapid increase in literary themes whose compass now became larger and larger. The principal part was still played by the manor and gentry tradition—a tradition which reached its height in Turgenev, Goncharov, and Tolstoy. A contrast to the manor school with its leisurely pace was provided by Dostoevsky, who took up the big city with its hectic tempo, its iniquities and enervating atmosphere. A third group of writers concentrated on the peasant and his problems— mainly from a populist standpoint. Meanwhile, Russian industrialism had sufficiently advanced to give rise to the proletarian novel in its early phases. There was plenty of material for the younger authors to draw upon. But whereas such names as Turgenev, Tolstoy, and Dostoevsky have become household words all the world over, other outstanding writers of that time are hardly known outside Russia. These include above all Alexey F. Pisemsky and M. E. Saltykov-Shchedrine, the two chief representatives of what might be called critical realism.

II

Pisemsky (1820-1881) was not outstanding as a stylist, but he combined a sharp eye with a sober mind, inaccessible either to sentimentality or to illusions. So he depicted the world he saw with the rancor of an outraged idealist who is no longer able to believe in ideals. His treatment of the gentry in particular is ferocious. In his first novel, *Boyarshchina*, he lays bare the fate of a sensitive but unhappily married woman, crushed by the atmosphere of the vile provincial gentry. The latter is exposed by him with an incredible condensation of all that is repellent in man and life. Pisemsky is no less hard on the new businesslike schemers. One of his narratives, *An Old Man's Sin,* shows the tragedy of an honest elderly official who falls in love and makes use of state money in order to help the woman he adores. But instead of returning the money in time as promised, the woman squanders it with her gigolo and then shamelessly makes the official her scapegoat. We mention this story as a proof that Pisemsky's realism derived quite a few of its ingredients from Gogol. The hapless official is a descendant of Gogol's Poprishschin (*Memoirs of a Madman*) and Akaky (*The Greatcoat*). The landowners he visits, during his attempts to borrow money, make one think of those in *Dead Souls*. Also Pisemsky's general attitude towards life and its vulgarity is akin to Gogol's. So is his cruel laughter, and even his capacity for comic situations. Yet unlike many Russian authors, Pisemsky never neglects the plot. On the contrary, he is fond of condensing it, of making it involved, even too involved at times, although he uses it mainly as a framework for what he regards as truth of life. And he spares no one except perhaps the peasant. As a descendant of impoverished gentry, Pisemsky knew and loved the peasant, but he was not blind to his failings. Apart from one of the best dramas of village life, *A Bitter Lot*, he wrote a number of narratives about the Russian moujik. And while refusing either to idealize or to approach him with populist blinkers, he still saw in him potentially fine and healthy material: infinitely superior to the gentry or to the corrupt bureaucracy, both of whom he heartily despised.

This scorn came out with unusual vigor in his *A Thousand Souls* (1858), which was proclaimed by Pisarev the best novel of that period. The novel still remains a masterpiece as a picture of manners, as a portrait gallery, and as a virulent criticism of life. Its central figure, Kalinovitch, is a bureaucratic Chichikov in quest of wealth and power. Having nothing to start with except his poverty, he becomes a "climber," ready to sacrifice everything to success, including the woman he loves. He actually marries a semicripple merely for the sake of money [1] and connections. Full of resources and enterprise, he soon reaches the top rungs of the bureaucratic ladder. But once he has succeeded, he only becomes aware of the futility of success for its own sake. As though ashamed of himself, he now tries to make up by his unflinching honesty in civil service. But this time it is his integrity which bars the way to his further advancement in a system corrupt to the core. Disgusted with the bureaucratic morass and with life as a whole, he finally gives up his career and returns to his old love, Nastya, whose strong personality is a sufficient compensation for all external losses.

In addition to a number of motives brought together in this novel, the one of unhappy marriage crops up, as it does in many of his other works, to begin with *Boyarshchina,* or *A Muff (Tufyak)* whose hero is a kind of Oblomov, but without a tinge of Oblomov's nobility. After *A Thousand Souls* Pisemsky's creative *élan* began to decline. His next long work, *The Stormy Sea* (1863), is brutal rather than strong. This scathing work about Russia before and immediately after the liberation of the serfs is one long indictment. Most of its characters hardly transcend the level of zoology. Because of its attacks on the radicals, the novel provoked much controversy and bitter criticism. From among Pisemsky's numerous works two further novels are notable: *The People of the Forties,* and *In the Whirlpool.* The first is an onslaught on the new acquisitive age (with valuable autobiographic touches), while the second is an apology for feminism—at the beginning of the 'seventies. His writings of the last period are of minor importance.

[1] The title, *A Thousand Souls,* means a thousand serfs.

III

As realistic as Pisemsky but much more topical was Michael E. Saltykov-Shchedrine (1826-1889). His external life was uneventful. For a number of years he was a civil servant in the provinces until, in 1868, he became one of the three editors of *The Fatherland's Annals*, acquired by the poet Nekrasov from its former proprietor Krayevsky. Shchedrine's first and rather weak story, *Contradictions*, had appeared in the same monthly as early as 1847. In the 'fifties he made a name among the intellectuals by his satirical sketches of provincial life, printed in Katkov's *Russian Messenger*, which, in those days, was not yet a reactionary periodical. At the beginning of the 'sixties he was associated for a while with *The Contemporary*. His greatest output coincided, however, with the years of his editorial functions in *The Fatherland's Annals* during the 'seventies and early 'eighties. It was in those years that he wrote his chief works, for the most part biting parodies and satires: *History of a Town, Pompadours Big and Small, The Gentlemen from Tashkent, A Contemporary Idyl, Poshekhonian Antiquity,* and above all his novel, *The Golovlyov Family* (1872-1876), which stands somewhat apart from Shchedrine's other writings.

The Golovlyov Family is one of the gloomiest and most powerful novels in Russian literature. As the title indicates, it is a family chronicle, but in a purely negative sense. Shchedrine took up one of those gentry families which, "having no work, no connection with public life, and no political importance, were at one time sheltered by serfdom, but now with nothing to shelter them, are spending the remainder of their lives in their tumbledown country houses." It is not the economic but the moral decay, the inner disintegration, of such a family the author is concerned with. And he shows it in all its nakedness.

The scene of action is the country manor of the Golovlyovs immediately before and after the abolition of serfdom. The central figure of the first part is the aged matron, Arina Petrovna—still a serf owner in all her habits. Greedy, callous, and bossy, she possesses two things no other member of the family can boast of—will and driving force. Unable to exercise them on the serfs who are now free, she practices them upon the members of her own family, all of whom she actually crushes. When her eldest son Stepan came back from Moscow—bankrupt and a complete failure, Arina Petrovna "met him sternly and solemnly, measured him from head to foot with an icy stare, but did not indulge in any useless reproaches. She did not admit him into the house but saw him on the backdoor steps and gave orders that the young master should be taken by the other entrance to see his father. The old man, white like a corpse, and wearing a nightcap, lay dozing on his bed covered with a white quilt. He woke up when Stepan Vladimiritch came in, and broke into idiotic laughter: 'Aha, my boy, you've been caught in the old hag's clutches!' he called out when his son kissed his hand. Then he crowed like a cock, laughed again, and repeated several times: 'She'll eat you up! She'll eat you up!'

" 'She will,' Stepan Vladimiritch repeated in his mind.

"His forebodings came true. He had a room assigned to him where the estate office was. They brought him there some underclothes of homespun linen and his father's old dressing gown, which he put on straightway. The doors of the sepulchral vault opened, let him in—and slammed to." [1]

This scene is typical of Arina's autocratic rule. Later, however, her power was cunningly usurped by her favorite off-

[1] Translated by Natalie Duddington (*Everyman's Library*).

spring Porphiry, nicknamed Iudushka (Little Judas). In shaping this character, Shchedrine reached the high-water mark of portraiture even in Russian literature. Iudushka is the prototype of an unctuous and pious scoundrel who cannot help being a liar and a schemer, because he is innocently hypocritical. The author himself puts us on the right track when saying that Iudushka was not hypocritical "in the same sense as Tartuffe or any modern French bourgeois who goes off into flights of eloquence on the subject of social morality. No, he was a hypocrite of a purely Russian sort, that is, simply a man devoid of all moral standards, knowing no truth other than the copy-book precepts. He was pettifogging, deceitful, loquacious, boundlessly ignorant, and afraid of the devil. All these qualities are merely negative and can supply no stable material for real hypocrisy. . . . We Russians," the author continues to elucidate, "have no strongly biased system of education. We are not drilled, we are not trained to be champions and propagandists of this or that set of moral principles, but are simply allowed to grow as nettles grow by a fence. This is why there are very few hypocrites among us and very many liars, bigots, and babblers. We have no need to be hypocritical for the sake of any fundamental social principle and do not take shelter under any of them. We exist quite freely, i.e. we vegetate, babble, and lie spontaneously, without any principles."

Iudushka is a spontaneous liar, bigot, and babbler of this kind. And it is he who wields power on the estate, after his "dear friend mamma" has been deprived of it and even compelled to take refuge in the house belonging to her granddaughters (Iudushka's nieces). But Arina without a whip in her hands feels like a fish out of water. She rapidly drifts towards the position of a hanger-on: a gossipy glutton and sybarite, willing to ingratiate herself even with Iudushka for the sake of a good meal. Iudushka has now become the wealthiest landowner in the district. But his wealth has only spurred on his greed, his meanness, his sneaky bigotry. He cannot do anything without moralizing, without God's name on his lips. It is through his callousness that his two sons are driven to death, but he remains just the same. When his irresponsible younger son, who has gambled away government money, implores him to help him out of the difficulty, Iudushka will not even listen: nothing on earth would make him part with his precious money.

"I am the only son you have left. Don't forget that," the exasperated young man exclaimed at last.

"God took from Job all he had, my dear, and yet he did not repine, but only said, 'God has given, God has taken away—God's will be done.' So that's the way, my boy."

Shortly after he learned of his son's death, but took it calmly. "God has given, God has taken away."

An even more terrible fate overtook Iudushka's two orphan nieces. Young and inexperienced, they decided to escape from the Golovlyov atmosphere in order to live an intense and useful life. Both started their career as actresses in the provinces. But provincial vulgarity proved stronger than their power of resistance. Sinking deeper and deeper in its mire, they became ordinary prostitutes. After a scandalous law case, one of the sisters poisoned herself, and the other returned consumptive to Iudushka's manor.

Iudushka himself is now an old half-crazy recluse, a parody of humanity. Doomed like his consumptive niece, he indulges together with her in drink. And she finds a vindictive pleasure in taunting and wounding him with reproaches. A tragic touch is added to it by the fact that in his dreary loneliness he actually becomes bewildered, and even something like conscience begins to stir in him at last.

"Iudushka groaned and, consumed with anger and restlessness, with feverish impatience waited for the evening, not only to get drunk like a brute but to drown his conscience in the vodka. He hated 'the wench' who so coldly and impudently probed his wounds but was irresistibly drawn to her as though something still remained unsaid between them and there were more wounds to be probed."

There were plenty of things left unsaid. Unable to formulate them, Iudushka yet felt that something was wrong with him and with his life—now that all was irretrievably lost. He died in a crazy impulse to atone for his subhuman past.

IV

Such is a very brief sketch of Saltykov-Shchedrine's best work, which is deservedly among the classics of Russian realism. Iudushka has become a nickname on a par with Gogol's characters and Goncharov's Oblomov. As for the basic impulse underlying Shchedrine's writings, it is the same as in Gogol, but with the addition of Belinsky's "social command." The same laughter through tears; the same indictment through jeering; the same fight with the vulgarity of existence. Shchedrine became, in fact, the most outspoken and the most versatile Russian satirist. Grotesque exaggerations, deliberate comic twists, and a mixture of art and journalism—such are the salient features of his "publicistic belles-lettres," as his other writings were referred to by his contemporaries.

Shchedrine's literary inspirations are to be sought in Gogol's *Dead Souls* and *The Inspector General*, in Pushkin's *History of the Village Goryukhino*, in Belinsky's articles, and in the works of George Sand. But in combining literature with pamphleteering, he brought to perfection the so-called Aesop's language, especially in his *Political Tales*. This language eluded the attention of the censor, but sharpened that of the readers. His suggestive dialogues, Swiftean lampoons and parodies taught people how to read between the lines, and his efforts were not in vain. But as he confined himself mainly to topical themes, he reflected the passing conditions of the period criticized to such an extent that the bulk of his work can hardly be understood at present without a commentary. This does not refer either to his great novel, or to his merciless indictment of the good old serfdom days in *Poshekhonian Antiquity*.

It was primarily Shchedrine's pamphleteering vein, his attacks on political and social conditions, on officialdom, on provincial Philistinism, that made him the mouthpiece of the radical intellectuals of the day. But even if he indulged at times in jeering for its own sake, his laughter proved at least a tonic if not a medicine. Whatever he did, he looked upon his own literary activity as a means of cleansing the Augean stables of Russian life. And in this task he persevered to the end.

CHAPTER VIII

Populists and Others

CRITICAL REALISM was by its very nature rather pessimistic. It would be wrong, however, to regard the entire Russian fiction as gloomy. The growth of the novel demanded that the latter should include all aspects of life, good and bad. It also approached them in a different light and from widely different angles. There was quite a conspicuous populist group of authors who tackled the village and the peasant, for example, with sympathy, or even idealized the moral and social instincts of the Russian moujik. Others paid more attention to the colorful ethnographic peculiarities of the provinces—a trend which made some of them introduce new types and themes into literature. The novel of the moneyed bourgeoisie, and even of the town proletariat, made its appearance. In short, Russian realism kept on growing and branching off in varied, often unexpected directions.

The dispassionate, quietly objective writings of P. I. Melnikov-Pechersky (1819-1883) are certainly surprising after the outbursts of such critical realists as Pisemsky and Saltykov-Shchedrine. In his early works, such as *The Krasilnikovs* (1852), he himself was one of them—he lashed officials and landowners. Later, however, he discovered a more congenial channel for his talent in his two long and rather remarkable novels, *In the Woods* (1871-1875) and *In the Mountains* (1875-1881). Both deal with a peculiar stratum of the Russian population: the so-called old believers whose ancestors, having rejected the reforms of the patriarch Nikon, preferred to abide by their own conservative rites and customs. Melnikov was the best connoisseur of those people, scattered in the woodlands along the upper Volga and in the Urals. And he unfolded a vast epic of their life. His characters are peasants, artisans, merchants—all of them attached to their faith, and generously supporting their illegal convents, monasteries, and hermitages, the demolition of which is described in the second novel. The pace of the narrative is slow and often crammed with ethnographic details. This is particularly true of *In the Woods*, which otherwise abounds in clear-cut characters. Its central figure, the village merchant Patap Maksimytch, is unforgettable. So are the abbess Manefa (his sister) and her illegitimate daughter Flenushka, not to mention scores of others all of whom fit into the curious background revealed by the author.

In addition to being painstaking, Melnikov-Pechersky is the quietest and the most placid among the Russian realists. He writes only from observation, but what he sees is usually worth seeing. Nor does he abstain from watching the inner conflicts of those simple people whose lives are conditioned by their old religious taboos, and whose God is fear rather than love. The only stumbling block is his excessive interest in ethnographic material, in which he often indulges (like his contemporary, the playwright Ostrovsky) at the expense of action. Thus at the end of the second book of *In the Woods*, the pathetic chapter of Nastya's death is encumbered by too detailed a description of an old-fashioned Russian burial with funeral songs and other customs. Nor is the author at his best when trying to imitate the picturesque folk language. However, faults such as these do not diminish the value, documentary and otherwise, of Melnikov's work. The life depicted in it is now a matter of the past. But this past continues to live in his writings.

II

One of Melnikov-Pechersky's partial followers was Nikolai S. Leskov (1831-1895). The range of his interest was, however, much wider. It covered the whole of provincial Russia. Yet unlike Pisemsky or Shchedrine, he preferred the brighter aspects of life, and his basic mood was one of sympathy. A commoner of mixed origin (clergy, merchants, petty gentry), he had ample opportunity of associating with all the strata of his nation, including the "old believers." These he described in *The Sealed Angel*—one of the finest longer stories in Russian. The variety of types, of themes, as well as of anecdotic material in his works is prodigious. His manner has, however, little in common with Melnikov's slow epic broadness. Leskov was fond of a bracingly told story and also of a well-constructed plot. In addition, he was a past master of the word and treated the folk language differently from the ethnographic realists. Instead of reproducing it externally, he recreated it into something new and rather individual. This brings us to one of Leskov's chief contributions to Russian literature: the so-called *skaz*. This is a stylized spoken tale, anecdote, or a series of anecdotes, usually told by a lower middle-class person in such a way that the accent and the inflection of the narrator himself are perfectly preserved. Leskov left a variety of stories of this kind. A classic example of the *skaz* is his humorous yarn, *The Left-handed Smith from Tula and the Steel Flea;* or—on a larger scale—his picaresque tale, *The Enchanted Roamer*. Equally clever are Leskov's stylizations of legends and apocrypha, so abundant in the Russian folklore. His *Sealed Angel,* on the other hand, breathes the most intimate atmosphere of the religious traditions and writings of the old believers.

This was one aspect of Leskov's prolific talent. Another aspect was his picture of Russian life as he had known it from personal experience. It was here that he showed his great understanding of the middle and lower class types: petty officials, merchants, tramps, peasants. His vivid stories become now and then—in his *Lady Macbeth of the Mtsensk District*, for example—also intensely dramatic. As a realist of manners, Leskov introduced into literature the Russian clergy through his best longer work, *The Cathedral Folk* (*Soboryane*, 1872). Hardly a novel in the conventional sense, this narrative is above all a lively panorama of a provincial cathedral town with a priest as its chief figure. Here we are far indeed from Shchedrine's jeering, or Pisemsky's resentment. Leskov's disposition is benevolent, full of warmth and humor. The contrast between the worldly-wise, externally pedantic but at the bottom kindly old priest Tuberozov, and his turbulent, childish assistant Akhilla (who secretly adores his superior), provides a number of comic situations, interlaced with genre pictures and delightful character drawings. We are plunged into a new unsuspected sphere of Russian country life in which we feel, for all its novelty, perfectly at home. *The Cathedral Folk* will remain, on account of its humanity and its art, among the major achievements of Russian realism.

Unfortunately, this cannot be said of Leskov's much weaker topical novels, *The Impasse* (*Nekuda*) and *At Daggers Drawn*. Despite his religious convictions, he was too intelligent and too balanced ever to become an opponent of progress. On the other hand, he could not help reacting against certain excesses on the part of the younger generation. In the first of the two novels he said plainly what he thought of it all. As a result, a hue and cry was raised in the radical camp. The critic Pisarev proposed to chase Leskov out of literature altogether. Irritated by this, Leskov wrote his deliberately antiradical novel, *At Daggers Drawn,* whose polemic character made his case even worse. The radical critics now began to ignore even his actual literary merits. He had to wait for recognition until the beginning of this century.

III

Various aspects of provincial and also of peasant life were dealt with by another realist of that period, Gleb I. Uspensky (1840-1902). A commoner by birth and therefore familiar with the lower classes, Uspensky wavered between documentary realism and the realism of indictment. Having adopted a more or less utilitarian attitude towards literature, he did his best to be as little artistic as possible. He preferred plain statements and photographic directness, without caring to work out a theme patiently. Quick jottings, diary notes, discussions, travel impressions and meditations, illustrated by documentary or by anecdotic material—such are his usual devices. But his literary talent came out even in his militant journalism.

Uspensky started writing in the 'sixties. His first successful work, *Manners of the Rasteryayeva Street,* is among his best. Begun in 1866 in *The Contemporary,* it was concluded in another periodical. It is a series of character sketches, disclosing all the ugliness and boredom of a slummy quarter in the provinces. Artisans, petty officials, publicans, and workers are its chief figures. Always a master of dialogue, Uspensky lets them speak for themselves. The general mood of the sketches is one of pity, disgust, irony, and tragedy, camouflaged at times by comic elements (as in Gogol). Another collection of similar character studies is his *Metropolitan Poverty.* Among the cases included is that of a destitute old woman whose only friend and companion in this world is a dog. After several months in the hospital, the woman returns. But meanwhile the dog has founded a family of her own in a more comfortable place, and refuses even to recognize the old woman when she comes to claim her only friend.

Motives of this kind were characteristic of Uspensky's first period. Later he turned all his attention to the peasant and the village. Here he showed strong populist leanings, but still remained unbiased enough to dismiss any blinkers or illusions. Even his best work about the Russian village, *Power of the Soil*, is mainly an illustration of how increased material well-being among the peasants invariably brings moral deterioration in its train. Uspensky was a skeptical populist, anxious to overcome his own skepticism. Looking at the postreformatory Russia, still weighted down by her old evils and at the same time threatened by the new evil of capitalism, he judged even the social-economic problems of his country from an ethical angle. From the same angle he scrutinized the tasks of the intelligentsia. His literary activities were thus an expression of his own lifelong quest. Owing to his sensitiveness, Uspensky the seeker gradually turned into a sufferer, bewildered by the contradictions and iniquities of life. Some of his narratives (for instance, *The Ruin*) anticipate the Chekhovian futility. Too honest to indulge in any ostrich sand, he was a helpless witness of how capitalism began to disintegrate the Russian village. His moral isolation eventually led him to suicide.

IV

Uspensky's mixture of art and topical discussion was quite a feature of the 'seventies—the decade of militant populism. The toiling masses were free at last, but they suffered from ignorance, from poverty, from lack of land. Their fate aroused a growing interest amongst the intellectuals. And there were populists who saw, or forced themselves to see, things in rosier colors than Uspensky. Nikolai N. Zlatovratsky (1845-1911), for example, described the peasantry in a naïvely idealized light. His first big work, *A Peasant Jury* (1874), is a paean to the high ethical instincts of the Russian moujik. Another of his novels, *The Foundations* (*Ustoi*) reflects the antagonism between the old peasant commune and the new disruptive elements brought into it by the *kulaks*—the greedy individual proprietors. Hardly exciting as a story teller, Zlatovratsky was inclined to indulge in didactic and ethnographic passages. It was due partly to his goodness, and partly to his acceptance of things at their face value that he remained to the end more sentimental than critical: the usual pitfall of confirmed populists. One of his most readable works, *How It All Happened*, is a book of memoirs of the 'sixties.

Peasantry, but different from Zlatovratsky's, is presented by F. M. Reshotnikov (1841-1871). His *People of Podlipnaya*, which appeared in *The Contemporary* in 1864, is a document of unrelieved village misery. In the first part we get acquainted with the hard, almost savage life in a northern hamlet; in the second we follow some of its inhabitants to a big river, where they work as boatmen and lose in a catastrophe their only enterprising and capable member. The commoner Reshotnikov was too much concerned with the subject matter itself to care for a high artistic standard in his writings. He was one of the first to take up also the proletarians and factory workers. His four novels, *The Miners, The Glupovs, Where It Is Better, One's Own Bread,* all written in the 'sixties, were allowed to appear only in fragments. Among the less-known authors describing the village life of the 'sixties and 'seventies are V. A. Sleptsov and A. I. Levitov. The tradition was continued in the 'eighties by S. Karonin (a populist) and N. I. Naumov.

Unadorned, even brutal is the realism of N. G. Pomyalov-sky (1835-1863), whose *Seminary Sketches* created a sensation at the beginning of the 'sixties. This work is primarily a document, but of the most embittered kind. It exposes the education in an old-fashioned clerical school, the pupils of which (for the most part sons of poor village priests) are at the mercy of their savage teachers. The atmosphere hovering over the life of the youngsters and over the entire institution is one of grotesque nightmare. The author—a commoner with a strong class feeling which came out even in his first narrative, *Molotov*—took to drinking and died at the age of twenty-eight.

Another victim of alcohol and poverty was Nikolai A. Kushchevsky (1847-1876). His sparklingly vivacious *Nikolai Negorev* (1871) is still regarded as an outstanding novel. He, too, shows up an old-fashioned secondary school; but he does it with a sense of humor, mixed with irony. Negorev, the hero of the novel, is a climber like Goncharov's Aduyev, or Pisemsky's Klinovitch. His chief aim in life is success, to which he sacrifices everything with good cheer, even with good conscience. Negorev and some of his companions are shown in their process of growth: from their boyhood up to their successful or unsuccessful starts in life. The novel is all the more readable because the author wrote it for its own sake, without any ulterior motives.

v

The bulk of the novels published in the 'sixties and 'seventies tended to be topical, often with a purpose. The populist novel in particular was much in vogue. So was the radical-intelligentsia novel, abundantly supplied by the now forgotten A. K. Sheller-Mikhailov (1838-1900). More interesting were the narratives reflecting the development

of Russia after 1861. In this respect the social novels of
N. D. Boborykin (1836-1921) were a creditable achievement.
Boborykin was familiar not only with the intelligentsia, but
also with the new moneyed bourgeoisie which he tackled
in *Kitay-Gorod*, *Vasily Tyorkin*, and many other works.
The theme of *Kitay-Gorod* is the fate of a nobleman who
had turned to business—quite the usual thing after the abolition of serfdom. Boborykin was one of the most prolific and
best-informed realists, but his very fluency made him somewhat superficial. He was a favorite with the more cultured
average readers, to whom he interpreted the signs of the
time. The manor novel itself assumed a purpose, even an
aggressive one, in the works of Evgeny L. Markov (1835-
1903): a defender of the village squire's mission against the
encroaching town civilization. His two novels, *Squirelings*
(*Barchuki*) and *A Black-earth Field*, both of which appeared
in the 'seventies, bear the stamp of an uncompromising class
consciousness.

A brief mention should also be made of the historical
novel of that period. The latter was represented by Grigory
P. Danilevsky, Count Salias, Vsevolod Solovyov, and by the
poet and dramatist Count Alexey K. Tolstoy whose historical
romance, *Prince Serebryany* (1862), enjoyed great popularity.
It is still read—partly because it deals with such historical
figures as Ivan the Terrible and Yermak (the conqueror of
Siberia). Unfortunately, its frequent pseudo-archaic language
and would-be folklore flavor strike a modern reader as
forced. So do the operatic effects—of the sort one finds in
the author's well-known "Shakespearian" trilogy. The historical novel was—from the 'seventies onwards—in great demand
by the petit-bourgeois readers, to whose tastes and escapist
tendencies it had to adapt itself. But for this very reason it
gradually lowered its standards until it ceased to count as
literature.

To sum up, in two or three decades the range of the Russian novel expanded beyond recognition. It included an enormous variety of themes and problems. The apex of Russian realism was reached, however, in the work of the two greatest novelists of the last century, Dostoevsky and Tolstoy, who must be discussed separately.

CHAPTER IX

Dostoevsky

No RUSSIAN author, not even Tolstoy, has had a greater influence on modern European literature than Fyodor Mikhailovitch Dostoevsky (1821-1881). It was he who added to the psychological novel the entire region of the subconscious. Yet he himself was interested not so much in psychology for its own sake as in those secrets of the human mind and spirit which lie beyond its bounds. Essentially a seeker, he scrutinized the human self with a merciless eye and with an intuition which was clairvoyant precisely when watching the most dramatic conflicts of man's inner life. At the same time, he was the first Russian author who concentrated all his attention on the big town with its haste, its tragic contrasts, its inner and external squalor. His chief characters are usually town dwellers. The city, or rather the capital, is his ever-recurring background.

While the manor literature reached its climax in Tolstoy, Dostoevsky introduced entirely new themes and problems. He also replaced the leisurely broadness of Goncharov or Tolstoy by a quicker pace and by a tension hardly paralleled in modern literature. In Dostoevsky everything is nerves and hurry. He was not interested in a static or even settled life. An unstable and unbalanced city dweller himself, he was anxious to unravel the chaotic urbanized man whose dilemmas and contradictions he explored to the end. With all this he combined three typical Russian features: a lack of restraint; a metaphysical attitude towards evil as something

inherent in the very nature of the universe; and a spiritual
thirst, directed towards the "city of God" for which he
fought all the more desperately the more his profound religious temperament was threatened by his own skepticism/
In his daring experiments he obliterated the line between
the rational and the irrational, between the normal and the
abnormal. Deliberately, he put his heroes into most unusual
conditions, in order to see how they would react and how
much travail their spirit could endure. He hoped to extract
the secret of man and life from the exceptional and the
abnormal rather than from the normal.

This can perhaps justify the pathology in his work. The
French author, Melchior de Vogüé, called him the "Shakespeare of the lunatic asylum." But such a statement is too
sweeping to be applied to Dostoevsky literally. The kernel
of his writings is and remains philosophic in the deepest
and most tragic sense. It also reveals so many hidden aspects
of man and life as to make the majority of other European
authors look somewhat superficial.

II

Dostoevsky's life was hardly less strange and agitated than
are his novels. Born in Moscow in a hospital for the poor,
where his father was a physician, he came at the very outset
into contact with misery, suffering, and disease—the three
companions he hardly got rid of again. At the age of seventeen he entered the Military College of Engineering in
Petersburg: that "most phantomlike city on earth." On finishing his studies, he obtained a commission which he soon
exchanged, however, for the life of a literary proletarian.
During that time he read a great deal, especially Gogol,
Balzac, George Sand, and Hoffmann. His literary debut
began, characteristically enough, with a translation of Bal-

zac's *Père Goriot.* In January 1846 his first original work, *Poor Folk,* appeared. Although inspired by Gogol's *Greatcoat,* this story (in the antiquated letter form) about the "insulted and injured," established at once Dostoevsky's reputation. Belinsky himself took him under his wing. Yet he failed to see the excellence of the young author's second and much better work, *The Double.* Prompted to some extent by Gogol's *A Madman's Diary,* Dostoevsky gave in it a fine study of a self-divided personality: a theme he continued to develop and to deepen until he reached some of the most involved processes of mind and spirit.

These two early works contain—in germ—practically all the elements of Dostoevsky's later writings. After a few more stories, however, his career was interrupted in an incredible manner. As a member of the semirevolutionary Petrashevsky circle, he was arrested and sentenced to death. In December, 1849, he and his comrades were taken to the place of execution. This is how he describes—in a letter to his brother Michael—the scene that followed: "Today, the 22nd of December, we were taken all to the Semyonovsky Square. There the death sentence was read to us, we were given the Cross to kiss, the dagger was broken over our heads, and our funeral toilet (white shirts) was made. Then three of us were put standing before the palisade for the execution of the death sentence. I was sixth in the row; we were called up by groups of three, and so I was in the second group and had not more than a minute to live. I had time to embrace Pleshcheyev and Durov, who stood near me, and to take my leave of them. Finally, retreat was sounded, those who were bound to the palisades were brought back, and it was read to us that His Imperial Majesty has granted us our lives."

The reprieved rebels were sent at once to Siberia. Dostoevsky spent four years among the worst criminals in the penal settlement at Omsk. Another four years he wasted as a soldier in a line battalion at Semipalatinsk. It was on his return to European Russia (in 1859) that he resumed his literary activities. The first two works to appear after his release were *The House of the Dead,* and his first large novel *The Insulted and Injured.* Both were published in the periodical *Vremya (The Time),* edited by Dostoevsky and his brother Michael. Another work of his, *Memoirs from the Underworld* (1864), appeared in *Epokha (The Epoch),* which the two brothers started without success after *Vremya* had been suppressed by the police.

The House of the Dead is a record of Dostoevsky's life among the criminals in Siberia and can be classed among the greatest human documents in literature. It is amazingly rich in observation, insight, and understanding. Far from seeing in those criminals mere wretches, Dostoevsky discovered among them unusually good material which had gone wrong for lack of a proper outlet and direction. It is known what a strong impression this book had made on Nietzsche. In his *Twilight of the Idols* Nietzsche, following up some of Dostoevsky's conclusions, says: "The criminal type is the type of the strong man made sick. . . . Concerning the problem before us, Dostoevsky's testimony is of importance. Dostoevsky, who, incidentally, was the only psychologist from whom I had anything to learn: he belongs to the happiest windfalls of my life, happier even than the discovery of Stendhal. This profound man, who was right, ten times over, in esteeming the superficial Germans low, found the Siberian convicts among whom he lived for many years—those thoroughly hopeless criminals for whom no road back to society stood open—very different from what even he had expected—that is to say, carved from about the best, hardest, and most valuable material that grows on Russian soil." And here is the final remark of Dostoevsky himself:

"How much joyless youth, how much strength for which use there was none, was buried, lost in those walls—youth and strength of which the world might surely have made some use. For I must speak my thought as to this: the hapless fellows there were perhaps the strongest and, in one way or another, the most gifted of our people. There was all that strength of body and mind lost. Whose fault is that?" Apart from being a literary masterpiece, this book stands as an almost unique record of criminal psychology.

Dostoevsky's novel, *The Insulted and Injured*, is nearly a failure. Its chief character is a self-divided aristocratic weakling, swayed by circumstances in the most contradictory directions. The heroine (his victim) has to pay for his weakness and also for the villainies of a typical Dostoevskian cynic, Prince Valkovsky.[1] The dominant elements of the novel are human misery and pity. Overdoing both, the author becomes garrulous, even sentimental. At times one is inclined to think that Dostoevsky enjoys his own pity like a voluptuary who is on the lookout for such suffering as would evoke in him a maximum of compassion. On the other hand, a man who had passed through the torments and humiliations of a Siberian prison could hardly refrain from exploring the limits of human endurance. Nor could he be indifferent to the problems, or at least the reactions, of a crushed personality.

It was this second theme that Dostoevsky tackled in his *Memoirs from the Underworld*, which provides a key to his post-Siberian work as a whole. This time the author probes (through the device of a would-be cynical confession) into the most intimate secrets of a thwarted ego. Rejected by life, his hero asserts himself by rejecting life on his part. For

---

[1] The fact that the narrator is sincerely in love with her and yet helps her lover against his own interest has a certain bearing upon Dostoevsky's love affair with his first wife, Mme Isayeva, whom he married in Siberia.

this purpose he transvalues all its values. With a cruel chuckle he unmasks our conventions, ideas, and ideals, reducing them to mere rags by which we cover our egoism and lust for power. He acknowledges quite frankly his own egoism and will to power. But unable to provide an outlet for them outside himself, he turns them against himself and even finds a perverted pleasure in self-laceration. Yet behind his nihilism of despondence one can feel a suppressed idealist and a weakling who is trying to transmute his very impotence into an illusion of strength. It was in this work that Dostoevsky probed into one of his cardinal problems: the problem of individual self-assertion. And the angle from which he scrutinized it goes far beyond a mere social "inferiority complex." It ominously leads up to some of those dilemmas which form the core of the author's next work, *Crime and Punishment*.

III

In this novel Dostoevsky explored some of the most paradoxical puzzles of human consciousness. Its chief character, Raskolnikov, is a product of the radical Western thought, but he goes much farther than Turgenev's Bazarov. As an atheist he rejects, quite consistently, the whole of that morality which has been built upon the belief in God as a Supreme Being and Lawgiver. He divides humanity into those few "supermen" who are strong enough to dispense with God and to accept the new gospel of "beyond good and evil"; and into the common herd who are too cowardly to discard the old beliefs and moral values. Moreover, he willfully murders a vile pawnbroker woman, not in order to rob her, but to prove to himself that he is "strong" enough to overstep line of the old morality. What he wants is to conquer the freedom of a "superman," who is a law unto himself, and to whom all things are lawful. His logic and reason are in agreement with such a step. Yet after the crime the irrational part of his personality comes forward with its own truth. And this reaction is so appalling that Raskolnikov is driven in the end to a voluntary confession. Unable to bear the "irrational" consequences of his crime, Raskolnikov ascribes his collapse to his weakness only, because logically he still refuses to regard himself as a criminal (in a higher, extra-legal sense). This is what he says to his sister Dounia, before surrendering to the authorities who have no evidence against him:

"I am going to give myself up. But I don't know why I am going to give myself up."

"Aren't you half expiating your crime by facing the suffering?"

"Crime? What crime?" he cried in a sudden fury. "That I killed a vile, noxious insect, an old pawnbroker woman, of use to no one! Killing her was atonement for forty sins. She was sucking the life out of the poor people. Was that a crime? I am not thinking of it and am not thinking of expiating it, and why are you all rubbing it in on all sides? Only now I see clearly the imbecility of my cowardice, now that I have decided to face this superfluous disgrace. It's simply because I am contemptible and have nothing in me that I have decided to, perhaps, too, for my advantage. . . . I am farther than ever from seeing that what I did was a crime. . . . But I wonder shall I in those fifteen or twenty years (of penal servitude) grow so meek that I shall humble myself before people and whimper at every word that I am a criminal. Yes, that's it, that's it, that's what they are sending me there for, that's what they want. . . . Look at them running to and fro about the streets, every one of them a scoundrel and a criminal at heart and, worse still, an idiot.

But try to get me off and they'd be wild with righteous indignation. Oh! how I hate them all!" [1]

He gave himself up even against his logic and reason. In his split personality the rational and the irrational truths worked simultaneously in opposite directions. Both were equally plausible on their respective planes, but these two planes not only did not meet—they actually seemed to exclude each other within one and the same consciousness. This inner conflict was rendered by Dostoevsky with such dramatic force as to make *Crime and Punishment* one of the great, but by no means pleasant novels.

As though anxious to create an antithesis to Raskolnikov, Dostoevsky gave us the portrait of Prince Myshkin in his next novel, *The Idiot* (1868-1869). If Raskolnikov is an impotent individualistic rebel whose reasoned-out superman is beyond the reach of his actual will to power, Prince Myshkin embodies the surrender to the irrational supra-individual values and intuitions. He is a Christ-like character, a "divine fool" in the old Russian style. An epileptic and former inmate of a lunatic asylum, he is so devoid of all rational cleverness that the first impression he makes on people is that of a simpleton and idiot. The more so because in all practical matters he is as helpless as a baby. At the same time he is endowed with "second sight" about things essential. His naïve, childlike wisdom transcends as it were our ordinary intelligence. Obeying the highest intuitions within himself, Myshkin is also a man of such goodness that even those who laugh at him at first are gradually compelled to admire him as a higher, unfathomable being. Yet even he is self-divided. Tossed between his love for Aglaya and his pity for Nastasya, he passes through a number of painful experiences the weight of which is too much for his brain. When the

[1] Quotations are taken from Dostoevsky's works, translated by Constance Garnett (Heinemann).

"offended and injured" Nastasya (an intensely hysterical character) runs away from him only to be murdered by his friend and rival, Rogozhin, Myshkin's mind is clouded, once again, and this time for good. The gruesome scene of his and Rogozhin's delirium beside Nastasya's covered body concludes the novel.

"When after many hours, the door was opened and people thronged in, they found the murderer unconscious and in a raging fever. The prince was sitting by him and each time that the sick man gave a laugh and a shout, he hastened to pass his own trembling hands over his companion's hair and cheeks as though trying to soothe and quiet him, and recognized none of those who surrounded him. If Schneider himself (Myshkin's former doctor) had arrived then and seen his former pupil and patient, remembering the Prince's condition during the first year in Switzerland, he would have flung up his hands despairingly, and cried as he did then: 'An idiot.'"

IV

Dostoevsky's preoccupation with crime was of a metaphysical nature. Such a trend was at least a partial reaction to the materialistic treatment of moral values (in the directions of "all things are lawful") attempted by Pisarev and other nihilists. And since his own personality was split into its irrational and rational tendencies, Dostoevsky was anxious to explore both to the very end in order to find an outlet or—if possible—a reconciliation. It was this quest and struggle in one that impelled him to create characters, passing through the same crisis of consciousness which he himself had to face—a process which reached a new phase in *The Possessed* (1871). In this novel Dostoevsky widened the dilemma into its far-reaching antitheses: religion versus materialist atheism; Christianity versus moral and social nihilism; Russia (that is, the Slavophil Russia as Dostoevsky understood her) versus Europe. The novel thus became a daring exploration of the metaphysical roots of nihilism and, incidentally, a mad attack on the radical Westerners. Even Turgenev was caricatured, and most maliciously, in the author Karmazinov.

The Possessed can be classed among the reactionary novels, like Pisemsky's *A Troubled Sea,* or Leskov's *At Daggers Drawn,* but it goes much deeper into the matter. Actually, it is an enlargement of *Crime and Punishment.* Its three principal characters, Stavrogin, Kirillov, and Verkhovensky, represent but three further aspects of Raskolnikov's dilemma, or better still—three further lines of its development. The principle, "all things are lawful," derived by Raskolnikov from the one-sided Western materialism, is here shown in its ultimate consequences not only in theory but also in practice. Some of its characters and episodes were based on real happenings, connected with the notorious Nechayev affair. The nihilist Nechayev, who was a follower of Bakunin, founded in Moscow (1869) a secret society of his own. His aim was to provoke a revolution by fostering all existing evils to their breaking point, and by cultivating destruction for its own sake. One of the members of his group, a certain student Ivanov, was actually murdered on suspicion of being a renegade. This happens also in *The Possessed.* The principal characters of this novel are demons of destruction rather than human beings. Destruction is not only their mania; it is their religion, or antireligion, spurred on by their own lust for power. "Listen," one of them raves, while expounding his visions of the future chaos, "first of all we'll make an upheaval. We shall penetrate to the peasantry. . . . On all sides we see vanity puffed up out of all proportions, brutal, monstrous appetites. . . . Do you know how many we shall catch by little ready-made ideas? Oh, this generation has only to grow up. One or two generations of vice are essential now; monstrous, abject vice by which a man is transformed into a loathsome, cruel, egoistic reptile. That's what we need. And what's more, a little 'fresh blood' that we may get accustomed to it. . . . We will proclaim destruction. . . . We'll set fires going. . . . We'll set legends going. . . . There's going to be such an upset as the world has never seen before. . . . Russia will be overwhelmed by darkness, the earth will weep for its old gods. . . . Listen, Stavrogin. To level the mountains is a fine idea, not an absurd one. Down with culture! The thirst for culture is an aristocratic thirst. . . . We will make use of drunkenness, slander, spying; we will stifle every genius in its infancy. We'll reduce all to a common denominator! Complete equality! Only the necessary is necessary: that's the motto of the whole world henceforward."

A more tolerant attitude towards the revolutionaries and the uprooted Russian intellectuals can be found in *A Raw Youth* (1871). This novel is above all a study of inner readjustment between the aristocratic intellectual Versilov and his illegitimate son Arkady, whose mother is a former serf, that is, from the people. The theme becomes significant when put against the background of the vital problems Russia was coping with in those days. The raw youth Arkady, chaotic though he be, is something of a symbol. Owing to his origin, he contains the promise of a new type, in whom the two almost antithetic elements—the gentry (or rather the gentry intelligentsia) and the people—are blended. Although badly constructed, *A Raw Youth* is psychologically subtle and profound, even if its numerous external devices often smack of a detective story. Still, it cannot be spoken of in the same breath as *The Brothers Karamazov* '1879-1880), Dostoevsky's last and greatest achievement.

v

In this work, too, the background of actual Russia serves only as a canvas for a powerful drama of human mind and spirit. The novel is a continuation of the Raskolnikov-Myshkin dilemma. As in *The Possessed*, the action takes place in the provinces, not in Petersburg. Its center is the Karamazov family whose head, the libidinous old roué, Pavel Karamazov, is nearer to an animal than to a human being. His crude passion has assumed, however, in his three sons—two by a different mother—different and nobler aspects. Mitya, the eldest, is as irresponsibly impulsive as his father, but his emotional chaos betrays a warm and generous heart. In Ivan the same force becomes intellectualized. The somewhat distressing purity of Alyosha points to an ethical sublimation. Karamazov's illegitimate offspring, the epileptic Smerdyakov, is, however, a regression and an antithesis of his half brothers in every respect.

The plot of the novel revolves round parricide and was based—according to recent investigations—on a real crime which had taken place much earlier, in the second half of the 'forties. The supposed criminal, Mitya Karamazov, was modeled by Dostoevsky on a certain Ilyinsky (convicted of parricide but later proved innocent) whom Dostoevsky had met in the Omsk prison. As for other influences, the Soviet critic L. Grossman points to *Spiridion*—a little-known philosophic novel by George Sand, where there are striking analogies between the monastic life as depicted in both works, and especially between the relationship of Alyosha and the elder Zosima (even George Sand's young monk is called Alexis, i.e. Alyosha). We should bear in mind, however, that whatever suggestions Dostoevsky may have received from other people's writings, he always based his novels on his own inner problems and on actual observations of Russian life. It is well known that in 1878 Dostoevsky, together with the young philosopher Vladimir Solovyov, visited the Optin Monastery, so well described by him afterwards in the novel. The elder Zosima was portrayed from an actual monk whom he met there and with whom he had several talks. One could find models for a few other characters as well. But to return to the plot of the novel, its crux is based on the rivalry between the old Karamazov and his son Mitya. There is not much love lost between the old voluptuary and his sons—Alyosha excepted. Mitya actually threatens to kill him on account of his advances to Grushenka with whom he himself is desperately in love. Ivan, too, loathes his father and wishes his death for his own secret reasons. So does Smerdyakov, who covets old Karamazov's hidden money and decides to acquire it by fair or foul means. A greater contrast than the one between Ivan and Smerdyakov can hardly be imagined. Yet the two have much in common—on the subconscious plane. Ivan moreover poisons Smerdyakov's brain and entices him indirectly, as though half unaware, to murder his father. Step by step he initiates him into the same logical sanctions which once prompted to Raskolnikov that "all things are lawful." In the end Smerdyakov murders the old Karamazov, but so cunningly that the guilt falls upon Mitya who is arrested, tried, and sentenced to penal servitude.

The repercussions caused by this murder form the second half of the novel. Mitya is in jail, where he accepts suffering and even undergoes, through it, a complete transformation. So does his capricious sweetheart Grushenka. The murderer Smerdyakov falls ill. His irrational reaction to his logical "all things are lawful" soon becomes so terrifying that he is driven to suicide. But a similar reaction besets Ivan, too, although the trend of his former conversations with Smerdy-

akov had been engineered surreptitiously by his "second self."
Ivan's inner distress grows so unbearable that, like Raskolnikov, he decides to give himself up to the authorities, even if
logically he believes neither in virtue nor in crime. "You are
going to perform an act of heroic virtue, and you don't
believe in virtue; that's what tortures you and makes you
angry, that's why you are so vindictive," his nightmare devil
taunts him on the night of Mitya's trial. "No matter if they
disbelieve you, you are going for the sake of principle. Why
do you want to go meddling, if your sacrifice is of no use
to anyone? Because you don't know yourself why you go.
Oh, you'd give a great deal to know yourself why you do!
. . . You must guess that for yourself. That's the riddle for
you."

Poised above the two antagonistic truths (Raskolnikov's
"all things are lawful," and its opposite), Ivan is too honest
a skeptic to accept entirely either of them. Half delirious
with fever and disgust, he yet denounces himself as the
instigator of the crime, knowing beforehand that the jury
will not believe him. The final result of his inner battle is
not shown, but the battle itself is symbolized in Ivan's dis-
pute with his nightmare devil—a section the depth of which
is matched only by the chapters of *The Legend of the Grand
Inquisitor*.

Ivan's negation is due neither to social rancor nor to a
thwarted will to power, but primarily to his moral sensitiveness. Unable to believe in any moral convictions, he still
retains a highly moral temperament and a passion for justice.
Like his Grand Inquisitor, he refuses to sing "Hosanna" with
the elect as long as millions of human beings are doomed
without any fault on their part. Even if he were compelled
to accept the existence of God, he would still reject the
unjust world created by Him. He would "return his entrance
ticket" from moral indignation. But no one can go on living

on rebellion. Dostoevsky had to indicate at least some outlet for Ivan's dilemma. So he created Alyosha and the monk Zosima, both of whom are at the opposite end of "Karamazovism."

In these two figures he indicated the process of self-realization, as distinct from the mere self-assertion of his metaphysical rebels. On a closer glance, however, the reader is not quite sure whether Zosima's and Alyosha's harmony represents a state before or after self-division. Is not the consciousness of Zosima only a contrast to Ivan's rebellion rather than a victory over it? The truth is that Dostoevsky himself was in desperate need of a figure endowed with his own potential acceptance of life, with his own "Hosanna." Hence the somewhat forced and didactic character of Zosima whose final conclusions are the reverse of those reached by Raskolnikov, Kirillov, or Ivan Karamazov. On the other hand, Father Zosima's affirmation of life in all its fullness was necessary to the general pattern of a novel in which Dostoevsky examined not only the extreme limits of lust and passion, but also the ultimate aspects of the problem of good and evil, of freedom and necessity, of Russia and Europe, of Christ and the destinies of mankind. And the final note of *The Brothers Karamazov* is not resignation but reconciliation; or at least a strong will to reconciliation.

VI

This point can best be understood if we regard Dostoevsky's creative process as a continuous endeavor to overcome his own latent nihilism. His work is one long struggle and at the same time a confession, a kind of "Pilgrim's Progress," on the part of a man who had to cope with all sorts of doubles within his own self, and also with his secret loathing of human beings as they are. He was too much of a psychologist to take these at their face value, or to respect them. Where there is no respect there can be no love in our sense either, but only pity, mistaken for love. And one insists on pity all the more vehemently the more one is afraid of being crushed by one's secret scorn. Like his Grand Inquisitor, Dostoevsky pitied, suffering with and for those whom he pitied. And on this roundabout way he was led to that new kind of sympathy which can dispense with respect. He himself tells us something about this in his allegorical *Dream of a Queer Fellow*, the contents of which may form a suitable postscript to a study of Dostoevsky.

A certain Queer Fellow dreamed that, on committing suicide, he was transferred to a planet which would have been a double of our earth but for the fact that its population was the blissful humanity before the fall. Welcomed by the inhabitants, the newcomer gradually infected that earthly paradise. He corrupted all and sundry "like an atom of pestilence." In the end they became deceitful, voluptuous, jealous, cruel. They started endless destructive wars for "mine" and "thine." Their former happiness became a dim legend at which they themselves laughed. Yet a suppressed craving for their lost harmony kept smoldering even amid their crimes and vices. These had transformed the once blissful planet into a hell—worse, into a picture resembling our own present-day earth to such an extent as to frighten the Queer Fellow himself. Having realized that he, and he alone, was to blame for it all, he was suddenly crushed by his awakened sense of guilt. He implored the inhabitants to punish him, to crucify him, but in vain. "I walked among them," he says, "wringing my hands, and wept over them, yet I loved them perhaps more than when there was no suffering in their faces, and they were innocent and beautiful. I loved the earth which they had polluted more than when it was a paradise, for this alone that sorrow had appeared upon it. . . . Their sorrow so mightily entered my soul that my heart shrank and I felt that I would die."

Dostoevsky adds that here the Queer Fellow awoke and began to preach. His preaching was of course that of Dostoevsky himself who well knew that without tragedy, sin, and suffering—however painful these may be—mankind would never reach its maturity. It is not without reason that the three occupy so much space in Dostoevsky's work. But he expressed quite a number of his views outside literature proper, notably in his *An Author's Diary*. Politically and culturally, he adhered to his own brand of Slavophilism which he vaguely defined, not as a gospel of national exclusiveness, but as a future synthesis of all Russian and European contradictions—in the name of a better and worthier humanity. This attitude was stressed in his Pushkin speech (1880) which was the swan song of his life. A few months later he was among the dead.

CHAPTER X

Tolstoy

DESPITE THE great contrast, or perhaps because of it, Tolstoy
and Dostoevsky complete each other in almost everything.
Whereas the literary proletarian Dostoevsky was concerned
mainly with the town, the landed aristocrat Count Lev
Nikolayevitch Tolstoy (1828-1910) was the last giant of the
manor realism. His *War and Peace* is an epic of the old
gentry class. His *Anna Karenina* tends even to canonize the
idyllic country life in all its hostility to town civilization. An
Epicurean by nature, Tolstoy put a moral strait jacket upon
himself and in the end wanted to abolish everything that
did not agree with his stern puritan principles. Dostoevsky,
on the contrary, preferred an intense life to a moral life. His
aim was the fullness of existence, deepened by religion, and
not the triumph of puritanism at the expense of both life
and religion. Dostoevsky slaved for nearly twenty years before he was able to enjoy moderate security and comfort.
Tolstoy, however, who was born into affluence, kept on
rebelling all the time against his own wealth and eventually
escaped, at the age of eighty-two, from his family, with
the object of spending the last stage of his life in loneliness
like a hermit.

Equally striking is the difference in their literary work.
Dostoevsky's genius is essentially dramatic; that of Tolstoy's
is epic. While Dostoevsky feels at home in the abnormal,
Tolstoy is at his best among the normal characters of a
normal three-dimensional world. And these he makes so

palpable, so concrete, that the reader moves among them as if they were his old acquaintances, whom he seems to know better than he knows himself. Both authors were seekers. Both looked upon their art as a means to go beyond mere art, but on different planes and by different methods. In Dostoevsky, for example, the physical, intellectual, and spiritual elements were mixed up in such a way that all the contrasts and antinomies existed in him simultaneously, side by side. In Tolstoy, however, there was an alternation, as well as a gap between the physical and the moral man. This gap is faithfully recorded in his writings which, in addition to being powerful as art, are also a great and moving human document.

The first feature likely to strike Tolstoy's readers, is a certain disparity between his genius and his intellect—a disparity which in him was even stronger than in Gogol, since it happened to be on a much bigger scale. Tolstoy's irrational genius drew its force from his acceptance of the instinctive biological life, not only within himself, but in the whole of creation. This enabled him to enjoy every aspect of existence as spontaneously and fully as though he were still a child, a savage, a part of nature herself. His artistic process at its best was mainly an intensification of this pagan joy of life, which tingled in him quite apart from and above any meaning of life. But parallel with this, his querying intellect always urged him to put the meaning of life (which he was able to interpret only in terms of morals) before and above life itself. What is known as the conflict between Tolstoy the artist and Tolstoy the moralist or even "prophet," can be reduced to the feud between these two elements in his consciousness. Until he was about fifty, the artist in him prevailed in spite of all the interference of the moralist. After that age, however, the moralist took the upper hand and kept Tolstoy the artist on a leash.

In all this Tolstoy's reasoned-out asceticism cooperated with one of his most instinctive, most irrational traits: his rootedness in the soil and in those patriarchal peasants who are a part of that soil. His worship of compact primitive masses continuously urged him to fight against individualism. And individualism meant to him separation from the compact collectives. It meant isolation and, finally, unrelieved loneliness. It also meant conflict; conflict not only between the individual and the group, but also between the individuals themselves, each of them eager for power, for property, for aggressive self-assertion. And since our civilization is based on such a war of all against all, Tolstoy turned against civilization itself. He wanted to reduce humanity to the pre-civilized conditions of a Utopian Golden Age in which there would be no division, no conflict, but only primitive tilling of the soil and what he regarded as universal love.

This static, antihistorical conception of humanity can provide a clue to a number of Tolstoy's other tendencies and ideas. Even his idea of God, of whom he talks so much in his later works, is a kind of deified group consciousness, or "group soul," in which all separate individual selves are obliterated rather than transcended. "Love one another" meant in Tolstoy's language: Suppress your own ego to such an extent as not to resist the evil inflicted upon you by another person, since every kind of resistance is active self-assertion. Tolstoy saw the only remedy in self-obliteration for the sake of others, for the sake of the group. And the more he was aware of selfish elements (such as pride, lust, vanity) within himself, the more he insisted on that de-personalizing Buddhistic Christianity of his own which was the final outcome of his conversion—so poignantly described in *My Confession* (1879). As a matter of fact, there was no sudden conversion in Tolstoy, but only a deliberate shifting of his inner center of gravity from one set of values to the other. Yet even after his attempt to cripple his exuberant vital force on the Procrustean bed of morality, his artistic genius was not entirely sacrificed to the moralist. Periodically it cropped up and made him write some of his best pages even in his old age. In this dualism consisted the tragedy of Tolstoy.

II

Tolstoy's first work, *Childhood* (1852), already reveals his power of making the simplest everyday happenings significant and alive. No matter how small the trifle, he identifies himself with it and imbues it with his own vitality. He also combines an unrivaled observation with an uncanny psychological intuition. At the same time, his descriptions preserve the freshness and the naïve intensity of a child, who notices at once an habitual tic and is thrilled by any physical peculiarities among grown-ups. Few artists had such an acute eye for individual peculiarities as was the case with the great anti-individualist Tolstoy. This is how he describes his father's steward in *Childhood:* "He (the father) stood at his writing-table and pointing to some envelopes, papers, and piles of money, spoke angrily—heatedly explaining to the steward, Jacob Mikhailov, who stood in his usual place between the door and the barometer with his hands behind his back, rapidly moving his fingers in all directions. The more vehement papa became the more rapidly the fingers twitched, and when papa paused the fingers too became still; but when Jacob himself spoke they were exceedingly restless and twitched desperately this way and that; by their movements one could, I think, have guessed Jacob's secret thoughts, but his face was always calm—expressing consciousness of his own worth, and at the same time subservience, saying as it were: 'I am all right, but let it be as you decide.' " [1]

This method was brought by Tolstoy to utmost perfection. He can indicate the entire character of a person by showing a few physical externals. One could quote a number of illustrations from his works, especially from *War and Peace* and *Anna Karenina*. Anna's bureaucratic husband with his large sticking-out ears and his cracking fingers has become a classical example. Another strong point is Tolstoy's clairvoyance with regard to all fundamental relations: those between man and woman, man and the group, man and nature. But to him everything is fundamental, even the simplest things of life. Or he knows at least how to intensify them to such an extent as to make them so. Take this description of the hunt in *Childhood*:

"Harvesting was in full swing. The limitless, brilliantly yellow field was bounded only on one side by the tall, bluish forest, which then seemed to me a most distant mysterious place beyond which either the world came to an end or uninhabited countries began. The whole field was full of sheaves and peasants. Here and there among the thick, high rye where a strip had been reaped, one saw the bent back of a woman reaping, the swing of the ears as she grasped the stalks, a woman bending over a cradle in the shade, and bundles of rye scattered over the reaped parts of the field which was all covered with cornflowers. In another place peasants in their shirts and trousers stood on the carts loading up the sheaves and raising the dust on the dry, scorched field. The village elder, in boots, and with a coat thrown over his shoulders and tallysticks in his hand, took off his felt hat when he saw papa in the distance, wiped his red-haired head and beard with a towel, and shouted at the women.

---

[1] Quotations are mostly from Tolstoy's Centenary Edition (Oxford University Press).

The little roan papa rode went with a light, playful step, sometimes bending his head to his chest, pulling at the reins, and brushing off with his thick tail the gadflies and gnats that settled greedily on him. Two borzois with tense tails raised sickle-wise, and lifting their feet high, leapt gracefully over the tall stubble, behind the horse's feet. Milka (the hound) ran in front, and with head lifted, awaited the quarry. The peasants' voices, the tramp of horses and creaking of carts, the merry whistle of quail, the hum of insects hovering in the air in steady swarms, the odor of wormwood, straw, and horses' sweat, the thousands of different colors and shadows with which the burning sun flooded the light yellow stubble, the dark blue of the distant forest, the light lilac clouds, and the white cobwebs that floated in the air or stretched across the stubble—all this I saw, heard, and felt."

Trifles such as these are not only presented but also deepened by Tolstoy in all their simple concreteness. He creates not in order to find an escape from life, but in order to make life fuller. Hence the opposition between art and life disappears in his work. Humans, plants, animals, trees, are blended: all of them equally important, equally divine (in the Homeric sense). The author's capacity of identifying himself with them infects the reader, too, whose life experience thus becomes enlarged and intensified. In *Childhood, Boyhood and Youth,* we not only witness the external and inner process of a boy's growth—we live it together with him as fully as though it were our own. The same applies to the experiences described in *Sebastopol Stories,* in *The Cossacks,* and in other works, most particularly in *War and Peace* (1862-1869) and *Anna Karenina* (1875-1877).

III

War and Peace can hardly be called a historical novel
in the accepted sense. It is simply a great novel, perhaps
the greatest novel ever written. As for the historical period
described (Napoleon's invasion of Russia in 1812), Tolstoy
chose it merely as a canvas on which to unfold, with gusto,
a tremendous panorama of life. He is concerned with the
latter not so much in its historical as in its universal aspect,
with which he interweaves an incredible variety of individual
existences—all of them subject to time, to change, and dominated by the immutable law of birth, growth, and death. The
novel is, moreover, a gigantic record of an entire nation
during one of its critical moments: a record which transcends
history. Home life with unforgettable pictures of growing
children, life in the army, at Court, in the two Russian capi-
tals, in the country manors, in the peasant cottages, in the
occupied and burning Moscow, in areas crammed with
refugees and with retreating soldiers—what a rich and varied
flux of people and events, all of them concrete, full-blooded,
more real than reality itself!

Like *A Captain's Daughter* by Pushkin, *War and Peace*
is in essence a family chronicle—at least in its framework.
The events described in it circle round two aristocratic
families, the Rostovs and the Bolkonskys (Tolstoy's grand-
parents and parents, on his father's and his mother's side)
whose destinies eventually intertwine. Each individual member of these two families is made intensely alive. So is each
character in the novel. We would look in vain for a more
fascinating portrait of a girl, developing into a woman, than
Natasha Rostova. Even her brother Nikolai—a mediocrity
in every respect, is shaped into something memorable. And

then the superb gallery of other figures: Pierre Bezukhov who typifies the charm of the good-natured Russian clumsiness; the smart careerist and climber Boris Drubetskoy with his fussy careworn mother; the old Prince Bolkonsky; the Russian Commander-in-Chief, Kutuzov; the Kuragins (especially Helen); Dolokhov; the youthful Petya Rostov; the eternal peasant, Platon Karatayev. One could mention hosts of others, each one more alive than the last. And while shaping them, Tolstoy remained objective in spite of his personal leanings and theories, which intrude into the novel as periodic interpolations.

The only character to whom he was not fair was Napoleon. And for obvious reasons. What Tolstoy could not stand was the Corsican's inflated egotism: Napoleon the hero and the leader of men. *War and Peace* was Tolstoy's opportunity of showing him up, which he did with an inimitable twinkle. Even so, he preserved a matter-of-fact method of description. This is how he first introduces him to the reader: "He had just finished dressing for his ride, and wore a blue uniform opening in front over a white waistcoat, so long that it covered his rotund stomach, white leather breeches tightly fitting the fat thighs of his short legs and Hessian boots. His short hair had evidently just been brushed, but one lock hung down in the middle of his broad forehead. His plump white neck stood out sharply above the black collar of his uniform, and he smelt of eau-de-Cologne. His full face, rather young-looking, with its prominent chin, wore a gracious and majestic expression of imperial welcome. He entered briskly, with a jerk at every step and his head slightly thrown back. His whole short, corpulent figure with broad, thick shoulders, and chest and stomach involuntarily protruding, had that imposing and stately appearance one sees in men of forty who live in comfort."

War and Peace presents a whole period of Russian life *sub specie aeterni*. And it is precisely this "unhistorical" substream of timelessness that turns its characters into our own contemporaries as well, into contemporaries of any epoch. Moreover, the younger characters grow before our eyes, and one generation replaces the other as naturally as spring replaces winter. It is true that Pierre Bezukhov and Andrey Bolkonsky voice many of Tolstoy's own burrowings and ideas; but as these are blended with the characters instead of being pasted upon them, they do not interfere, as yet, with Tolstoy's art. Also the idealized peasant Karatayev, into whom Tolstoy projected one of his basic tendencies, remains fully convincing and alive. Quite a different matter are, however, his own interpolated discourses upon the unconscious urges of the masses as the only agents of history—an attitude which is the exact opposite of Carlyle's hero worship. When proclaiming the peasant Karatayev as a greater man than that "puppet of circumstances"—Napoleon, Tolstoy only affirms, once more, his anti-individualistic trend; his worship of the static "group soul" and of the undifferentiated precivilized masses. At the end of the novel, the vegetative principle of existence actually triumphs: in the married life of Pierre and Natasha, both of whom are so much submerged in the cares for their increasing family (especially Natasha) that they hardly have time for anything else. The individual is sacrificed to the race, to the species. This exaltation of the biological continuity of life, with all those processes which are beyond or outside human will and control, is in itself profoundly antihistorical. Yet Tolstoy the artist was great enough to blend even such an attitude with the material provided by history into an artistic pattern. What is more, he did this in the very teeth of his growing inner conflict, which might be defined as one between the biological and the ethical affirmation of life.

IV

The clash between the two became apparent in *Anna Karenina* which in several respects anticipates the Tolstoy of *My Confession* and of the moralizing pamphlets he wrote after 1880. The very structure of this masterpiece is based on a Rousseauesque impulse: on the antithesis between the idyllic country life and the artificial city existence. In the brooding seeker Levin, Tolstoy depicted himself as he was before his conversion. The happy love marriage between Kitty and Levin is contrasted by the "sinful" free union between the adulterous Anna Karenina and her lover Bronsky, both of whom are duly punished. Tolstoy the moralist has meted out a particularly heavy punishment to Anna. At the same time, Tolstoy the artist could not help describing her feminine charm with incomparable skill and admiration. And who could ever forget his other portraits—from the incorrigible Epicurean, Stiva Oblonsky, or the frozen bureaucrat, Karenin, to the most casual characters! But what now mattered to Tolstoy even more than art was the moral lesson. It is significant that his cultured squire Levin was saved from an inner blind alley and from suicide by an illiterate peasant. The peasant—a child of nature—knew by instinct what was good and what was right. Consequently, he alone was able to reveal to Levin not only the true meaning of the Gospel, but also of life. Here again, Tolstoy's tendency to merge with the group soul, with the masses, and with the truth of the masses came to the fore. This is what he says in *My Confession:* "Thanks either to the strange physical affection for the real laboring people, which compelled me to understand them and to see that they are not so stupid as we suppose, or thanks to the sincerity of my conviction that I could know nothing beyond the fact that the best I could do was to hang myself, at any rate I instinctively felt that if I wished to live and understand the meaning of life, I must seek this meaning not among those who have lost it and wish to kill themselves, but among those milliards of the past and present who make life and who support the burden of their own lives and of ours also. And I considered the enormous masses of those simple, unlearned, and poor people who have lived and are living."

With this he combined his equally powerful fear of death, which was only a negative expression of his biological vitality. That vitality prompted to him, now and then, words and acts which were quite beyond good and evil. Thus, at the height of his family prosperity, Tolstoy wrote to his wife in 1865, i.e. after the murderous suppression of the Polish rising: "I am not in the least interested in knowing who is oppressing the Poles, or who has conquered Schleswig-Holstein. The butcher kills the ox we eat, and I cannot be compelled to blame him or to express my sympathy." These words sound too callous to be ascribed to the great moralist Tolstoy. Yet if we bear in mind the fact that in some respects he was a force of nature, we must not be surprised that he could be also as indifferent, at times, as nature. Or that he could dread death with the same intensity with which he felt life throbbing in his own veins. This dread was latent in him since his very childhood, but became overpowering after 1879, i.e. after his conversion. "If a man has learned to think, no matter what he may think about, he is always thinking of his own death. All philosophers were like that. And what truth can there be if there is death?" he complains in *My Confession,* and in a later pamphlet (*What I Believe*) he is even more categorical about it: "Death, death, death awaits you every second. Your life passes in the presence of death. If you labor personally for your own future, you yourself know that the one thing awaiting you is—death.

And that death ruins all you work for. Consequently, life for oneself can have no meaning. If there is a reasonable life it must be found elsewhere; it must be a life, the aim of which does not lie in preparing further life for oneself."

This is how the pagan Tolstoy rationalized his own fear of death in order to use his philosophy of altruism and puritanism as a screen, behind which he could hide from his bogy. And the more he was afraid of his own latent impulses the more he turned all his theories into a Procrustean bed and chopped off everything that did not fit into his quasi-Christian scheme. Having accepted Christ's teaching like a Russian peasant, Tolstoy yet lacked the mental simplicity of a peasant to be able to follow it spontaneously and without sophistications. So he reasoned out each point and tried to improve upon the Sermon on the Mount in the name of his own private Christianity. In the end he turned Christ Himself into a Tolstoyan. The result was a slackening of his artistic activities. Regarding himself primarily as a preacher, he now issued one moralizing pamphlet after the other: *What I Believe, What Then Must We Do?, On Life, The Kingdom of God Is within You, The Slavery of Our Time, What Is Religion?*, etc. Turgenev, who had visited Tolstoy during that time, said about him in a letter: "He has plunged headlong into another sphere—has surrounded himself with Bibles and Gospels in nearly all languages, and has written a heap of papers. He has a trunk full of these mystical ethics and various pseudo-interpretations. Very probably he will give nothing more to literature, or if he reappears, it will be with that trunk. . . ."

v

Fortunately for literature, the artist in Tolstoy was not entirely crushed by the moralist. Nor did he ever bridge over his inner split. This little incident, recorded by Gorky in his *Reminiscences of Tolstoy* [1] is significant. Tolstoy walked with a friend in the Moscow streets, when all of a sudden two guardsmen came walking in the opposite direction. "The metal of their accoutrements shone in the sun; their spurs jingled; they kept step like one man; their faces, too, shone with self-assurance of strength and youth. Tolstoy began to grumble at them: 'What pompous stupidity! Like animals trained by the whip! . . .' But when the guardsmen came abreast with him, he stopped, followed them with his eyes, and said enthusiastically: 'How handsome! Old Romans, eh? Their strength and beauty! O Lord! How charming it is when man is handsome, how very charming!' "

His former duality remained the same after his conversion, but with the moralist on top. Still, there are splendidly written pages even in his pamphlets—those in particular in which he attacks our capitalist system and civilization. But what he offers us in exchange for our present mode of life proves that, instead of overcoming civilization he only wants to run away from it—back to an amorphous precivilized community, and to a puritanism which he adopted in order to check his own latent sensuality of which he was so afraid. Had he been less afraid of it, he would never have written his *Kreutzer Sonata*, with its curious message that even man and wife should abstain from sexual intercourse. His perverted puritanism came out rather unpleasantly in his last big novel, *Ressurrection*. We read there how a refined and cultured girl—a political exile, befriended the former prostitute and murderess, Katyusha Maslova, on the ground that they were "united by the repulsion they both felt for sexual love. The one loathed that love, having experienced all its horrors; the other, never having experienced it, looked on it

[1] Translated by M. Kotelyansky (Hogarth Press).

as something incomprehensible, and at the same time as something repugnant and offensive to human dignity."

The same puritanic furore which made him degrade sexual love to the level of prostitution was responsible for his attacks on his own art, on Shakespeare, on modernism (in *What is Art?*), on all beauty devoid of a moral or didactic purpose. Yet the great master of the word refused to capitulate. Splendid narratives were still coming from under his pen.

He, moreover, simplified his language so as to make it accessible to the peasants whose parables and legends he successfully imitated in his *Folk Tales*. One of his notable works of that period is his *The Death of Ivan Ilyitch*—an overpowering treatment of the theme of death. Another attempt to exorcise fear out of death is his great story *Master and Man*. Even his *Resurrection*, encumbered though it may be by Tolstoy's moralizing mania, is a remarkable novel—remarkable even in its defects. And as for his posthumous works, one cannot help admiring his *Father Sergius*, *The Devil* (with its autobiographic touch), *The False Coupon*, *Hadji Murad*, and the refreshing peasant story *Alyosha Gorshok*.

Tolstoy was the most puzzling and the most conspicuous literary figure in Europe during the last two decades of the nineteenth and the first decade of the twentieth century. The universal interest in his writings may have suffered an eclipse of late, but this does not diminish their value. Whatever one may think of Tolstoy the moralist and thinker, Tolstoy the artist will always be looked upon as one of the giants of world literature.

CHAPTER XI

The Chekhov Period

THE SOCIAL and political impetus of the 'sixties spent itself in a comparatively short time. Reaction began to creep into Russian life once more, and triumphed completely after the assassination of Alexander II (on March 1, 1881). Under his follower, Alexander III, there was a rapid development of industry. As the freed peasants had not received enough land to live on with their increasing families, many of them were compelled either to emigrate to Siberia, or else to invade the towns where they were employed in the factories as cheap labor. Industrialization went on at such a pace that even the die-hard populists failed to see how Russia could avoid the capitalist phase of evolution. The more so because all around there was an orgy of money-making, while the intellectuals seemed to have lost all orientation. The superfluous man was now enlarged into a superfluous intelligentsia. Higher purposes of any kind had become remote and impossible. The former idealists were driven into the morass of Philistine existence, into cynicism, or into helpless nostalgia. Some of them found a refuge in alcohol, others in Tolstoyanism with its cult of moral self-perfection. Society as a whole submitted almost willingly to the bureaucratic pressure from above.

Paradoxically enough, this mood, so typical of the 'eighties, favored a detached aesthetic attitude towards art and literature. The very absence of obligatory slogans and purposes brought more freedom into literary creation, but the creative *élan* itself was much weaker than in the previous two decades. Russian thought, too, now less dogmatic and categorical, was able to branch off in new directions. The best sociological publicist and critic of that period, N. K. Mikhailovsky, kept to his populist convictions to the end. But Marxism had already appeared on the horizon and was only waiting for its chance. As a contrast, the conservative Russo-Byzantine trend, with a strong admixture of the land-owner type of "Nietzscheanism," found an expression in the writings of Konstantin Leontyev—one of the fiercest crusaders against the democratic tendencies in modern society. Something different emerged, however, in Vladimir Solovyov's attempt at a synthesis of culture, religion, and life—an attempt which was responsible for the rather active neo-idealist trend in the Russian school of thought. Despite these quests and gropings, the inner stagnation continued unabated. What the moods of that decade were, can be gathered from the work of Vsevolod M. Garshin (1855-1888) and even more from those of Anton P. Chekhov (1860-1904), so much so that the period we are now dealing with can justly be called the "Chekhov Period."

II

Garshin's sensitiveness was equaled only by his Dostoevskian feeling of personal responsibility for all the evil, for all the "insulted and injured." Hence the morbid intensity of his stories. Unable to separate his artistic and his human (or rather humanitarian) selves, he recorded, in a series of stories, not only the stifling age he lived in, but also his personal vexation of spirit which in the end drove him to madness and suicide. A disposition such as this is reflected in his style: condensed, nervously impressionistic, but devoid of affectation. He wavers between the carefully worked out short *nouvelle* and the agitated diary form. The tension, which is always there, is due not to the intricacies of the plot but to the rankling of some wounded idea or ideal. Although not large in bulk, his work is incisive. It opened up, moreover, further possibilities in the same direction.

Garshin made his debut with *Four Days*—a longish, excellently told story from the Russo-Turkish War in which he had taken part (1877) as a volunteer. *Four Days* is a rendering of impressions, thoughts, and emotions he himself had passed through, while lying wounded on the battlefield beside the corpse of a Turk, shot by him in the battle. It was the nervous vigor of his style, and partly also his hidden antiwar tendency that accounted for the success of the story. The same antimilitarist spirit came out in some of his further narratives, in *A Coward*, for instance. Soon, however, Garshin turned to tragic themes, to the problem of evil in its social and moral aspects. His *Nadezhda Nikolayevna* is an example. This story of a somewhat idealized prostitute depicts a human tragedy as viewed by two dramatically contrasted attitudes. A similar contrast is worked out in one of his best-known narratives, *The Artists*. One of the characters is a talented young painter, who becomes so overwhelmed by his pity for the dehumanized slaves of modern industry that he abandons his artistic vocation in order to help the "insulted and injured" as an ordinary schoolteacher. But the irony of it all is that his sacrifice proves of no use either to the workers or to himself: the roots of the social evil are too deep to be solved by such isolated efforts. Garshin's horror at the injustice of life came out in his little gem, *The Red Flower*. Its hero is a madman who dies in the happy delusion that by plucking a certain red flower he has destroyed all the evil in the world. Garshin's own end was devoid even of this delusion.

Such moods were often prevalent among the best intellectuals of the 'eighties. Yet there were exceptions. Vladimir

G. Korolenko (1853-1921), whose first works coincided with that decade, definitely refused to succumb to its oppressive atmosphere. A Pole by his mother, a Ukrainian by his father, and a Russian by education, Korolenko combined his quest for justice not only with a sunny disposition towards life, but also with a strong sense of humor. He even persevered in the populist idealism of the 'seventies, although he saw clearly some of those evils which had so dismayed his older contemporary, Gleb Uspensky. He bravely stuck to his guns and had to pay for it with a six-year-long exile in the remotest parts of Siberia.

Korolenko is one of the most genially humane Russian authors. His impressionism and the musical flow of language are in the tradition of Turgenev. So are his descriptions of nature. These are blended not only with the moods of the characters, but with the action itself, as for instance in his *The Frost*, or *The Wood Rustles*. His mellowness may verge now and then on sentimentality, from which he is saved by his humor, his common sense, and most of all by his personality—simple and lucid as the style of his prose. Korolenko's best-known narratives, such as *Makar's Dream*, *The Frost*, *The Blind Musician*, *The Wood Rustles*, *At Night*, *The Judgment Day*, etc., are based either on his Siberian experiences and impressions, or else on his reminiscences of South Russia. In both cases he often deals with peasants. But whatever theme he chooses, he invariably imbues it with that human warmth which compensates one for a certain lack of creative verve in his works. Like so many of his characters he, too, was a seeker for truth and justice. Divided between the task of an author and a publicist, he did not mix the two like Uspensky. Technically, he separated these activities. But in the second half of his life, the militant pamphleteer took the upper hand.

This may have been due to his connection with *The Russian Wealth (Russkoe Bogatstvo)*—the populist monthly which replaced *The Fatherland's Annals*, suppressed in 1883. During the last thirty years of his life, Korolenko's voice commanded attention. Some of his pamphlets (for example, the one attacking the executions after the abortive revolution of 1905) stirred the entire public opinion to righteous indignation. Lastly, Korolenko's autobiographic *History of My Contemporary* should be mentioned. It consists of three volumes, bringing the author's life up to 1881. Full of vivid pictures of his childhood, youth, student years, and early manhood, this panorama of distilled memories is shown together with the epoch the younger generation of those days had to tackle and to cope with.

Before passing to Chekhov, a few other authors should be dealt with in brief, to begin with the already mentioned Boborykin. He showed the unpalatable new bourgeoisie and the generation of the 'eighties in a naturalistic manner, not devoid of sensationalism. Two other able representatives of realism, A. I. Ertel (1855-1908) and D. Mamin-Sibiryak (1852-1912), both had populist sympathies. Ertel, a mild Tolstoyan by his views, described the provinces and also the business world after 1861: the period in which the bourgeois and the capitalist elements were beginning to intrude into all the walks of life. His novel, *The Gardenin Family*, is still regarded as a masterpiece of its kind. Ertel excels in portraits and in landscapes. But he is inclined to indulge in description of nature for its own sake. On the other hand, many a page of his is enlivened by his fine humor. As for Mamin-Sibiryak, he is a regional and social novelist in one. He wrote mainly about the mining industries in the Urals, or else about the corn trade with its magnates and victims. Anxious to point out the destructive side of capitalism, he successfully portrayed its devotees in such novels as *Privalov's Millions, Bread, Gold,* etc. One of his most powerful stories depicts thousands of starved boatmen, mercilessly exploited by a bogus firm in the Urals.

Another author who came into prominence in the 'eighties was Nikolay N. Kazin (1842-1908). A favorite theme of his novels is the invasion of Siberia by all sorts of spurious businessmen, whose rivalries had a disastrous effect. It is a pity that his writings are spoilt by melodramatic touches. A solid realist was N. G. Garin (his name was Mikhailovsky, 1852-1906) whose trilogy, *Foma's Childhood, High School Boys, Students,* is a disguised autobiography, turned into good literature. It is also a reliable documentary picture of the development of Russian youths in those days.

The method employed by these authors conformed to tradition. Garshin was an exception, but even his technical innovations were not startling. A departure on new lines was, however, made by Chekhov.

III

Anton Pavlovitch Chekhov is the most conspicuous transition figure between the great age of prose and the modernist wave. He was a commoner by birth and started writing while studying medicine in Moscow. His first stories were for the most part potboilers for humorous papers: amusing and ironical anecdotes, influenced by Gogol, and probably by Ivan F. Gorbunov (an excellent anecdotic *diseur*). Chekhov's *Motley Stories* (1886) were written mainly in this vein. Sometime about 1887, however, or soon after, a sudden change took place in him. This change was first apparent in his play, *Ivanov* (1888), and in his second collection of stories, *Gloomy People* (1890). Both testify to an awareness of that blind alley of life which dominated the moods of the 'eighties. It was Chekhov's art as a whole that gave a powerful diagnosis of contemporary Russian society, and particularly of the intelligentsia. He expressed their stagnation in accents of suppressed and muffled tragedy—accents which reach their climax in such longer narratives as *A Tedious Story, My Life, Ward No. 6, The Duel, Three Years,* etc.

In the first of these the reader is plunged into an atmosphere of hopeless futility. Its victims, an aged professor who has known fame, and his sensitive girl relative who has just started life, are both crushed by the muddle, stupidity, and emptiness of existence. They understand, they sympathize with each other. Yet the moment they crave for mutual warmth and confidence, neither is able to open up or to overcome the barriers of personal isolation. In the end they part like two bankrupts: with no hopes, no prospects, even without understanding why they are crushed, or why they must part. But they accept their fate with resignation. The final chord is that of perplexed sadness for which there is no remedy. In his *My Life* we see again the fate of a high-minded youth, compelled to put up with a futile provincial existence. Another variation on a similar theme is *Ward No. 6.* Its hero, the doctor of a lunatic asylum in the provinces, is cultured and intelligent, but has become utterly passive in practical matters. The only other sane inhabitant of the town is an inmate of the asylum. The doctor befriends the patient and spends hours with him, talking about things that matter. These eccentric conversations soon arouse suspicion about the doctor's own sanity. Finally, his assistant (a thick-skinned, unscrupulous vulgarian) usurps his place by declaring his chief a lunatic and forcibly turning him into an inmate of the asylum where he dies.

In *The Teacher of Literature* a young intellectual marries, overflowing with joy and happiness. And this is how the story ends, about a year later: "The March sun was shining brightly in at the windows and shedding its warm rays on the table. It was only the twentieth of the month, but already the cabmen were driving wheels, and the starlings were noisy in the garden. It was just the weather in which Masha (his wife) would come in, put one arm round his neck, tell him the horses were saddled or the chaise was at the door, and ask him what she should put on to keep warm. Spring was beginning as exquisitely as last spring, and it promised the same joys. . . . But Nikitin was thinking that it would be nice to take a holiday and go to Moscow, and stay at his old lodging there. In the next room they were drinking coffee and talking of Captain Polyansky, while he tried not to listen and wrote in his diary: Where am I, my God? I am surrounded by vulgarity and vulgarity. Wearisome, insignificant people, pots of sour cream, jugs of milk, cockroaches, stupid women. . . . There is nothing more terrible, mortifying, and distressing than vulgarity. I must escape from here, I must escape today, or I shall go out of my mind." [1]

Cruelly pathetic, *The Black Monk, In the Ravine,* and scores of other stories show the same principal moods and motives of Chekhov. They also illustrate his cult of frustration—a feature which is so totally different from the Anglo-Saxon cult of success. This may be one of the reasons why Chekhov prefers the stagnant and drab provinces as the setting for his writings. Gogol was driven to despair by that drabness, and Chekhov—to resigned melancholy. But whereas Gogol tried to save himself in religion, in pretentious moral outbursts, Chekhov is much too honest in his knowledge of life to champion any highfalutin ideas or ideals. At the same time he does not subscribe to any black pessimism either, at least with regard to the future. Everything in him is strangely noncommittal and understated. If Gogol hid his

---

[1] Translated by Constance Garnett (Chatto & Windus).

despair behind "laughter through tears," Chekhov knows how to hide his behind a smile—a nostalgic smile, full of tolerance and warmth, but devoid of respect for man. Often it is not what he says that matters, but what he transmits through his silence, or through a casual conversation which camouflages more disturbing things underneath. Nor does he ever raise his voice, but remains quiet, fastidious, and always observant of small but important details. Even a passage taken at random, the beginning of his *A Misfortune*, is enough to convey the suggestive casualness or even baldness of his descriptions. "Sofya Petrovna, the wife of Lubyantsev, the notary, a handsome young woman of five and twenty, was walking slowly along a track that had been cleared in the wood, with Ilyin, a lawyer who was spending the summer in the neighborhood. It was five o'clock in the evening. Feathery-white masses of clouds stood overhead; patches of blue sky peeped out between them. The clouds stood motionless, as though they had been caught in the tops of the tall old pine-trees. It was still and sultry. Farther on, the track was crossed by a low railway embankment on which a sentinel with a gun was for some reason pacing up and down. Just beyond the embankment there was a large white church with six domes and a rusty roof."

IV

In Chekhov's stories (and plays) the monumental Russian realism began to disintegrate. It was Maxim Gorky who guessed that after Chekhov it was hardly possible to write in the old orthodox manner and said this clearly in a letter he wrote to him in 1900: "Do you know what you are doing? You are slaying realism. And you will slay it pretty soon, you will murder it, and for good. Realism has outlived its time, that's a fact. No one can follow this path beyond you, no one can write so simply about such simple things as you know how to do. After any of your stories, however insignificant, everything appears crude, as though written not by a pen but by a cudgel. . . . So there you are going to dispatch realism." [1]

But the very manner in which he was "dispatching" it, assumed in Chekhov's writing a style of its own. For one thing, the old narrative with a well-developed plot was replaced in his stories by a number of apparently casual bits, incidents, patches, and slices of life, welded together not so much by the plot as by the atmosphere. This can be said also of his longer stories, especially of *The Steppe.* Chekhov's impressionist atmosphere becomes in fact the very core of his writings whose nostalgia reflects so poignantly the basic moods of his generation. His method of suggestive understatement found a powerful medium also in the rhythm of his language, full of minor notes and subdued echoes, capable of rendering some of the most elusive shades of human sensitiveness. And the tragedy of so many of his characters is essentially one of sensitiveness in its conflict with vulgarity. The real motive of *Ward No. 6, My Life, Three Years, A Tedious Story,* and numerous other narratives is sensitiveness versus vulgarity. The same applies to his plays. But vulgarity always wins. And the more smug, practical, and brutal it is, the more is it likely to be crowned by what is regarded as success in life. Hence Chekhov's cult of failure is not devoid of logic.

If Chekhov is partial at all, it is towards the victims of their own simplehearted warmth and generosity. Even when amused by them (in his masterpiece, *The Darling,* for example), he still watches them with an understanding smile whose secret tenderness is as inimitable as the atmosphere conjured up by such of his plays as *The Seagull, Uncle*

[1] Quoted from the *Slavonic Review,* vol. XVII.

Vanya, Three Sisters, and *Cherry Orchard.* This tenderness found its indirect expression also in his loathing of self-satisfied Philistines. The antiphilistinism of Gogol was continued by Chekhov, who exposed it as sham life, as antilife. Approached from this angle, one can perhaps better understand his vogue among the advanced British intellectuals a few years ago.

Chekhov's genius is of a smaller caliber than the genius of Tolstoy or Dostoevsky. His language, on the whole, is less racy than that of his great predecessors. Yet on his own ground and within his limits he is unique. Apart from being a notable playwright, he ranks, together with Maupassant, as one of the greatest short-story writers in world literature. And like Maupassant, he died at the early age of forty-four.

CHAPTER XII

Maxim Gorky

THE DESPONDENCE and stagnation of the 'eighties could not last indefinitely. The next decade opened with several signs of a new and different era. The famine of 1891-1892 was in itself enough to arouse the intelligentsia from lethargy. On the other hand, with the growth of industrial enterprises in Russia (there were 40,000 of them by 1890), the town proletariat had increased accordingly. This new force soon began to play its part in the social and historical destinies of the country. Both the old manor type and the populist type of novel now practically ceased to count. What remained of the first was largely a negative attitude towards the manor, while the cult—whether populist or Slavophil—of the peasant was replaced by such grim village narratives as Chekhov's *The Peasants* and *In the Ravine*. Town motives began to predominate. The hopes of a new future were pinned to the town worker rather than to the conservative moujik. In the violent polemics between the Marxians (led by P. B. Struve) and the populists of the 'nineties, most of the principles and institutions, dear to the latter, were discredited. Even the famous *obshchhina* or the village commune was proved to be only a device to enslave the individual peasant all the more firmly.

The important thing, however, was that the town workers no longer formed an amorphous mass. They were being organized into a conscious class movement. The Marxian doctrine, introduced into Russia in the 'eighties, was making headway. It soon provided a link between the workers and those intellectuals who had rebelled against the passive "Chekhovian" twilight. The Russian social-democrat party found able leaders in Plekhanov and later in Lenin, whose personal integrity was itself a powerful propaganda for the socialist creed. But at the same time, the self-indulgent individualism of the 'eighties bore its fruits in decadent currents, which deliberately ignored the social element in literature and gave themselves to the cult of aestheticism and of the ego. In this way a split was produced in the literature of the 'nineties. It led to modernist trends on the one hand, and to a renewal of Russian realism on the other. If the former appealed mainly to the highbrows—to men with literary culture and with the *fin de siècle* mentality, the latter had its readers among the average intellectuals. The more so, because by that time a new type of intellectual or half intellectual from the working classes began to assert himself. But his needs had little to do with those of the highbrows. The most outstanding young author of that decade, Maxim Gorky, was himself one of those self-made intellectuals from below. This explains not only his meteoric rise to fame, but also the part he was destined to play in the history of Russian culture during its most critical years.

II

The real name of Maxim Gorky (that is, Maxim the Bitter) was Alexey Maximovitch Peshkov. Born into a family of artisans in 1868 at Nizhny Novgorod, now called Gorky, he lost his parents at an early age and had to undergo all the humiliations of a frustrated childhood. As he had no regular education, his only teacher was life. From his boyhood on, he followed one profession after the other and tramped all over Russia, either in search of work or simply as a vagrant.

This brought him into contact with countless people and conditions. The nature of his experiences can be gathered from his autobiographic books, which are mainly about his ordeals and adventures before his spectacular entry into literature.

Gorky made his debut in 1892 with *Makar Chudra*. The story appeared in Tiflis, where he was working at the time. Three years later he was introduced to the general public by Korolenko's monthly, *The Russian Wealth*. But it was from 1898 on that he continued to rise to the height of fame more quickly and more triumphantly than any author before him. Each new narrative of his was an event. In 1900 he tried his luck also as a dramatist. His play, *The Philistines*, was produced by the Moscow Art Theatre, while his *Nether Depths* had a successful run also in the theaters of Europe and America.[1] A year or so later, he became an active member of the Russian social-democrat party and played a prominent role in the revolt of 1905. His writings of that period are marked by his attacks on the bourgeoisie and intelligentsia. All his sympathies were with the workers, struggling for a better future. After the abortive revolution of 1905, Gorky left for abroad. Later he settled down in Capri, where his villa became a center of revolutionary exiles. In Capri he wrote *A Confession* (1908), marked by a curious quasi-mystical exaltation of the Russian people— those eternally restless seekers and "God-builders." It is interspersed with vigorous landscape painting and with pictures of provincial manners which he amplified—but in a different, i.e. critical spirit—in his *Chronicle of the Town Okurov* and in its continuation, *Matvey Kozhemyakin*.

During all that time, that is, from 1904 to 1913, he was director of the publishing company "Knowledge" (*Znanie*).

---

[1] Gorky's dramatic technique is a not very successful imitation of Chekhov.

This firm was a rallying point of the younger authors, whose realism was imbued with social significance and was opposed to the decadent and symbolist currents, especially to the *fin de siècle* subjectivism and pessimism. But in spite of the varieties of his duties and activities, Gorky wrote, from now on, a number of books, the best of them (*Childhood, In the World, My Universities*) being about himself. Others depict Russian life and manners and particularly the decay of the Russian bourgeoisie.

When the war broke out he was frankly defeatist. During the revolution of 1917 he did not commit himself entirely to any party, but it was mainly he who saved numerous art treasures from destruction. He did everything he could in order to help those writers and scientists who had remained in Russia. Involved in some bitter polemics, and afflicted also with lung trouble, he went abroad in 1922. Meanwhile, his prestige kept growing all over Russia. On his return in 1928, he was generally looked upon as the greatest moral and cultural force in the Soviet Union. His mysterious death in 1936 was due to poison, administered to him by his own doctors.

III

Gorky's creative urge came from his impulse to overcome his feeling of social inferiority, and the drabness of the life he saw around. He started to write as a self-assertive romantic, full of defiance. Instead of submitting to "Chekhovian" resignation, he sounded a warlike clarion, in which there vibrated strength, self-reliance, and a youthful will to live fully and dangerously. Untrammeled by any taboos, traditions, and conventions, he chose characters most likely to express the same attitude towards life: tramps and roamers whose only home was the endless expanse of the steppes, and whose favorite melody—the song of the winds, of the sea. The old gypsy Izegril, Tchelkash, the breezy Malva, or Varenka Olyosova are some of them. To those he added the social outcasts of the towns, the "people who once were humans." In both cases he protested either against the drabness of life, or the injustice of our present system. Hence the scorn, the naïvely "Nietzschean" insistence on the pride of the social underdog, in so many stories of his earlier period.

His flouting of all the bourgeois "good and evil" was not devoid of nihilism. But even when his arguments were not convincing, his temperamental language appealed to those intellectuals who were tired of the moody impressionists. For there was vigor even in Gorky's rhetoric. In addition, he insisted on a change of life; on new aims and ideals, which could not fail to influence the younger generation. In the already quoted letter to Chekov, Gorky wrote these words which might well be applied to his own writings: "Truly, at this moment one feels the need of heroics: there is a common desire for stimulating, brilliant things, for life, better, more beautiful. It is absolutely necessary for present-day literature to begin embellishing life a bit, and as soon as it begins to do so, life will take on color; I mean men will begin to live a quickened, a brighter life."

It was his romantic propensity to "embellish life a bit" that was responsible both for his criticism of the life he saw around him and for the revolutionary character of his work. As the stormy petrel of the revolution, he naturally adopted an appropriate manner. His style of that period was saturated, often rhetorical, full of color, and at times irritatingly didactic. Here are a few typical passages from one of his early stories, *Tchelkash:* "The jingle of the anchor chains, the rattle of the links of the trucks that bring down the cargoes, the metallic clank of sheets of iron falling on the stone pavement, the dull thud of wood, the creaking of the carts plying for hire, the whistles of the steamers, piercingly shrill and hoarsely roaring, the shouts of dock laborers, sailors, and custom officers—all these sounds melt into the deafening symphony of the working day, that hovering uncertainly hangs over the harbor, as though afraid to float upwards and be lost. And fresh waves of sound continually rise up from the earth to join it; deep, grumbling, sullen reverberations setting all around quaking; shrill, menacing notes that pierce the ear and the dusty, sultry air. The granite, the iron, the wood, the harbor pavement, the ships and the men—all swelled the mighty strains of this frenzied, impassioned hymn to Mercury. But the voices of men, scarcely audible, were weak and ludicrous. And the men, too, themselves, the first source of all that uproar, were ludicrous and pitiable: their little figures, dusty, tattered, nimble, bent under the weight of goods that lay on their backs, under the weight of cares that drove them hither and thither, in the clouds of dust, in the sea of sweltering heat and din, were so trivial and small in comparison with the colossal iron monsters, the mountains of bales, the thundering railway trucks and all that they created. Their own creation had enslaved them, and stolen away their individual life. As they lay letting off steam, the heavy giant steamers whistled or hissed, or seemed to heave deep sighs, and in every sound that came from them could be heard the mocking note of ironical contempt for the gray, dusty shapes of men, crawling about their decks and filling their deep holds with the fruits of their slavish toil. Ludicrous and pitiable were the long strings of dock laborers bearing on their backs thousands of tons of bread, and casting it into the iron bellies of the ships to gain a few pounds of the same bread to fill their own bellies—for them, worse luck, not made of iron, but alive to the pangs of hunger. The men, tattered, drenched with sweat, made dull by weariness, and din and heat; and the mighty machines, created by those men, shining, well-fed, serene, in the sunshine; machines which in the last resort are, after all, not set in motion by steam, but by the muscles and blood of their creators—in this contrast was a whole poem of cruel and frigid irony." [1]

It was precisely these working men, "tattered, drenched with sweat," that were eventually singled out by Gorky as the only hope for the future. In the smug Philistines he saw nothing but decay. He despised them and their bourgeois ways with every fiber of his soul. His outraged sense of justice and his human pride rebelled against the capitalist order of life. It was partly through such an attitude that the former romantic Gorky arrived at the straightforward and rugged realism which links him to one of the basic traditions of Russian literature as a whole. Equally strong is his emphasis on the quest for higher values; on the innate yearning for beauty and decency among the lowest: among those stepsons of life, who have no chance to gratify such an urge. Gorky's *Twenty-six Men and a Girl* is one of the finest stories of this kind.

Unfortunately, the seeker and reformer was too strong even in Gorky the artist to be able to abstain from reasoning or preaching. He often turned his characters into heralds of his own messages and ideas. Hence the impression as though a number of them were only acting their appointed parts. And what is more, those reasonings, discussions, and admonitions are often carried on in a bookish language. This duality intrudes too much into Gorky's plays and longer prose works, especially those he wrote after 1905. It is disturbing in his first novel, *Foma Gordeyev* (1899), which presents an agitatedly drawn picture of the provincial trading bourgeoisie—with the uprooted Foma, rebelling against his own class, in the center. Like his less compact novel,

---

[1] From *Twenty-six Men and a Girl, and Other Stories,* by Maxim Gorky (Duckworth).

The Three of Them (Troe), it has for its background a busy Volga town towards the end of the century. His *Mother* (1907-1908), on the other hand, is crammed with socialistic outbursts and with protest. Full of defects, it preserves all the same its value as an epic of the Russian working-class life and struggle. The brewing revolutionary forces are strongly felt also in such long novels of manners as *The Artamonov Business* (1925) and his unfinished last novel. Yet Gorky's socialist propaganda is only another proof of his craving for justice which comes out in most of his works. It intrudes even into his lyrical descriptions—such as this, taken from *In the World*.

"I walked up to the town and came out in the fields. It was midnight, heavy clouds floated in the sky, obliterating my shadow on the earth by their own black shadows. Leaving the town for the fields, I reached the Volga, and there I lay in the dusty grass and looked for a long time at the river, the meadow on that motionless earth. Across the Volga the shadows of the clouds floated slowly; by the time they had reached the meadow they looked brighter as if they had been washed by the water of the river, everything around seemed half asleep, stupefied as it were, moving unwillingly, and only because it was compelled to do so, and not from a flaming love of movement and life. And I desired to cast a spell over the whole earth and myself, which would cause everyone, myself included, to be swept by a joyful whirlwind, a festival dance of people, loving one another in this life, spending their lives for the sake of others, beautiful, brave, honorable." [1]

IV

It was from 1902 (after having joined the social-democrat party) that Gorky became didactic almost from a sense of

[1] *In the World* (Werner Laurie).

duty. His descriptions of the commercial bourgeoisie are particularly scathing. And if his novel, *The Life of Klim Samgin*, with its background of the chaotic revolutionary Russia is much too long and uneven, he becomes highly condensed in his truly fine *The Artamonov Business*: a tale about three generations of commercial prosperity, stained with a crime, and destroyed by the recent revolution. But even at its best, Gorky's style looks somewhat improvised, if not careless. The structure of his works, too, is often motivated rather by his ideals than by his artistic urge. He is prone to simplify not only ideas, but also psychology. In his lack of shades he mistakes, now and then, brutality for strength, and his love of glaring colors forms the greatest contrast to Chekhov's art. On the other hand, his observations are acute and shrewd.

This is particularly clear to a careful reader of the four-volumed *Klim Samgin*—a chronicle of Russian life during some forty years preceding the Revolution of 1917. It is done on an enormous canvas, and the principal character, Klim, is a masterpiece of psychological dissection. He is depicted as a Russian middle-class Hamlet, typical of that critically thinking intelligentsia which, "educated by the pamphleteers and the *littérateurs*," had already finished its part in history and was unable to accept or even to understand the new tasks demanded from it. He is decidedly clever, but in a destructive sense. His cold and prying mind is always suspicious and too much on its guard to allow him to trust even his good impulses. It is, in fact, that sterile and self-conscious intelligence which leads to the blasé kind of egotism and makes one unable to go beyond or outside oneself. Even when Samgin acts, he does so without real faith: his thought "oxidizes everything, covering it with the monotonous rust of criticism." As his skeptical mind is divorced from his deeper emotional life, he becomes morbidly ambivalent and therefore even less able to find that focal point which would absorb him completely. He confuses his inner aimlessness with mental freedom, and this itself goes far to explain his sterility. Behind his intelligentsia mask there is a hidden Philistine who emerges during the Revolution. Proofs of Gorky's psychological shrewdness are also his studies of Tolstoy, Chekhov, and Korolenko. His impression of Tolstoy in particular gives an interesting clue to that great and puzzling figure.

Gorky can be regarded as a symbol of the transition period between the old and the new Russia. A restless intellectual nomad looking for an anchorage, he became a romantic of the revolution and incidentally a precursor of what is called at present "socialist realism." When the revolution broke out, he did his best to humanize it, to prevent it from degenerating into mere revolution for its own sake. It was here that his personality and his work served as a bridge between the creative values of the old intelligentsia culture and the culture of the risen masses, anxious to build up a new world.

CHAPTER XIII

The Modernist Movement

THERE WERE several reasons why, towards the end of the century, modernism prevailed in Russia. The growth of economic and social complexities in Russian life brought in its train a marked cultural differentiation, with the high-brows as the vanguard of the latest literary fashions. Inspired by the French *décadents,* from Baudelaire to Verlaine, from Rimbaud to Maeterlinck and Mallarmé, these Russian modernists were determined to sever literature from all utilitarian or social purposes. They frankly adopted the formula of "art for art's sake"—in which effort they found an ally even in Oscar Wilde. Parallel with this, they were apprehensive about the organized masses or collectives, in whom they saw a danger to the sovereign rights and caprices of the individual. The gospel of aestheticism thus merged with the gospel of self-sufficient egotism, the highest expression of which was Nietzsche's philosophy of the superman. But once the two had become one, they landed many of their votaries in the blind alley of a sterile self-centeredness. So it was necessary to find some outlet. An emergency outlet was provided by the revolution of 1905. But the hopes aroused at first were crushed by its failure. The aftermath had a disastrous effect upon literature. It increased the cult of decadence, of despair, and of literary dopes.

The banner of modernism was first raised by two not very promising poets: Merezhkovsky and Minsky. Its starting point was Merezhkovsky's provocative book of essays, *About the Causes and Decay and the New Currents in Russian*

Literature (1893). It was followed two years later by a collection of modernist poems, *The Russian Symbolists,* largely
influenced by Maeterlinck and Verlaine. In spite of general
derision, the current kept on growing. Such decadents as
Hippius, Balmont, Bryusov, and Sologub, established their
reputation on public resistance. But even before the century
was out, that resistance turned into applause. Modernism
became the leading trend, its center being Diaghilev's extrav-
agantly lavish monthly, *The World of Art,* founded in 1898.

It did not take long, however, before a certain split was
noticeable in this trend. The aesthetic cliques, hothouses, and
"ivory towers" struck a few adepts of art for art's sake as
leading to sterility and individual disintegration. A change
of attitude was imminent. As the latter could not be achieved
except by a change of consciousness, the boundaries of art
had to be enlarged accordingly. Modernism began to grope
for an alliance with religion, mysticism, and would-be mysticism. Eventually, a small group aimed at turning art into
"theurgy," which would create new myths, a new type of
consciousness, new forms of life. It was at this juncture that
the influence of Dostoevsky, Solovyov, and of the early
"Dionysian" Nietzsche (of *The Birth of Tragedy*) became
paramount.

One of the books responsible for the cult of Dostoevsky
was Vasily V. Rozanov's (1856-1919) *The Legend of the
Grand Inquisitor* (1890), in which the author analyzed Dostoevsky's works from the standpoint of the new religious consciousness. But Rozanov himself fell a prey to certain decadent propensities, especially to his mystical cult of sex. At
times one can definitely feel in him latent exhibitionism,
peering through his intensely personal prose—a prose full of
winks, suggestive inflections, and quaint grimaces.[1]

---

[1] Rozanov's cult of sex is reminiscent of D. H. Lawrence. Both have a
number of points in common, including their propensity for mixing biology
and mysticism.

Dostoevsky's religious trend affected also some of those ex-socialists who eventually rejected Marx in the name of a more spiritual interpretation of man and life. In the course of the polemics, started by P. Struve, Bulgakov, and Berdyayev, certain problems of Dostoevsky and of the Slavophils were raised once more, but in a new form. This religious spirit was fostered by the philosophy of Solovyov, whose influence was soon noticeable even in the character of Russian symbolism itself.

II

Vladimir S. Solovyov (1851-1900) was a kind of Don Quixote of active idealism in an age of materialistic thought. As an opponent of mere reasoning "armchair philosophy," he was something of a mystical visionary, as well as a poet, aiming at a synthesis of religion, philosophy, science, art, and life. He wanted to achieve this through a change of man's consciousness and its gradual ascent towards God-man or Christ. His standpoint was the reverse of Nietzsche's deified man-God. So it is hardly surprising that some of those Russian moderns, who wanted to get out of their decadent egotism, should have found in Solovyov one of their guides. It was mainly under his banner that they made the passage from decadence to symbolism. And symbolism with them was not a matter of mere literary technique (as was largely the case in France), but of a new world perception, of a new interpretation of life and of man. Yet the symbolist period, which gave the finest harvest of poetry since Pushkin and culminated in the work of Alexander Blok (1880-1921), cannot be dissociated from decadence. The two trends continued to mix and overlap, until the revolution of 1917 left both behind as products of the old society. As our task is only the prose of that period, we

can perhaps best approach it through its single representatives, such as Merezhkovsky, Hippius, Sologub, Bryusov,
and Bely.

Dmitry S. Merezhkovsky (1865-1943) is essentially an
erudite whose will to create is stronger than his talent. After
an indifferent start as a poet, he switched over to philosophic
criticism, historical novels, plays, and pamphlets. In all this
he showed a great eclectic knowledge and the dogmatism
of a seeker, inclined to turn his pet ideas into fixed ideas,
into reasoned-out schemes. For he is essentially a rationalist
—an agitated and temperamental rationalist, rebelling against
his own rationalism which he is unable to overcome. His
secret is his inner coldness—the coldness of a man, anxious
to persuade his readers and himself (especially himself) that
he is a modern prophet, full of divine fire. The result is a
forced agitation, an overloud grating note which often
verges on hysteria. However cleverly constructed some of
his writings may be, in the end he is more at home in the
archives and theories than among living characters or in
living life. Even his famous three novels, *The Death of the
Gods, Leonardo da Vinci, Peter and Alexis,* upon which he
worked—from 1893 onwards—for twelve years, are based on
a scheme which is not his own. Its idea of the "Third Kingdom" is the same as in Ibsen's *Emperor and Galilean:* flesh
and spirit as the two antitheses whose conflict should be
superseded by the Christian synthesis to come. In spite of
the dry Hegelian development of the theme underlying this
trilogy, the novels show much erudition, especially the second in which Leonardo is treated as a Nietzschean amoralist.
The most schematic of them is *Peter and Alexis,* dealing
with the conflict between Peter the Great and his conservative son, whom he is supposed to have strangled.

Novels were not Merezhkovsky's strong point. He probably knew this when taking up his philosophic quest. It was

he who preached most vehemently that decadence should be superseded by a new religious consciousness. A number of essays followed. One of them, *Tolstoy and Dostoevsky* (in two volumes), was epoch-making. It can still be regarded as his best work. Notable are his studies of Gogol, Lermontov, and Gorky. In 1903 and 1904 he edited *The New Path*—a journal dedicated to symbolism in its "Russian," i.e. religious, sense. This journal was replaced, in 1905, by its short-lived but stimulating successor, *The Problems of Life*. Merezhkovsky was also one of the founders of "The Religious-Philosophic Society" which provided, towards the end of the last century, a meeting ground for the "God-seeking" intellectuals and the more advanced representatives of the Church. It had no marked success. His attempts to imbue the revolutionary movement of 1905 with a religious depth and meaning were also a failure. And since the revolution of 1917 was not in keeping with his religious-philosophic scheme, he would have nothing to do with it: it was all the work of Antichrist. In 1919 he and his wife emigrated to France where they wrote some of the most vitriolic indictments of the bolshevist régime. His more recent studies (of Napoleon, Atlantis, etc.), and his quasi-philosophic novels, *Tutankhamen in Crete, The Messiah,* are pretentious and hardly readable. Still, his work as a whole provided a ferment at a period when the Russian intelligentsia, or rather the entire Russian culture, found itself in a cul-de-sac, hardly suspecting the gravity of the impending storm.

Less pretentious but more complex is Merezhkovsky's wife, Zinaida Hippius (1868-1945). She was the most gifted woman poet of the decadence period, although the intensity of her introspective poetry was intellectual rather than lyrical. If we assume that there can be a certain antagonism between intelligence and genius, then Mme Hippius was almost too intelligent to be a genius. Spiteful, restless, and fastidious, she is inwardly frozen rather than cold by nature —a kind of Russian Hedda Gabler, inclined to avenge her disappointment not only upon life, but also upon herself.

Endowed with a protesting temperament, Mme Hippius joined her husband in his crusade against materialism and positivism. This step influenced most of her later literary work, beginning with her sensational novel, *A Devil's Doll*, which depicts the deadlock of the younger intelligentsia after 1905. As the first part of a trilogy about the revolution, it is interesting by its theme, but devoid of spontaneity. It only proves that the authoress is less at home in narrative prose than she is in poetry. Her critical articles, however (under the nom de plume of Anton Krainy), are incisive, very aggressive, and often to the point. Her finest book in prose, *Living Faces*, was written in exile. It consists of a gallery of portraits (Rasputin, Rozanov, Blok, Sologub, etc.), prejudiced at times, but full of subtle if malicious observation.

III

The interest in religion, before the last revolution, became quite a vogue. So did the interest in occultism, or rather in inverted religion, indulged in by the most talented of all the Russian decadents, Fyodor K. Sologub (1863-1927). Sologub, whose real name was Teternikov, was the son of a peasant woman, employed as a servant in Petersburg. His early years were far from happy, but he managed to get some education and to obtain a schoolteacher's diploma. While teaching in God-forsaken provinces, he wrote much poetry and prose of a morbid type. As though under the weight of an irreparable injury, he adopted a Manichean attitude towards life, in the name of which he rejected the entire visible world as something unworthy of acceptance. In this manner he carried Gogol's aversion to reality to those limits where negation passes into rancorous antireligion of a Satanic kind. To this he adapted his own theory of aestheticism, conjuring up in its hothouse atmosphere a compensatory world—dreamy and ghostlike, over which he ruled like a necromancer. "I am god of a mysterious universe, and the entire world exists only in my dreams." This was the only world in which he felt perfectly at home. The world of our everyday actualities aroused in him nothing but disgust and negation. The symbol of his romantic negation was Satan—the Satan of Baudelaire rather than of Carducci.

Sologub's writings thus became largely an apology of a decadent who looks upon art as a shelter from the ugliness and vulgarity of life. Not only his poems, but also his novels and stories are, in a sense, autobiographic. His method is distilled realism of indictment, mixed with symbolic and allegorical fancies. His somewhat diluted first novel, *Heavy Dreams,* reflects his unpleasant experiences as a teacher in a small provincial town. It is realistic and very subjective in its realism. Like Gogol, he regarded vulgarity as something which has a metaphysical existence of its own, and is beyond man's control. But if life be devoid of beauty, man is still free to create a beautiful legend of his own—both as a refuge from and a reproach against life as it is. Such deliberate quixotism became a cult with Sologub, threatening now and then to pass into aesthetic sentimentality, at least after his remarkable novel, *The Petty Demon* (*Melky Bes*) 1907.

This work is one of the masterpieces of Russian modernism, most of whose ingredients it contains. Indictment, strengthened by several Dostoevskian elements (the very title of the novel was taken from Ivan Karamazov's nightmare), is deepened into a frightening symbol of human vulgarity and squalor. Their embodiment is a certain provincial schoolmaster Peredonov—a slimy, hypocritical nonentity, suffering from persecution mania, until he goes mad. Perverted and vulgar in all his doings, he is displayed against an equally vulgar provincial background, until the novel resembles a delirious nightmare. Even the two young lovers, who evidently are meant to provide a relief, are likely to strike the reader as unconscious perverts. The climax is Peredonov's madness. The gloomy and pessimistic atmosphere of the novel is redeemed only by its literary perfection. Peredonov, in particular, is so well presented that he can be added to the gallery of such figures as Gogol's Chichikov, Goncharov's Oblomov, Shchedrine's Iudushka, and Dostoevsky's old Karamazov.

In his intense aversion to actual life, Sologub turned aestheticism into a cult and built out of his dreams a legend, an imaginary counterreality of his own. The series of novels in which he embodied this attitude bears the general title, *The Legend in the Process of Creation* (*Tvorimaya Legenda*). Its first part, *The Magic of the Dead* (*Navyi Chary*) brims over with all sorts of necromantic spooks. Trirodov, the chief character of the series, is a Russian des Esseintes [1] and a modern Prospero in one—with a magic power over nature and human beings. Interesting as a transposed confession, this series is a pastiche of allegorism, reality, and sentimental-romantic fancies of a decadent escapist. Sologub sums up life as a disgusting fat slut, whose touch makes everything appear gross and ugly. This is the leitmotiv of most of his stories and novels. In *Sweeter than Poison*, for example, he depicts in his best vein the tragedy of a lower middle-class girl whose dreams of love are defiled by a vulgarian from the gentry. The same attitude pervades Sologub's plays—most of them rather forced and therefore inferior to his novels, as well as to his poetry in which he achieved real greatness.

Another decadent poet with a few stories and novels to

[1] The hero of *À Rebours*, by Huysmans.

his credit was Valery Y. Bryusov (1873-1924). Endowed with more sensuality than passion, he was a disciplined and cultured eclectic, inclined towards erotic amoralism, and rather fond of nightmarelike themes. Always a competent craftsman, he was yet much too self-conscious and *voulu*, even in his technical perfection. Whereas Sologub is aloof, Bryusov is cold. Otherwise he suffers from an equally incurable individualism. This comes out in his fantastic *The Republic of the Southern Cross*—a story permeated by the cult of ego and the cult of death. Bryusov's most ambitious prose works are his novels, *On the Altar of Victories* and *The Fiery Angel* (1907-1908). The second of these two decadent works is a cleverly stylized excursion into occultism and witches' lore. Its form is that of a diary from sixteenth-century Germany. The chief character is a hysterical woman who implicitly believes that she is a witch and is finally burnt at the stake. Bryusov's numerous critical writings (he was the editor of the symbolist monthly, *The Balance*, and the leader of the Moscow group of modernists) need not be discussed here.

IV

The author who made a strong effort to overcome decadence in the name of a new symbolist view of life was Andrey Bely: a nom de plume of Boris Bugayev (1880-1934). Together with the poets Alexander Blok and Vyacheslav Ivanov, Bely became one of the chief exponents of Russian symbolism. A poet, a novelist, a critic, an essayist, a first-rate authority on Russian prosody, he yet remained a brilliant experimenter whose genius failed to crystallize entirely—perhaps on account of its very wealth. Anxious to overcome his gloomy tiredness of the *fin de siècle*, he looked for an ally in his own metaphysical irony, in the philosophy of Vladimir Solovyov, and later even in the anthroposophy of

Rudolf Steiner. Kant, Nietzsche, and Maeterlinck affected him also. In his four *Symphonies* in prose between 1902-1908, to which he applied the principle of musical counterpoint, one feels the influence of the Polish decadent, Stanislaw Przybyszewski.[1] Yet the two authors who left a lasting mark on Bely's prose were Gogol and Dostoevsky. He worked out the possibilities of Gogol's ornate and musical style in so many directions that he became, together with Remizov, one of the masters of the word in modern Russian fiction, the Soviet fiction included. What brings him even closer to Gogol and Dostoevsky is his peculiar view of the world, by virtue of which he mixes—often with amusing grotesqueness—two planes of existence: the actual and the fantastic, that is, irrational. Like Gogol, he too dissociates reality, alters its proportions, and then creates a strange subjective world of his own: a blend of naturalism and apocalyptic mysticism, often seasoned with delightful puckish bouts, in which his talent for parody finds its full scope.

Bely's first novel, *The Silver Dove* (1910), was one of the most remarkable products of the symbolist period. Its prose goes back to Gogol, but Bely applies to it a conscious technical discipline and pattern. What makes this work so modern (in a morbid sense) is the subtle mixture of mystic and erotic exaltation which, on a lower level, would decidedly have led to Rasputin and Rasputinism. With care and insight, Bely discloses to the reader some of the most elusive irrational roots of a sect, to which the chief character falls a prey. In spite of its high technical standard, *The Silver Dove* is written with such unflagging verve as to be a source of delight even to people who are used to lighter fare.

More puzzling and difficult is Bely's next novel, *Petersburg*

[1] Przybyszewski's works had a great vogue in Russia immediately after 1905.

(1913). Its stammering language and deliberate confusion of reality with hallucination are reminiscent of Dostoevsky's *The Double.* Worked out according to a definite ideological plan, *Petersburg* is charged with peculiar rhythm, euphony, and verbal instrumentations. Its chief character is a revolutionary intellectual in whose consciousness the Russian metropolis—or rather Dostoevsky's irrational Petersburg— looms and haunts him as a phantom of his own diseased brain. Whatever happens to him is immediately turned into a series of spooks and inner conflicts. All proportions are altered, distorted, until the hero is lost in the mazes of his own psychic chaos. This novel is too ingenious to be really enjoyable. Its very subtleties become tiresome in the end. What one admires in it is above all the tour de force of Bely's narrative technique.

Bely continued his experiments also after the revolution. In his autobiographic *Kotik Letayev* (1922) he even used some of Proust's and James Joyce's devices in order to penetrate into a child's early stages of consciousness, including his prenatal period. But in this work his prose is truly difficult and involved. A few lines from its prologue are enough to give the reader an idea of Bely's style.

"Here, on this sheerly-dividing line, I cast dumb and lingering glances into the past. . . .

"I am thirty-two years of age; consciousness of self has rent my brain and rushed headlong into infancy; with my rent brain I watch the spirals of events rise up in smoke before me; and watch them running back. . . .

"The past is threaded into the soul; on the threshold of my third year I confront myself; we converse with each other; we understand each other.

"The patch of the past stretches back with precision: from the défilés of the early infant years to the steeps of this self-conscious instant; and from the steeps to the défilés before the portals of death rolls down the Future; in them the glacier will surge again: in torrents of feelings.

"Thoughts of that instant will charge as an avalanche in my pursuit; and that vortex of snow will blot out the overhanging sky that is so close to me overhead: I shall grow faint on the edge of the precipice; the path of descent is terrible. . . .

"I am standing here, in the mountains: so I stood, among mountains, having fled from people; from the distant, from the near; and left myself, in the valley, with arms stretched . . . towards the far peaks, where:—rocky peaks threatened; jutted under the sky; called one to another; formed a vast polyphony of the cosmos in creation; and vertiginously, vertically, enormous masses massed themselves; mists climbed the crags of chasms; stricken clouds reeled; and rains poured; rapid lines of peaks ran in the distance; the fingers of the peaks moved, the azure, jagged ridges dripped in pale glaciers and faint nervous lines combed everywhere; the relief gesticulated and postured; torrents gushed and foamed from enormous thrones; and the reverberation of a thundering voice followed me everywhere: for hours on end my eyes danced with running walls, pine-trees, torrents and precipices, boulders, cemeteries, cottages, bridges; the purple of ragged heather stained all the landscapes in blood, whirls of damp vapor sprayed, began whipping my face; a cloud fell at my feet, into riots of torrent; the turbulently churning foam hid under the milk; beneath it, everything quivered, sobbed, thundered, groaned and smashed its way through the thinning milk in the same watery riot. . . ."[1]

Those interested in Bely's personality will find his *Memoirs of a Queer Fellow* enlightening. His two Moscow novels, *The Moscow Original* and *Moscow under the Blow*, show—

[1] *Soviet Literature, An Anthology* (Wishart).

with all their nervous vivacity—the author's lesser skill in handling events on a broad canvas. Good without reservations, however, is his *Reminiscences of Blok* (1923). Apart from being a noble tribute to his great poet-friend, it provides an excellent picture of the social, literary, and spiritual atmosphere of the modernist movement in Russia. What a pity that its cantankerous and gossipy continuation, *Between the Two Revolutions,* fails to keep up such a high level!

Prolific as he was, Bely published several volumes of essays: *The Green Meadow, Symbolism, Arabesques*, etc., and also travel sketches. In contrast to so many intellectuals, Bely—like his friend Blok—welcomed the revolution, but in a Messianic spirit. Seeing in it the harbinger of a new era, of a new humanity, he even hailed it with a few appropriate but not very good poems, under the title, *Christ is Risen*. He was intensely active during the first four or five years after the revolution. But as time went on his physical and mental nervousness increased, until it brought him to a premature end. Even so he survived the Russian symbolism. The latter had left the literary stage years before his death.

v

No discussion of decadence and symbolism can leave out Leonid Andreyev (1871-1919), who rose to fame mainly as a cheap popularizer of these trends. His first influences were those of Korolenko and Gorky. Later he found his own place and achieved success by exploiting certain moods and dispositions after the abortive revolution of 1905. While Gorky, with his aggressive common sense, was more and more popular among the workers, Andreyev became the idol of the nerve-racked intellectuals, especially of those who indulged in their own pessimism with gusto and were on the lookout for literary dopes. Andreyev specialized in the latter, making clever use of all sorts of horrors—physical and metaphysical. Having taken up various Dostoevskian and Tolstoyan problems, he spiced them with posterlike effects, borrowed from Poe, Maeterlinck, Przybyszewski. The narratives of his first, predecadent period (1898-1904) are good, often excellent. In one of them, *In the Fog,* he treats even such a motive as the sexual tragedy of an adolescent with tact and restraint. But from his *Father Vasily Fiveysky,* or rather *The Red Laugh* onwards, Andreyev's talent gradually became entangled in the jungle of glaring overstatement and would-be modernist tricks.

This is only partly true of his *The Seven Who Were Hanged* (1908). Its characters are five revolutionaries and two murderers—all of them condemned to die on the gallows. The author analyzes their thoughts and emotions during the last few days before the execution, and also during the execution. Strong as it is, the narrative affects the reader's nerves and testifies to Andreyev's principal weakness— the weakness to choose themes which are bigger than his creative power. Hence his propensity for rhetoric, for spiritual melodrama, and for what might be called "colossalism." This is typical not only of his stories, but also of most of his plays. Highfalutin allegories, hyperbolism of contrasts, smart oleographic effects—such are his usual pitfalls. His pretentiousness is indicated even by the titles he uses: *Towards the Stars, King Hunger, The Life of Man, He Who Gets Slapped, Black Masks, Anathema,* etc., are some of them.

In his attempts to melodramatize the inner tragedy of life, Andreyev found abysses everywhere and became one of their self-appointed explorers. In the end, nihilism became not only his habitual attitude, but his profession. His novel, *Sashka Zhegulyov* (1911), proclaims utter futility even with regard to revolutionary efforts. But however striking at first, his ebullient pose could not be taken seriously very long, and was bound to be found out in the end. As a matter of fact, its secret is simpler than it looks: it is rationalism gone hysterical. Andreyev would first brood upon some colossal theme or other, during which process he would whip himself into an adequate emotional state. Once this state has been reached, he becomes forced rather than strong—forced and artificial. The hero of his *My Memoirs,* for example, has spent his best years in prison. But when released, he immediately builds a private prison of his own, in which he intends to spend the rest of his life voluntarily. During his seclusion he had discovered that the whole world was a prison. So he prefers his own small prison to the one at large, in which he is supposed to be free.

Andreyev's work may be little read at present. Yet as a distorted symptom of that period it still claims our attention. Less attention is deserved by his contemporary, N. Artsybashev (1878-1927), whose novel, *Sanin* (1907), had an enormous vogue, mainly on account of its gospel of emancipated sex combined with a cheap provincial brand of "beyond good and evil." In another novel, *On the Last Line,* Artsybashev's decadent mind indulged in a voluptuous cult of death and putrefaction. The reason of it all was that nihilism of despair which often finds its outlet in an exaggerated scorn of man and life. It would be wrong, of course, to approach the entire Russian fiction of those years from such an angle. There were other trends also, represented by a number of talented authors, some of whom were strong enough to resist even the pleasures of pessimism.

CHAPTER XIV

Some Later Realists

MODERNISM, with all its striking achievements, was confined to a comparatively small group of authors, many of whom prided themselves on keeping aloof from the political and social questions of the day. There were, however, a number of gifted prose writers anxious to continue the realistic tradition in close contact with the social tasks of that period. Maxim Gorky's publishing firm, *Znanie,* was particularly keen to bring before the public the best socially minded realists of their generation. Once known under the nickname of "podmaximki" (those under Maxim's cloak), some of them —Muizhel, Skitalets, Chirikov, etc.—have now ceased to count. Others have achieved a more lasting fame: Kuprin, for example, Bunin and Shmelyov. Also the early works of the well-known Yiddish author, Sholom Ash, were published (in Russian) by the *Znanie.* Quite a number of realists with modernist leanings stood, however, outside that group and their works were published elsewhere—chiefly by the firm *Shipovnik* ("Wild Rose"). Sergeyev-Tsensky and Count Alexey N. Tolstoy were among them. So was Alexey Remizov.

The technical level of this prose, whether realistic, impressionist, or symbolist, continued to be high. The range of themes, too, was considerable. As most authors connected with the two firms mentioned were still fairly young, they had to face the revolution of 1917, by which their subsequent fate was decided. Some of them accepted the new régime at once. Others did so later and somewhat half heartedly.

Others again emigrated as its uncompromising enemies, and founded an interesting *émigré* literature abroad: in Paris, Berlin, Prague.

This fact alone illustrates the difficult dilemma of those authors whose maturity coincided with the greatest cataclysm in Russian history. Whereas Veresayev and Alexey N. Tolstoy, for example, adapted themselves in time, such important realists as Kuprin, Bunin, Shmelyov, Zaitsev, and Remizov preferred to emigrate and continue their work abroad.

II

V. V. Veresayev (Smidovitch, 1867-1943) can be regarded as the most reliable chronicler of the moods and dispositions of the intelligentsia between the 'nineties and the present period. A doctor by profession, he made his entry into literature by his story, *Pathless,* printed in 1894 in Korolenko's *Russian Wealth.* Towards the end of the 'nineties he joined the Marxian group of periodicals and analyzed the crisis of the Marxian intelligentsia in his *At the Turning Point.* Something of a sensation was caused by his *A Doctor's Sketches* (1901). This was due to its sincere tone and its documentary character; for Veresayev is by his very nature the quietest and least sensational of authors. He started as a conscientious observer and such he remained also after the revolution. He is one of the few prerevolutionary authors whose more recent novels, *The Deadlock* (1922) and *Sisters* (1933), have been widely discussed in the Soviet press. The first depicts the civil war as seen and experienced by the intelligentsia; the second, the new socialist Russia as viewed by two young sisters of utterly different temperament. Apart from fiction, Veresayev wrote lengthy studies of Tolstoy, Dostoevsky, Nietzsche, and Pushkin.

More complex in his mentality and his career is Sergeyev-

Tsensky (born 1876). His early writings are full of mannerisms. His *Bogland* (*Lesnaya top,* 1907), for instance, could have been written by Leonid Andreyev. In addition, his novel, *Babayev,* which appeared in the same year, displays a contempt for the lower classes. The First World War freed him, however, from his mannerisms and even from his class snobbery. His *Captain Konyayev* (1917) may still profess little or no faith in the revolution; but he showed a different spirit six years later, when working upon his ambitious *Transfiguration.* This masterpiece was conceived as a series of ten novels: the first three dealing with the prewar period, the next three with the war, the last four with the revolution and the early stages of the new society. The author had matured by then as artist. His new style has that simplicity which comes from constant exertion.

The first volume of *Transfiguration* introduces us to a remote Crimean coast town, inhabited by somewhat casual intellectuals whose daily routine is disturbed by the intrusion of a tragedy. An offended husband, mourning his dead wife and taking revenge upon her former lover, constitutes the backbone of the plot. The important thing is, however, the author's insistence on the irrational side of life; on those "strange moments when one's life ceases to be clearly distinguishable and when we can grasp it only as it retreats in the distance." The second novel of the series (*The Doomed Ones*) contains a ghastly picture of the disintegrating prewar intellectuals. He also wrote a novel about Pushkin which is not among his creditable achievements.

Although younger than Sergeyev-Tsensky, Count Alexey N. Tolstoy (1882-1945) came into prominence before 1914 as a painter of the gentry. He depicted them without any wistful looking back *à la* Turgenev. In fact, he took no pains to conceal his somewhat hostile, even spiteful attitude towards his own class. Mentally less accomplished perhaps than certain highbrow intellectuals, he yet possessed a thirst for life and an instinct for the right thing and the right touch in art. He is also a keen observer and one of the raciest storytellers. Always on the lookout for new material, he was naturally drawn towards the revolutionary turmoil, of which he made such good use as to be now regarded as one of the important and certainly one of the best-read Soviet authors. His narrative talent came into its own after he had reconciled himself to the new régime. He, too, forms a link (although in a different sense from Gorky) between the old and the postrevolutionary realism. But since his finest works appeared after 1924, they must be discussed in connection with Soviet literature proper.

A special place in literature can be claimed by Mikhail Prishvin. Although a veteran of letters (he was born in 1873), he is still looked upon as a master of Russian at its best and raciest, which like Leskov before him, he had learned from the people. In his early writings, consisting of travel descriptions of northern Russia, his ethnographic interests and love of nature were prominent. Then he was carried away by stories of provincial life, of animals, of hunting, and of nature in general. His *Beast of Krutoyarsk* (1912) is still considered the finest animal story in Russian. One could add to it his more recent *Yen Chung* (*The Root of Life*)—a narrative about the successful taming, by the author and his Chinese host, of a spotted deer called Khu-a-lu in the wilds near the border of Manchukuo. While reading it, one cannot help wondering which to admire more: the author's feeling for the beauties of nature, or his amazing understanding of animals. But his range of interests does not end here. In 1924 he published his *Karymushka*—a transposed and refreshingly simple account of his childhood and boyhood, which was later incorporated in his *Bony's Chain* (1927). Planned as a series of novels about Russian life be-

tween the assassination of Alexander II and the fall of
Nicholas II, this ambitious work does not advocate any
particular ideology or "ism," but the author's tacit message
is always there. It can be defined as the unity between man,
nature, and society, and it is from this unity that Prishvin
derives his own artistic vitality, his healthy optimism, and
his love of life.

III

Among the authors who declined to collaborate with the
Soviets or to remain in Soviet Russia, Kuprin should be
mentioned first. A partial follower of Gorky, Alexander
Kuprin (1870-1938) was endowed with a boisterous but
good-natured vitality. He is a born storyteller: clear, direct,
and always attracted by life in its more elementary aspects.
Apart from Gorky, he learned quite a lot from Tolstoy,
Maupassant, and Knut Hamsun. As an ex-officer, he wrote
a number of stories about the army which he knew well.
His first successful novel, *A Duel* (1895), shows or rather
shows up the life of officers in a stuffy garrison town near
the Western frontier in all its unattractive grayness. Its
realism anticipates some of Kuprin's best qualities, above all
his capacity for combining a vivid plot with equally vivid
character drawing.

Kuprin's strength and weakness lies in his inner simplicity.
He is attracted by simple natures, although his insatiable
curiosity often drives him into the most unexpected corners
of human existence. A closer scrutiny may reveal in him a
hidden romantic, even a sentimentalist—a feature implied
in a few of his themes rather than in his style, which remains
manly, robust, and straightforward. This is why some of
his long and short stories—*The River of Life, Gambrinus,
Captain Rybnikov, The Garnet Bracelet,* and many others—
are among the best told of that period. He deteriorated

only when embarking upon such a tedious problem novel
as *The Ditch* (*Yama*): a naturalistic and unpleasantly moralizing picture of the life of prostitutes in a house of ill fame.
With all his broad curiosity, Kuprin was essentially a man
of the prewar Russia. He emigrated, but his output after
the revolution was small. It included, however, his pathetic
short novel, *Jeannette, or the Princess of Four Streets,* the
chief character of which is a quaint Russian *émigré* in Paris.
His vitality sapped, Kuprin returned to Russia in 1938 where
he died a few months later.

In contrast to Kuprin, the great talent of Ivan Bunin
(1870-1942) has not diminished either in quantity or in quality during his years of voluntary exile in France. Bunin is a
master of the short story, a novelist, and a poet. Yet it is
difficult to place him. As a narrator he is intensely introspective, but his introspection is of a contemplative—not of
an analytical character. It often seems that none of his heroes
has an existence entirely independent of Bunin. At the same
time you accept them all and find them convincing, because
you accept Bunin's plane of creation. An heir of Turgenev
and Chekhov, he possesses a strong lyrical vein, which often
intrudes into his descriptive passages. As though aware of
this danger, Bunin must have deliberately disciplined his
prose before achieving such graphic terseness as we find in
his famous story, *The Gentleman of San Francisco* (1915).

The concise style of some of Bunin's narratives thus resulted from a resistance to his own lyricism. In the same
way his apparent detachment is often due to the struggle
with his own subjectivity. The surprising thing, however, is
that—like Maupassant—Bunin knows how to awaken the
readers' emotions precisely by suppressing them in his stories.
He can also weave a tale, or even a novel, out of next to
nothing. A few casual moods, observations, descriptions,
meditations, and the pattern is there—without a complicated

plot, even without a plot at all. And from behind everything he writes there peers at you a perplexed seeker and a fastidious romantic whose eye sees too much to leave him any facile optimism. His early novel, *The Village* (1910) is one of the gloomiest books about the Russian peasants—the period is 1905. Hardly less gloomy is his *Sukhodol* (1912) in which he gives a picture of manor life with its drifting types even before serfdom came to an end. Yet if you read some of his stories (such as his excellent *Sunstroke*) or his exotic travel sketches, you cannot help feeling that he is a man passionately fond of the unusual of romance. of life in all its variety.

Widely traveled, Bunin found plenty of material on which to exercise his descriptive talent. As his attitude towards the revolution was negative, he went to France where he became one of the chief pillars of the *émigré* literature. It was abroad that he wrote two of his best and most subjective things, *Mitya's Love* and *Arsenyev's Life*. The first is the age-old love tragedy of a disappointed youth; but however old in itself, it sounds new when told by Bunin. The second is a fine example of a transposed autobiography—this time up to the age of seventeen. The skill with which it is told proves that his talent has not been impaired by exile. Bunin is one of the difficult authors to translate. In spite of that he enjoys considerable international prestige, enhanced by the Nobel prize for literature, which was awarded to him in 1931.

IV

However great the difference between Shmelyov, Zaitsev, and Remizov, they all owe much to the modernist technique, of which they made ample use. The oldest of them, Ivan Shmelyov, was born (in 1875) into a merchant family and made his name before the war by his *A Man from the*

Restaurant. This is an intensely human story of a waiter in a restaurant *à la française*—an honest, simple soul who looks upon the world through his profession. He gets into difficulties in the restaurant and in his home life. His daughter goes astray, his son becomes an active revolutionary, and he himself loses his job. But in the end everything comes out satisfactorily and he is reinstated in his modest profession.

Shmelyov's short stories, too, were much appreciated—partly because of the dexterity with which he handled social motives. Yet his best and maturest things appeared after the revolution, which he detested. His attitude towards it can be seen in his novel, *The Sun of the Dead* (1923), with its almost apocalyptic pictures of the civil war in the Crimea. The novel sums up the spiritual, moral, and economic devastation caused by the collapse of the old order in that part of Russia. Less objective than Veresayev's *Deadlock,* which deals with the same period and the same region, it is overwhelming by its nightmarish cruelty and its evocative visionary power. The intensity of the novel is increased by the author's emotionally overcharged style.

Among Shmelyov's many short and long stories, *The Inexhaustible Cup* (1918-19) can be singled out on account of its old-world manor atmosphere. Its theme is the frustrated love between a serf—a painter of genius, and his owner's young wife. The tenderness of the narrative, suggestive of Leskov's *Sealed Angel* and of Turgenev, verges on but does not pass into sentimentality. In contrast to its contemplative quiet, so remote from the revolutionary chaos, *That Which Never Was* (1923) symbolizes—with its atmosphere of a lunatic asylum—the First World War. An uncompromising enemy of the Soviets, Shmelyov occupies a conspicuous place among the *émigré* writers.

Equally hostile to the Soviet régime is Boris K. Zaitsev (born 1881)—an oversensitive, moody, and lyrical descendant of Turgenev and Chekhov. He is also one of the last representatives of the manor literature. Spiritually, he is an aristocrat, spiteful of contemporary bourgeoisie. This explains his gentleness towards the intellectuals of the doomed gentry class.

Rooted in the prewar Russia, he first made his name with short stories, consisting almost entirely of lyrical atmosphere. In 1922 he emigrated, traveled a great deal in Italy, went to Mount Athos, and finally settled in Paris. There he continued his literary activities which include stories, travel sketches, and a few novels. The first of these, *The Golden Pattern* (1925), describes the fate of uprooted Russian intellectuals after the revolution. The story is told by a woman singer, and the scene of action is Russia, Paris, and Italy. This work can hardly be called a successful novel. whatever its other merits, if any.

Stronger, even powerful at times, is Zaitsev's shorter novel, *Anna*. It is the story of a sensitive girl, living on her uncle's pig-breeding farm in a remote corner of Soviet Russia. The plot, though slight, is one of sentimental entanglements which cause Anna's death. In spite of its lyrical tone, this novel (if you call it a novel at all) is more restrained than the author's previous works. The characters, too, are more tangible, not only the representatives of the former gentry, but also those of the new Soviet system. Less significant and much weaker in construction is his *A House in Passy* (1935)—a novel about the Russian *émigrés* in Paris. His *Gleb's Journey,* on the other hand (the first part appeared in 1935), can be regarded as the best thing he has written. Like *Arsenyev's Life* by Bunin, it is a scarcely veiled autobiography. Its background is a manor house in central Russia, and its hero—a shy, sensitive boy whose eyes are opening to the wonder of the world and the people around him. This part represents, of course, only the first stage of his journey through life.

Zaitsev's impressionist talent comes out best, perhaps, in his fine renderings of the Russian landscape. Resigned and contemplative, he is prone to burrow in the inner contents of things—a feature which brings him close to the symbolist-religious trend in Russian modernism. During his exile his Christian God-seeking moods increased. But he turned his very Christianity into something antibourgeois and exclusive: into a religion of the free aristocratic poor. Always restless and homeless, he recorded his roamings in a series of travel sketches, notably about Italy and Mount Athos.

v

A rather puzzling artistic personality is Alexey M. Remizov (born 1877). His talent bears the stamp of Dostoevsky, decadent modernism, Leskov's *skaz,* and folklore. Steeped in the folk legends, tales, and Apocrypha, he paraphrased them with an uncanny feeling for the pattern and inflection of the spoken word in his *Tales of the Russian People,* as well as in several other books. Remizov is a sophisticated modern and a child in one—a child whose toys are words and the spooks of folk tales. Yet he combines his childlike vision with a shrewd, humorous twinkle and with a craft of which he is always sure. His language is "Russian unbound," based on the living folk speech rather than on the accepted syntax. This is why he is so good at handling the *skaz.* His mastery of words and word patterns places him beside Bely as one of the great stylists in recent literature.

Such is, however, one aspect only of his work. Its other aspect is his realism as exemplified by his novels. The first of these, *The Pond,* is still somewhat diffuse. So is the marshy character of the life it presents. The realism of his

Sisters of the Cross (1910) is more condensed and deepened into a painful symbol of human existence. Remizov, like Bely, applies the same care to prose which is usually applied to poetry. He stylizes, with great skill, even his realistic narratives, such as *The Fifth Pestilence,* or *The Story of Stratilatov,* both of which are accessible only to those readers who are familiar with the intricacies of the modernist technique. But some of his later works—for example the novel, *Olya*—are distinguished by utter simplicity.

Another feature, typical of Remizov, is his sense of the irrational forces mixed up with human fates. In this he resembles Gogol and Dostoevsky—with elements of Rozanov. He blends most dexterously the real with the unreal, the actuality with the dream, by means of a symbolic or quasi-symbolic vision in which several planes are intertwined, sometimes deliberately confused. Surprising effects of this kind can be found in his *Whirlwind Russia* and in *Fiery Russia,* dealing with the revolution. The manner in which he reconstructs his dreams is equally admirable. But he is and remains a great stylist, whatever he touches. No wonder that he is one of those prewar writers whose influence upon the Soviet prose has been enormous. And this in spite of the fact that he, too, emigrated as an enemy of the Soviet system.

Like Merezhkovsky and Zinaida Hippius, these authors continued the former intelligentsia tradition also in their exile. Later, in 1931, they were joined by the modernist, Evgeny Zamyatin (1884-1937). A naval engineer by profession, Zamyatin made his literary debut in 1908 as one of the ablest followers of Leskov and Remizov. Endowed with irony and with a satirical vein reminiscent of Gogol and Saltykov-Shchedrine, he wrote chiefly about provincial backwaters, especially in his *District Tales* (1911). His temporary stay in England during the last war resulted in two scathing stories about English life, *The Islanders* and *The Man-hunter*.[1] After the revolution he became a great influence among the younger Soviet authors. He himself supported the formalist school of literature, led by Shklovsky and Professor Zhirmunsky. Refusing to have anything to do with bolshevist ideas, he joined the "inner emigration," i.e. those intellectuals who had remained in Russia but stood aloof from revolution. One of such "inner *émigrés*" was Sologub. But Zamyatin proved more aggressive than that high priest of decadence.

His aversion to the revolution came out in his *The Cave*—a powerful story about a married couple (former well-to-do intellectuals), freezing and starving in their Petrograd flat during the catastrophic months, like two ice-age troglodytes. His *Story about Many Things* is even more frankly anti-revolutionary. A disciplined and whimsical skeptic, he had a predilection for gruesome episodes. Yet his skepticism did not prevent him from fighting anything that threatened his individual independence. And the climax of this fight was his Utopian novel about the mechanized future, *We* (1922)—a strange anticipation of Aldous Huxley's *Brave New World*. A cruel satire upon all equalizing tendencies as Zamyatin understood them at the time, *We* often reads like a deliberate blend of Dostoevsky's Grand Inquisitor, Shigalyov (in *The Possessed*) and the Man from the Underworld—jeering at the Crystal Palace of the thoroughly planned-out and thoroughly dehumanized future. The novel was only partly published in Russian, but this was enough to discredit him with the Soviets. Eventually, in 1931, he obtained permission to become a real *émigré*. He left for France where he died in 1937.

---

[1] His play about the English, *The Society of Honorary Bell Ringers*, is equally scathing.

VI

A thorough study of the Russian *émigré* literature would be a fascinating subject. But while this is beyond the scope of the present book, we cannot omit Aldanov (Landau), the author of several notable historical novels. Mark Aldanov's trilogy about the end of the eighteenth century—*The 9th of Thermidor* (1923), *The Devil's Bridge* (1926), and *The Plot* (1927)—shows that he combines a well-informed skeptical mind with a strong narrative verve and plastic power. His portraits of Robespierre, Catherine II, Suvorov, and Paul I are worthy of the fine traditions of Russian realism. Aldanov now lives in America.

Another *émigré* who has settled in America is the Siberian writer, George Grebenshchikov (born 1882). A peasant by birth, he has been active in literature since 1905 but became more widely known during the First World War when his two volumes of stories, *In the Spaces of Siberia* (1914-1915), appeared. The bulk of his work can be defined as an epic of the Siberian peasantry whom he loves and knows well. This refers to his series of novels, *The Churayevs* in particular, which first appeared in Paris in 1922 and has since been reprinted in America, where also his realistic-symbolic *Mikula Buyanovich* (the title of its American version is *A Turbulent Giant*, 1940) came out.

An interesting point about the Russian *émigrés* is that they can boast of even a new literary generation, reared and educated abroad. The young author Vladimir Sirin (V. Nabokov) is one of them. Very much up-to-date, cold, inquisitive, and intelligently self-conscious, he is above all a brilliant experimenter, taking delight in unusual pathologic types and situations. Sirin's themes may remind one of Dostoevsky, but the resemblance is superficial, for he treats them in his own utterly detached manner. For this reason several of his novels, such as *King-Queen-Knave*, *Pilgrim*, *Luzhin's Defense*, *Spy*, are difficult to place. Even when they fail to be profound, they strike one as intriguing products of an author who is not properly rooted anywhere—of a typical distinguished foreigner, writing in Russian.

CHAPTER XV

Revolution and Civil War

APART FROM yielding an abundant literary harvest, the symbolist period was responsible for a number of technical innovations, which widened the gap between the average reader and the highbrow. But its aloofness from life, its subjectivism and obscurity of language soon provoked a reaction on behalf of concreteness and clarity. Among the currents which challenged it, between 1910 and 1912, futurism was particularly loud and aggressive. Challenge and experiment were the order of the day. Restlessness filled the air. In addition, public opinion was stirred by a series of political events, such as Austria's annexation of Bosnia and Herzegovina in 1908, and the Balkan War in 1912-1913. Russia's backing of Serbian aspirations in the Balkans led to a tension between Austria and Serbia. The assassination of Francis Ferdinand was followed by the First World War.

The first phase of the European War brought, for a while, the entire Russian nation together. But the gulf between the government and the rest of the population was too big to be bridged. Court scandals, Rasputinism, administrative incompetence, corruption, official hostility towards the Provincial Councils or *zemstvo* organizations (which were doing splendid war work), lack of food, lack of ammunitions, and, last but not least, lack of faith in the integrity of Russia's allies—all this contributed to the revolution of 1917. Its first portent was the murder of Rasputin; its climax—the Bolshevist *coup d'état* a few months later. There followed a complete dislocation of all former values and ways of life. The bulk of the intellectuals either refused or else failed to adapt themselves to the new conditions, so they had to bear the consequences of their own maladjustment. The intelligentsia period of Russian culture came to an end.

The world was slow to realize the tremendous significance of the revolution. It was equally slow to see that the upheaval itself had not been imported from outside, but was due to inner causes, some of them rooted in the entire Russian history. The difficulties to overcome were enormous, almost insuperable. Still, one could not but admire the determination with which one sixth of our globe asserted, not only its will to live, but also to put human existence on a new basis. The change was radical. It affected the whole pattern of life. It gave a new coloring, a new trend, to thoughts and emotions. It also provided new channels for literature.

II

The first few years of revolutionary struggle were too hectic to leave much time for literary activities. Lengthy prose works were out of the question through lack of paper. The years between 1917 and 1922 were mainly years of poetry which was full of abstract slogans about revolution, brotherhood, a new heaven and a new earth. Most of it was not even printed, but publicly recited at various gatherings or in semi-Bohemian cafés. The greatest poetic product of that period was Alexander Blok's swan song, *The Twelve,* which, incidentally, was also the swan song of Russian symbolism. New trends and poets were in the ascendant. The man who sprang into sudden fame was Vladimir Mayakovsky—the leader of Russian futurism. He combined certain ideas of the Italian futurist Marinetti with dadaist experiments upon the Russian language, first undertaken by a very

able young poet, Velemir Khlebnikov. In contrast to his
Italian maestro, who later turned into a supporter of fascism,
Mayakovsky became the mouthpiece of the new socialist
order. He even worked out a posterlike platform poetry,
suitable for propaganda. His chief rival was Sergey Esenin:
a peasant by birth and a bard of the village in its opposition
to the industrialized town. While Mayakovsky appealed to
the workers, the former intelligentsia adored Esenin's
pathetic "back-to-the-village" lyrics, although Esenin, too,
welcomed the revolution.

But Mayakovsky and Esenin were only the two highest
peaks, surrounded by a number of lesser talents—many of
them of proletarian or peasant origin. There was a tendency,
supported by Lenin, Gorky, Trotsky, and Lunacharsky, to
encourage the poets and writers from among the workers, for
which purpose special studios were established. The Prolet-
Kult (Proletarian Culture) organization, founded in 1920,
even aimed at liquidating the remnants of bourgeois culture
not only in Russia, but all over the world. Poets of proletarian origin (Obradovitch, Gastev, Zharov, etc.) failed to
produce anything new or outstanding, but this did not
matter. What mattered was the fact that the general consciousness which arose out of the revolution was entirely
different from the one reflected in the intelligentsia literature.
Gone now was the former sense of tragic futility. It was
replaced by a brave acceptance of life, and by a practical
activism in which there was little room for the "superfluous
man." Literature began to insist on its social tasks and
duties. This often led, however, to tendentiousness pure and
simple. The professional communist authors even demanded
a definite class literature. Grouped round the periodical, *On
Guard* (*Na Postu*), founded in 1923 by the "October Association," they were anxious to turn literature into a vehicle
of communist propaganda. Fortunately, quite a few promi-

nent communists, including Trotsky and Lunacharsky, rose against such a narrow view.

Parallel with that, there existed a strong nonpolitical literary group of "Serapion Brothers." Founded in 1921, it took its name from a romantic work by Hoffmann. The chief aim of its members, largely intellectual *déclassés*, was to produce works of a high artistic value and to disregard any pressure upon the creative freedom of the individual. Anxious to liquidate the remnants of symbolism, they usually stressed the external anecdotic perfection, and were addicted to the *skaz*. The group comprised a variety of young talents: Zamyatin, Fedin, Vsevolod Ivanov, Kaverin, Zoshchenko, and others.

A number of Soviet authors, whether within or outside the Serapion Brothers group, accepted the revolution as an accomplished fact, even when they did not personally adhere to communism. Among these "fellow travelers," as Trotsky labeled them, were some of the best Soviet novelists, such as Pilnyak, Leonov, Katayev. They were not hostile to the revolution or to Bolshevism; they only looked upon both with a dispassionate or even critical eye. Most of them showed, sooner or later, their sympathy with the new régime or even accepted it completely. The critic Voronsky was sagacious enough to invite them to collaborate in the largest Soviet monthly, *The Red Virgin Soil* (*Krasnaya nov*). They were actually responsible for the revival of the novel under the Soviets.

During this revival, which coincided with the N.E.P. (New Economic Policy, 1922-1929) period, a number of talents came to the fore and kept the novel on a rather high level. When Stalin inaugurated, in 1929, his first Five-Year Plan, he naturally called for enormous sacrifices. The writers, too, were expected or even urged to contribute towards its success. Literature was deprived of the relative freedom it had enjoyed during the preceding six years or so. The result was a certain lowering of the former level by mixing art with direct social tasks and with propaganda. In 1932, however, the government itself took the initiative and granted a Charter of Liberty to literature. The intolerant proletarian groups were dissolved. Their mouthpiece, the critic Averbakh, even fell into disgrace. The General Union of Soviet Authors was now formed instead. It included all the writers, whether Russian or those belonging to national minorities, who were in agreement with the general trend of the Soviet policy. Through Maxim Gorky's endeavors the first congress of this Union took place in 1934. One of its important items was the affirmation of socialist realism as the chief literary vehicle of Soviet Russia.

III

Even before such a decision was made, Soviet fiction had passed through an interesting process of development. This began with the end of the civil war. Once life was returning to more or less normal conditions, a demand for prose fiction (at the expense of poetry) became inevitable. It was equally inevitable that the first phase of this fiction should deal with the cataclysm which had just taken place. Revolution and civil war offered countless themes which were eagerly seized upon by the younger writers—most of them describing their own personal experiences. Pilnyak, Babel, Fadeyev, Vsevolod Ivanov, Furmanov, Fedin, and scores of less distinguished authors could not help writing about the events which had turned the tide of history. They even found an appropriate style for it: a somewhat disjointed, nervously lyrical, dynamic prose. The psychological intricacies of the prewar literature were neglected: they seemed almost out of place amidst the elemental happenings described. Yet stylistically, this dynamic period learned a great deal from two prewar authors: Alexey Remizov and Andrey Bely, especially from Bely. The influence of Bely's agitated and ornate prose formed a link between the new Soviet fiction and the tradition of Gogol, whereas Remizov's *skaz* (sprinkled with peasant idioms and provincialisms) joined it to Leskov. On the other hand, the material dealt with was so overwhelming that it defied, as it were, any individual imagination. Facts were more fantastic than fancy. What was needed was not to invent, but to organize, to chronicle all the happenings in such a way as to turn actuality into art. The revolution and civil war were thus responsible for a number of documentary works, to begin with those of Pilnyak, Furmanov, Vsevolod Ivanov, Babel, Fedin, and Leonov.

Boris Pilnyak (born 1894) is partly of German extraction, his real name being Wogau. He achieved fame in 1922, when he published his novel, *A Bare Year*—one of the earliest gruesome pictures of revolutionary turmoil. Influenced by Bely and by Remizov, he indulges in impressionist patches, in a dithyrambic, jerky, and romantic prose. His construction, too, is jerky and loose, like a quick sequence of effectful film shots. A few passages from his description of a train, crowded with famished people in search of corn, can be quoted as an example.

"Mixed train No. 58, creeping across the inky plains.

"People: human legs, arms, bellies, heads, backs and droppings; people as thick in lice as the wagons are in people. People herded in it maintain their right to travel by sheer force of their fists, because out there, in the famine districts, scores of famine refugees rush the train at every station, struggling inside over heads and backs and necks and legs over other people—and these strike out, and those strike out, tearing off and throwing down those already aboard. The scrimmage going on till the train starts and bears off those that happen at the moment to be stuck on—and then those that had got in the last time get ready for another fight at the next station. They travel for days twixt filth and cleanliness, and have learned to sleep sitting, standing, or dangling. The horsebox, lengthwise and crosswise in several layers, holds wide shelves, and on these bunks and under them, on the floor and on the shelves and in every crevice, sitting, standing, lying, are people, huddled, silent—storing up their noise for the stations. The air in the coach is shattered by human bowels and home-made tobacco. At night the wagon is in darkness; the doors and ventilators are all closed. It is cold in the wagon; the wind whistles through the cracks. Somebody croaks as he breathes, somebody scratches; and the wagon creaks like an old swung four-in-hand. It is impossible to move in the wagon, as one man's legs are on another's chest and a third sleeps on top of them both, with his feet on the first one's neck. And yet— they do move. . . ." [1]

While mixing the most daring naturalism with a modernist technique and a highly personal temper. Pilnyak is attracted not by the ideology, but by the chaos of the revolution—by its incredible sweep. Its inhuman, or rather prehuman, side appeals to him. He is fascinated by it, as he is fascinated by everything primitive, rooted in the elements, in nature. He has an instinctive loathing for civilization, for a settled industrialized existence, as we can gather from his *Wolves and Machines,* or *Mother Damp Earth.* The essential Pilnyak is certainly nearer to the earth than to machines. It was on this ground that he came into conflict with the Soviet

[1] Translated by Alec Brown in *Soviet Literature: An Anthology* (Wishart).

authorities. His *Mahogany* (1927) only increased the mis-understanding. He tried to make up for it by his "loyal" novel, *The Volga Flows into the Caspian* (1931), which deals, however, with a different period of Soviet life and will be mentioned in a later chapter.

Another painter of the romantic side of the revolution and civil war is Vsevolod Ivanov. Born in Turkestan (1895), he had no regular education. Like Gorky, under whose auspices he made his literary debut in 1915, he wandered about, exchanging one profession for another. Even his exuberant style, his impressionistic naturalism, makes one think of young Gorky. With this he combines Bely's fondness for ornate prose and that snappy film technique which is noticeable in his narratives about the civil war in Siberia and Turkestan. He came into prominence as early as 1923 with his *Partisans* and *Armored Train No. 14-69*. His other well-known works are *Blue Sands, The Return of Buddha, God Matvey*—all of them striking by a mosaiclike construction, flowery language, unusual situations, and elemental characters. Their general attitude toward life is one of adventurous fatalism. More sober are his tendentious novels, *North Steel* (1925) and *Ferghan Cotton,* dealing with the constructive period of Russia. So are his two Five-Year-Plan contributions, *A Journey to a Non-existent Land,* and *The Stories of Brigadier Sinitzin.* His later writings, to begin with his collection of scathing village stories, *The Mystery of Mysteries* (1927), are marked by psychological preoccupations. Of great biographic interest is his more recent work, *The Adventures of a Fakir.*

A very able chronicler of the civil war—against Kolchak, in the Ural region—was Dmitry Furmanov (1891-1926). His best book, *Chapayev* (1923), is an authentic document: somewhere halfway between thrilling raw material and good literature. Chapayev, the hero of the narrative, was a peasant of thirty-five who had learned how to read and write only four years before the events described, and who became an immensely popular commander of a whole division: one of those leaders who seem to be extemporized by history. The height of his career came when he saved Uralsk from the "white" Cossacks, during which action he lost his life. The whole book is a matter-of-fact description of his strong, enthusiastic, and yet peasant-like, or rather childlike personality. The background of the civil war is well rendered and also well blended with this amazingly Russian figure. Furmanov's second novel, *The Revolt,* is equally outspoken in its Bolshevist sympathies.

More noncommittal is another chronicler of the civil war, Isaac Babel. Born (1894) into a Jewish family in Odessa, he made his first appearance in literature at the age of twenty-two. His early stories came out in 1925, but he owed his reputation to his *Red Cavalry* (1926). This book is a collection of authentic documents about the civil war (during which he was attached to Budyonny's army), turned into short stories or *nouvelles* with that directness which avoids all rhetorical or flowery touches. Endowed with the quick observation of a reporter and the terseness of a Maupassant, he often dwells on the crudest physiological aspects of life, which he organizes so as to achieve a maximum of effect. His very detachment seems to grow in direct ratio to the cruelty of the scenes described. His stories of Odessa are different in character, but they are well told, no matter whether they record his early reminiscences and memories of Jewish pogroms, or else describe the Odessa underworld—with the enterprising Jewish gangster and smuggler, Benya Krik, as its central figure. After a considerable vogue, Babel's productivity and fame began to decline.

IV

Somewhat apart from the authors mentioned stands Konstantin Fedin (born 1892), whose *Cities and Years* (*Gorodá i Gody*) is one of the landmarks of Soviet fiction. This novel appeared in 1924 and aroused interest not only because of its contents but also on account of its construction. The narrative begins not at the beginning but at the end. This device enables the author to give a restrospective picture of war and revolution as seen by the chief character of the novel, Andrey Startsov: a civil prisoner of war in Germany, and later an active revolutionary in Russia during her most tragic months. The author develops an intricate plot, but the stress is on the inner drama of Startsov—a revolutionary Hamlet, not unlike Nezhdanov in Turgenev's *Virgin Soil.* Having become unfaithful to his sweetheart and to the revolution, this vacillating, self-centered intellectual is eventually killed by his own fanatical friend, Kurt Wahn. One of Fedin's memorable figures is the good-natured peasant Lependin, who returns a legless cripple from German captivity and is callously sacrificed, by his own fellow villagers, to the fury of the "Whites."

In spite of his sympathies with the revolution, Fedin is too much of an intellectual imbued with the flavor of Bunin's or even Chekhov's Russia. He treats revolution not as a thrilling event, but as a disturbing psychological problem. So much so that the clash between the old and the new is his cardinal theme, and introspection his usual method of approach. Both come out in his second and more conventional novel, *The Brothers* (1928). Here, too, civil war forms but the background against which the author analyzes the attitude of the intellectuals towards the great upheaval. The chief character reminds one of Startsov but is less carefully worked out. As for Fedin's much discussed novel, *The Rape of Europe*, which began to appear in 1934, it falls below the level of *Cities and Years*. The action covers Russia, Norway, Germany, Holland, and its theme is the antithesis between two irreconcilable worlds: Russia and the capitalist West. The novel is diluted, slow, and loose in construction. At the same time it is decidedly friendly to the Soviets. It also contains some well-deserved criticisms of our money-grubbing civilization. In the much shorter novel, *The Sanatorium Arcturus*, Fedin seems to vie with Thomas Mann in tackling the theme of *The Magic Mountain* (Davos) but remains far behind in size and in quality.

Perhaps the most conspicuous figure among the Soviet writers is Leonid Leonov (born 1899). After his debut in 1922 he attracted attention by his stylized Tartar tale, *Tuatamur,* and even more by his Dostoevskian narrative, *The End of a Small Man* (1924). The hero of the latter is a savant, starved to death during the famine period after the revolution. Its actual theme is Revolution versus Culture: at least in so far as it implies that the gains of a destructive revolution are hardly worth all the suffering and human wastage incurred. Leonov learned much from Gogol, Dostoevsky, Shchedrine, and technically—from Bely and Remizov. His excellent first novel, *The Badgers* (1925), is stylized in the manner of an amplified *skaz*. But like Fedin, Leonov, too, weaves into the revolutionary background the psychology of his characters. In this novel he contrasts—through two brothers—the old antagonism between town and village. One of them, brought up in the town, is an active communist, while the other is a village *kulak*. But this time the author's sympathies are with the revolution as against the peasant conservatism. The village with its stagnant outlook, that is, as an enemy of civilization, is stressed also in his *Unusual Stories about Peasants* (1928).

Leonov consistently treats the revolution and the period after it in their more complicated and deeper aspects. His psychological propensity, on the other hand, is quite in the tradition of Russian fiction. In his subsequent and less stylized novels, *The Thief* (1928), *Sot* (1929), *Skutarevsky* (1932), and *The Road to the Ocean* (1936), his talent reaches out in new directions which will be discussed in the next chapter. It is enough to say that the Soviet critic Vorovsky proclaimed Leonov a bridge between the Soviet realists and the classics of the prewar realism.

It is important to note that such a statement was meant as a compliment. After the early iconoclastic stage, during which practically all traditions were disparaged or even repudiated, the idea that organic continuity in Russian fiction should not be lost began to assert itself instinctively, as it were. The more so because such a prewar author as Alexey N. Tolstoy became one of the prominent Soviet writers, and a link in that continuity.

Alexey N. Tolstoy enjoys a theme above all on account of its anecdotic value. As long as he deals with concrete facts and people, he is excellent; he ceases to be so when taking up abstract themes, ideas, or ideologies. This is why his Wellsian Soviet novel, *Aelita*, whose action takes place on Mars, is weak and unconvincing. A different matter is his trilogy, *The Path of Suffering* (its English title is *Darkness and Dawn*) in which he describes concrete Russia before, during, and after the Revolution. The two central figures, Ivan Telegin and Dasha, are at first two typical intellectuals of the old school; but, having passed through the ordeals of the Revolution, they see also its constructive points and accept all it stands for. A. Tolstoy's picture of the bourgeois intelligentsia on the eve of the Bolshevist rising is hauntingly incisive. So are his incidents of the revolution and the civil war—a real path of suffering, even when his descriptions verge at times on the sensational.

Less satisfactory is his novel *Corn* (*Khleb*), which is a modified chronicle of civil war in the Don and Volga region. It comprises the period between the Brest-Litovsk treaty and the victory over the "white" Cossacks near Tsaritsyn, the defense of which was in the hands of Stalin. His history of the first workers' army and of those guerrilla fights which —under the leadership of Voroshilov and Budyonny—saved that key town, vital for the provisioning of Moscow and Leningrad, is based on official data. He also introduces to us the chief promoters of the revolution in person, especially Lenin and Stalin. But why is Trotsky presented as an incompetent blockhead, and even as a traitor? Whatever Trotsky's faults may have been, they were hardly those of a blockhead. Still, the main thing is Tolstoy's talent, and not Tolstoy's judgment. And at its best his talent is worthy of the traditions of the past. The influence of those traditions can be traced in several Soviet authors, who deal with the period described: Neverov, for example, Fadeyev, and Sholokhov.

Alexander Neverov (1885-1923), a peasant by birth and a village teacher by profession, had done some writing before the war, but came into prominence in 1921—with his *Tashkent, the City of Plenty*. The period described is one of famine after the revolution, and Neverov confines himself to the village only, which he knows well. The hero of his narrative is a peasant boy who leaves his starving family in order to bring back food and corn. His errand takes him as far as Russian Turkestan, whence—after many adventures— he returns home, steeled for the fight with hard realities. One of Neverov's strong points is his love of children. He also admires Russian peasant women, of whom he speaks very highly in some of his works. Death prevented him from finishing his best work—the extensively planned novel, *Swan-Geese*, about village life under the stress of war and revolution. His language, though mingled with savory peasant idioms, is of a quiet traditional type.

Alexander Fadeyev (born 1901) is a Siberian by birth. As a youth he fought against Kolchak and has since been an active member of the Bolshevist party. His first novel, *The Débâcle* (1926), gave a broad, full-blooded picture of the civil war in Siberia, and at once assured him a prominent position in literature. Avoiding any deliberate experiments, Fadeyev models his style on the vigorous simplicity of Tolstoy, trying to balance a well-told external incident with psychological insight. His biggest work so far is his unfinished novel, *The Last of the Udeghé*, which began to appear in 1928. It is mainly about the civil war in a remote corner of Siberia, and also about the effects of the revolution upon a primitive nomadic tribe, the Udeghé. The author has woven into this background a variety of motives and problems: love, family, the ineradicable bourgeois spirit, etc. There are a number of intricate psychological situations—especially those connected with the chief heroine of the novel, although her behavior is not always sufficiently motivated.

Another link with the Tolstoyan tradition is Michael Sholokhov's well-known novel, *Quiet Flows the Don* (1929-1930). It is a Cossack counterpart of *War and Peace*, but within a narrower compass and on a lower level. Sholokhov sets out to show—in fine and fluent language—the panorama of Cossack life on the eve of the war, during the war, and especially during the Revolution. On the surface he certainly achieves his aim, for he is a vivacious observer of the outer side of people and things. Deeper and more enduring aspects of life seem, however, beyond him, in spite of his psychological bent. Nor is he able to resist scenes which lend to some of his pages a spicy flavor. He is more tempered in his next big novel, *The Virgin Soil Upturned* (1932-1933), dealing with the transition from the individual to the collective farming among the same Cossacks. Although diluted at times, the author shows the economic contrasts and antagonisms in a Cossack village, while competently portraying the individual peasants and their womenfolk—from the "kulaks" downwards. This novel has a literary and documentary value. It refers, however, to a considerably later period (Stalin's policy after 1930) than the one with which we are now concerned.

The civil war provided Soviet literature with so much material that we must confine ourselves—and very briefly—to some of its other products only. *The White Guard* by Michael Bulgakov (born 1891) should be mentioned as an outstanding work. The author shows the "Whites" fighting for Kiev against Petlyura, whose savage rule ended with the arrival of the Bolsheviks. In the dramatized form of the same work (under the title, *The Days of Turbin*) he shows the "Whites" in a sympathetic light, as fighters for their own ideals. Uncompromising in their pro-Bolshevist sympathies are two excellent novels about the civil war: *The Heavy Brigade* by Lebedenko, and Alexander G. Malyshkin's *The Fall of Dair*. The latter deals with the conquest of the Crimea by the "Reds." Malyshkin's language is rhetorical, even ecstatic, but his descriptions of the revolutionary masses and of the red army are masterly. His chief weakness lies in his mixture of naturalism, poetry, and symbolism. His subsequent novels, *The February Snow* and *Sebastopol,* are more disciplined. Both are interesting on account of their theme: the individualist intellectuals wavering between revolution and counterrevolution. The hero of *Sebastopol,* for example, finds an outlet in merging completely with the collective consciousness of the proletariat. It is not so much the psychological depth as the sincerity of the author that infects and even carries one away.

The effect of the revolution upon the intellectuals found a further expression in *The Lavrovs* by Michael Slonimsky. Another early novel by the same author, *The Middle Avenue,* is concerned mainly with the lower middle-class people in Petrograd and their reactions to the revolutionary events. Among the notable painters of the civil war is Boris Lavrenev (born 1894) whose first collection of stories, *The Wind,* appeared in 1925. Lavrenev is a bracing storyteller. No matter whether he writes his gruesome romance of the civil war, *Forty First,* his satirical *The Downfall of the Republic of Itle,* or his war novel, *White and Blue,* he is always full of verve and vitality. The same applies to his later work.

The majority of these authors vary in their technique. Yet it is significant that a tendency to return to the traditional realistic manner was on the increase and became general after 1927. A few followers of Remizov and Bely persisted in their experiments. Others continued to use them discreetly and with profit. Thus Artyom Vesyoly's (born 1899) best-known works, *The Native Land* (1927) and *Russia Washed in Blood* (1928), bear a strong influence of the *skaz,* as well as of the colorful peasant language. Vesyoly is weak in construction. But he feels the lyrical or rather dynamic quality of words and is perfectly familiar with the rich idiomatic speech of the lower classes.

Such are a few of the principal works recording the revolution, the civil war, and the period immediately following. Our task is now to examine the Soviet fiction under less strenuous conditions.

CHAPTER XVI

Soviet Life in Literature

QUITE a number of Soviet writers first took up the revolution as a thrilling phenomenon rather than a problem and described it as such. But as time went on, a new system of life began to emerge out of the turmoil. This system was itself a great problem and harbored, moreover, countless special problems of all sorts which were eagerly taken up by the younger authors. There were two phases in particular which left a strong mark on literature. One was the N.E.P. period, and the other the first Five-Year Plan, inaugurated by Stalin in 1929. Both offered plenty of material—it all depended on how the writers approached and used it. Some of them entirely identified their aims with those of the Bolshevists, whom they supported with enthusiasm. Others adopted a humorous, benevolently satirical attitude. Others again tried to preserve their artistic independence, whether they agreed or not with the Bolshevist system. This applies above all to such fellow travelers as Leonov and Pilnyak.

Leonov's second big novel, *The Thief* (1928), deals with the N.E.P. period. Its background is the disorganized, ruined Russia, doing its uttermost to settle down. Mitka Vekshin, the hero of the novel, is a former revolutionary who finds it impossible to come to terms with the new tasks and conditions. Thrown out of gear, he becomes a drifter and a gangster. He passes from one unpalatable experience to the other, until he is staggered by the magnitude of his own fall. Eventually, he decides to abandon his bad ways. The final note of the novel is a promise of regeneration. Vekshin moves in a curious motley world, littered with the wreckage of the old system, and with its parasites still clinging to it. The author's skepticism with regard to the revolution protrudes now and then, and his digs at the Soviet bureaucracy are malicious. Otherwise this work bears the stamp of Dostoevsky. Leonov's interest in the inner man is absorbing. He is also fond of complicated situations. Technically, the novel is not unlike André Gide's *Les Faux Monnayeurs*—in so far at least as the author's mouthpiece, Firsov, collects and groups the entire material before the reader's eye.

Leonov's next two novels, *Sot* and *Skutarevsky,* are about the reconstruction period, which the author approaches sympathetically. In *Sot* we witness the transformation of a northern wilderness, beyond the Ladoga lake, into a busy center of the paper industry. Hampered by sloth and ignorance, by nature, by *saboteurs,* the pioneers of the new socialist Russia persevere and triumph in the end. *Skutarevsky,* too, illustrates an enormous constructive task: the large-scale electrification as devised by Lenin. Yet in this novel attention is centered on the character and the inner life of Skutarevsky—the scientist responsible for the completion of this undertaking. The somewhat grumpy Skutarevsky is at first diffident with regard to the Soviets. Gradually, however, he becomes their staunch supporter. In spite of his self-conscious cut-and-dried manner, he is alive and convincing. So are most of the author's characters, ranging from the degenerate bourgeois wreckers to the fanatical workers for the new social ideal, which now seems to appeal to Leonov. Unfortunately, the novel is so overladen with technicalities that some of its pages resemble a manual for specialists. The author's predilection for psychology comes out also in his more recent novel, *The Road to the Ocean.* This time, the chief hero is an ardent communist, and the author's sympathies are decidedly on the side of the Soviets. But the Soviet actualities are not entirely blended with the Utopian dream of the sick hero. The novel is excellent in details rather than as a whole.

Pilnyak's *Volga Flows into the Caspian* (1931) is another novel about the reconstructive period. Like Leonov's *Skutarevsky*, it is full of technical details. The plot is based, however, on the family tangles and tragedies of the three engineers entrusted with the diverting of the course of a river in the Moscow district. Pilnyak's language is simple, this time, and more disciplined. But at the bottom he is still in love with the revolutionary chaos and cannot accept wholeheartedly the industrialization now imposed upon Russia. After his Far Eastern tales and impressions (the result of a journey to China and Japan), he made a trip to America which he recorded in his book, *O.K.* (1933). One need hardly say that he is not enthusiastic about America. Some of his pages—those about Hollywood, in particular—read like a parody of humanity.

Pilnyak's will to adapt himself to the new conditions, even against his deeper convictions, makes some of his pages rather forced. His story, *The Birth of Man*, may strike one as a jumble of insincere rhetoric. It is even possible that this conflict has been responsible for the slackening of his talent. In his recent book, *The Ripening Fruits* (1938), he seems reconciled to Stalin's Russia and to the constructive work that is going on all over his vast country. Yet, strangely enough, the pretext for writing it was his holiday in Palekh: a village of primitive peasant artists from times immemorial. It is a bit of pre-Petrine Russia which would have fascinated Melnikov-Pechersky or Leskov. Pilnyak's record of his stay there is, however, not a work of art, but only a pastiche: about Palekh itself, art, politics, literature, motor cars, marriage, education, and even the Turk-Sib (Turkestan-Siberian railway). He is quite enthusiastic about the Soviets, although one may hesitate to accept his change of attitude at its face value. If we want unadulterated enthusiasm, we must go to a different type of writer. And this brings us to Gladkov, Seifullina, S. Semyonov, and others.

II

One of the most discussed early Soviet novels was V. Gladkov's *The Cement* (1925). Its author (born 1883), who is of poorest peasant stock, had an unhappy childhood and after it the usual proletarian existence. But he rebelled against it all, was exiled, and—under Gorky's influence—started writing about the workers and political exiles. After the revolution he published his nervously rhetorical novel, *The House on Fire* (about the civil war in the Kuban region), which failed to attract attention. *The Cement,* on the other hand, took the public and the critics by storm: not as a work of art, but as a document, a problem novel, and enthusiastic reportage in one. Uneven, sometimes indifferent technically, it yet reflects the zest with which the workers embarked upon the social and economic reconstruction of Russia, once the civil war was finished. Workers, intellectuals, and Soviet officials form a lively background for the actual thread of the novel: the love tragedy of a married couple faced by an unexpected dilemma. Dasha, the heroine, eventually kills her personal love in order to be free to serve what she regards as her social ideal and duty. The new mentality with its new scale of moral values is strongly pronounced in this work, which is—in some respects—a modern counterpart of Chernyshevsky's *What Is to Be Done?* Gladkov's Five-Year-Plan novel, *Power* (1933), shows on the whole the same virtues and defects as *The Cement* but aroused less enthusiasm.

Another novel about a common Soviet woman, who abandons the standardized code of values in order to serve the new constructive life of her country, is *Virineya,* by Lydia Seifullina (born 1889). The authoress first came into prominence in 1921 by her narrative, *The Lawbreakers,* in which she took up the waifs and strays, made homeless by the revolution. Her *Golden Childhood* is of the same kind. Both are full of sympathy and understanding. Fame came to her, however, in 1923, when her *Mulch* caused something of a sensation—perhaps on account of the vivid naturalism with which she depicts the civil war on the border of Asia and its salutary effect upon a rather degraded village community. She followed up her success by *Virineya,* after which her initial popularity began to decline. Seifullina's best passages are those describing the village poverty. Otherwise she is prone to be voluble, with a propensity for melodrama and for erotic realism. She rendered undoubted service by introducing into literature those strayed children whose fate was later well described by the young author F. Olyosov in his novel, *The Return* (1925). A fine documentary book about them is Anton Makarenko's *The Road to Life,* which shows how the little half savages were turned into decent human beings simply by human treatment and sympathy.[1] Readers interested in wider aspects of Soviet education in those early transition years should read *Kostya Ryabtsev's Diary,* by N. Ognyov. It is a good example of documentary facts, turned into literature "on the wing," as it were.

There was hardly any side of the new Soviet era that remained neglected by the writers. This gave them the great advantage of being close to realities—often too close, in fact, to be able to turn them into smooth literary works. More-

---

[1] This work was responsible for one of the finest documentary films under the same title. The Russian title is *An Educational Epic.* Important from an educational point of view is also Makarenko's *Book for Parents.*

over, as Gladkov had already indicated, a new conscience was growing among the Russian masses—a socialist conscience. The latter claimed an ever larger share in literature —even at the risk of lowering its artistic quality. Any work that illustrated this new conscience was sure to find plenty of readers who were quite willing to overlook artistic defects as long as the spirit was of the right kind and in the right direction. This explains the enormous success of *The Cement* or of such a novel as *Natalia Tarpova* (1927-1929) by another proletarian author, Sergey Semyonov. Like Gladkov, Semyonov is a staunch communist, describing the eagerness of Soviet workers in a big factory. His chief heroine, Natalia, represents—like Dasha in *The Cement*—the type of Soviet woman who solves her erotic difficulties in the light of her socialist conscience.

From 1928-1929 on, that is, from the inauguration of the Five-Year Plan with its motto, "Socialism in one country," the enthusiasm for the new constructive period became general and almost religious. This was possible mainly because the psychology of the Russian workers had meanwhile undergone a radical change. Western Europe can hardly realize what it meant to millions of former proletarians to know that they were working no longer to fill the pockets of their exploiters but in order to raise the general prosperity, the economic, social, and cultural level of the entire nation, of one-sixth of our globe, in fact. Their attitude towards the tasks they were coping with was no longer a matter of mere wages, but one of principle. Ideologies apart, it was something more vital, more intimate and at the same time more idealistic than anything the Western workers have known hitherto.

Whether this was good for literature is a different matter. For no sooner had the Five-Year Plan been launched than the professional communists, with the critic Averbakh at their head, began to exercise a kind of literary dictatorship. This was the heyday of the Russian Association of Proletarian Writers, putting propaganda before art. For a while, at any rate, the former freedom was gone. Direct or indirect pressure was used in order to make the writers comply with the party line. Even literary "shock brigades" were formed with the object of dictating to the authors what to do and of seeing to it that it was done. This situation lasted until 1932.

However excellent the results of the Five-Year Plan may otherwise have been, in literature they were unsatisfactory. It was during that period that the propagandist, the Prolet-Kult enthusiast, and the second- or third-rate novelist asserted himself with unchecked power. A sort of standardized Five-Year-Plan novel made its appearance. Its heroes are the communist workers, while the bourgeois wreckers are the villains of the piece. Needless to say, the *saboteurs* are always discovered in the nick of time, and virtue triumphs with no less certainty than in the old melodrama. Novels conforming to a similar pattern were manufactured in huge quantities, but the bulk of them had little to do with literature. Notable exceptions are, of course, such works as *Sot* and *Skutarevsky* by Leonov, Pilnyak's *The Volga Flows into the Caspian*, Gladkov's *Power*, Sholokhov's *Virgin Soil Upturned*, and a few others, two of which, Panferov's *Bruski* and Kartsev's *The Main Line*, can be mentioned.

The first-named voluminous novel began to appear in 1930, and its instantaneous success was due to its topicality: collectivization of a Volga village at a time when collective farming was the order of the day. Written without literary pretensions and in an extemporized style, *Bruski* bears the mark of authenticity. It may be uneven, frowsy at times, yet it is a proof that the author—an ardent communist—is thoroughly familiar with the peasants and the problems presented.

The Main Line (1934) by Alexey Kartsev was a novel written by a talented newcomer. Its subject matter is the building of a huge railway line, and the young author treats his theme not only with sincere admiration, but also with that objectivity which is devoid of official or any other bias. A follower of Tolstoy's method, Kartsev has a keen eye for what is permanent behind the external forms of life. Novels of this kind coincide, however, with the socialist realism, which came into power after 1932, and will be discussed later.

III

During all these developments, Soviet literature was far from confining itself to a serious tone only. Humor and satire were bound to come into their own as soon as conditions were sufficiently settled to withstand criticism through laughter. As for satire, its early stage was directed chiefly against the capitalist civilization of Europe rather than against the new society that was in formation in Soviet Russia. This is why such a novel as Zamyatin's *We* was banned altogether. Irony and sneering skepticism could not be tolerated in a period which needed a maximum of faith and effort in order to prove that human society can be founded on a new and different basis. On the other hand, such a biting satire of the European postwar civilization as Ilya Erenburg's (born 1889) *Extraordinary Adventures of Julio Hurenito* was welcomed, in spite of its hidden skepticism. This extraordinarily sneering book is a modernized *Candide,* covering Soviet Russia and the European West, after the stress of the war years. Its chief character Hurenito (he is supposed to be a portrait of the famous Mexican painter, Rivera) and his Negro servant travel, observe, comment and make the reader roar with laughter at the idiotic inconsistencies of our capitalist civilization. A prolific and smart journalist by nature, Erenburg combines a satirical vein with a snappy, terse language, and a flair for topical themes with very unsentimental eroticism. Another satirical book of his is *Thirteen Pipes*, telling the history of each particular pipe in the possession of the author, in the same antibourgeois spirit. His attitude towards Western capitalism is negative in the extreme, but he lacks the enthusiasm of faith, whether this be faith in revolution or in anything else. Erenburg is a skeptic whose will to accept whole-heartedly the new ideal of life seems to be as sincere as is his inability to do so. In his novels and stories he touches upon all sorts of important themes and plays upon many strings—cleverly, amusingly, at times even poignantly, but never very deeply. As a rule, he seems to give more than he actually does—a defect for which the general reader is always grateful.

In spite of the real or official enthusiasm (which almost became a duty) over the new building-up period, there was plenty of room for both humor and satire, especially during the N.E.P. period. What is more, both conquered an important place in Soviet literature almost at once. The demand for humor kept on growing. And even violent satire was tolerated as long as it refrained from attacking the basis and the general trend of the new ideal of life. Thus Michael Bulgakov's *Diavoliada* (*The Devilry*, 1925) is a collection of stories, ridiculing not only Soviet life, but also Soviet officialdom. Satirical as well as humorous pictures of Soviet life abound in the writings of Valentin Katayev, of the joint authors Ilya Ilf and Evgeny Petrov, and in the sketches by Michael Zoshchenko.

Valentin Katayev (born 1897) is fond of the picturesque side of existence. As a writer he seems to have learnt much from Bunin and from Tolstoy. His best early work is *The Embezzlers* (1926)—a tragicomic novel about two Soviet officials who embezzle state money, not from greed, but from infantile irresponsibility which is too naïve to make any distinction between good and evil. Having pocketed a considerable sum, they roam—like Gogol's Chichikov—from place to place, until they are caught and brought to justice. The plot is full of incidents illustrating the N.E.P. period in some of its less palatable aspects.

Of a different kind is Katayev's refreshing novel, *Lonely White Sail* (1937). It is retrospective, and its heroes are two boys (one of whom is a fisherboy of ten) and a sailor from the rebellious battleship *Potyemkin*. The background is Odessa during the first revolution of 1905, with its nervous tension, its mutinies, and its pogroms. The sailor is sought by the police, but with the help of the two boys he manages to hide and even to escape to Rumania. The novel is simply and well told. Permeated by the atmosphere of the sea, it breathes the adventurous spirit of early boyhood. It is noteworthy that Katayev—a fellow traveler—became fully converted to socialism in his excellent Five-Year-Plan novel, *Speed Up, Time!* (1933). It covers Russia at work during a period of twenty-four hours, depicting enthusiastic shock brigades competing with each other in the new socialist society. The book is a proof of the author's own enthusiasm. So is his next novel, *A Son of the Working People* (1937), although its literary standard is not so high. Katayev, who is one of the best Soviet authors, is fond of external action. The structure of some of his works shows American influences.

The two collaborators, Ilya Ilf and Evgeny Petrov, have scored a lasting success with their satirical novels, *Twelve Chairs* (1927), *An Exalted Personage*, and *The Golden Calf*, not to mention their short stories from provincial life. Their usual device is the picaresque novel, crammed with adventures and with delightful comic characters, the principal figure being Ostap Bender—the great schemer in *Twelve Chairs* and *The Golden Calf*. He is a new kind of rascal, produced by the N.E.P. period. Actually, Bender's exploits are art for art's sake, whether it be the search for the jewels hidden in the lost chairs, or a series of such ingenious attempts to enrich himself as are depicted in *The Golden Calf*. A cheat, an artist, and a child in one, he is resourceful and reckless. But he can also be as broad and magnanimous as a grandee. The contrast between him and the petty scoundrels of the pocket-picking variety in the latter novel is both subtle and exhilarating. No less exhilarating are the humorous touches with which the authors view the Russia of that particular period. Their later book, *One-storeyed America*, is amusing journalism, illustrating a Soviet citizen's reactions to the American capitalist society.[1]

One of the most widely read Soviet humorists is Michael Zoshchenko (born 1895). He is of gentry origin and became a writer—after a number of other careers—in 1921, when he joined the Serapion Brothers. Some of his early sketches are about the civil-war period. Later he concentrated entirely on literary snapshots of Soviet life. His genre can best be defined as a lively anecdote (with the inflection of a lower middle-class narrator) turned into a *skaz*. In spite of the influences of the early stories of Chekhov, Remizov, and the once very popular Arkady Averchenko, Zoshchenko has worked out a type of sketch of his own. And this gives him an almost unlimited opportunity for criticizing through humor. Most of his jottings are small incidents and comic trifles, shaped into a kaleidoscope at which the author himself chuckles—sometimes with amusement, sometimes with

---

[1] Ilya Ilf was killed in 1941 (during an air raid on Moscow), and Evgeny Petrov in 1942 in Sebastopol.

hidden sadness, and sometimes with a purpose. His earliest success was his *The Tales of Nazar Ilyitch—Mr. Sinebryuk-hov*. And since then he has proved to be one of the most prolific Soviet authors. Such volumes of his as *A Merry Life, Hard Times, What the Nightingale Sang, Reminiscences about Michel Sinyagin*, etc., have enjoyed an enormous circulation. His favorite target is the eternal Philistine in man and in life. Like many a short-story writer, Zoshchenko is less successful when tackling a longer narrative. His seminovel, *Restored Youth* (1933), is in essence a sequence of anecdotic fragments, connected by one and the same character. It tells how a Soviet man (in this case an aged professor) burdened with years, diseases, and melancholy sets out to regain his lost youth. Half of the book tells of the professor's escapades with a silly tart; but this more or less rejuvenating process does not last long. When the professor finds his mistress in the arms of a younger lover, the shock gives him a stroke of paralysis. After due treatment in a hospital, the learned man recovers and, like a prodigal son, returns to the bosom of his rightful family. The other half of the book is a would-be scientific, popular pastiche on rejuvenation, which the author must have written with his tongue in his cheek. Something of a departure from his ordinary genre is *Story of a Life*, describing the regeneration of a criminal through taking part in a great social task—the building of the White Sea Canal.

IV

A few words should be said here about some of those writers who scrutinized Soviet life from the angle of ethical problems, but in the light of the new communist conscience. One of them was Panteleimon Romanov (1884-1936), a straightforward, often pedestrian, but always principled realist. In his broadly conceived novel, or series of novels, *Russia*, he wanted to show—not unlike Sergeyev-Tsensky— the transition from the old bourgeois Russia to the new Soviet society. But as though feeling that such a modern *Comédie humaine* was too big a task for him, he took up less complicated aspects of the early period of Soviet life. In his novel, *Comrade Kislyakov* (*Three Pairs of Silk Stockings* in English), he gives a depressing picture of moral disintegration produced among the intellectuals by the revolution, especially among their women. In his longer but indifferently written novel, *Property*, he shows how the old bourgeois mentality persists, and how the devil of property, thrown out by the door, comes back through the window. But while Romanov's longer novels deal with the lingering shadows of the old generation, his stories are concerned with his younger socialist contemporaries, and most particularly with their attitude towards love and sex. It should be remembered that in the early stages of the N.E.P. period even love and marriage were often derided as old bourgeois prejudices, while the former marriage conventions were actually breaking up. It was then that Romanov became an advocate of a chivalrous and romantic-idealistic conception of love, but from the new Soviet angle. The theme of one of his best longer stories, *A Woman's Letters*, is the failure of a Soviet marriage, because the young Soviet woman's ideal of married life is infinitely higher than that of the former bourgeois society—so high in fact that her husband, a postwar intellectual, is unable to rise up to it. In some of his shorter stories he is concerned with sexual life among the Soviet students. On the whole, Romanov feels at home amidst documentary material of everyday life, especially when he can interpret it in the light of his own ethical idealism.

Another communist writer, Yury Libedinsky (born 1898),

took up social and ethical problems of Soviet life, but in connection with the communist party. His fervent belief in the creative side of the Bolshevist revolution came out even in his early stories, such as *A Week*, or *Tomorrow*, in which there is a curious blend of lyrical language, psychology, and party rationalism. One of his narratives, *The Commissars*, affords us valuable glimpses into the life within the communist party itself, even if the author is too much in the grip of reasoning. Libedinsky's most interesting work so far is *The Birth of a Hero* (1930). This is a novel about Soviet society from the angle of love, family, and especially education, in which the author still sees a few sinister remnants of the old influences. He is an ardent idealist, full of problems, but his ideology does not always tally with his psychology. Nor did he please the orthodox Soviet critics on account of showing the heroes of the new Soviet Russia through their erotic and emotional experiences rather than through the party ideology. He came under suspicion, and his literary career had a temporary setback.

Another painter of early Soviet life and manners is Vladimir Lidin (born 1894). Influenced by Chekhov and Dostoevsky, Lidin is an individualist and a roamer, but he sympathizes with the Soviet system of life. He wrote a number of short stories and sketches about ordinary Soviet folk. Yet his chief work, *The Tomb of the Unknown Soldier* (1932) has only an indirect bearing upon Russia. It is about Paris and the European bourgeoisie, the very sight of which gives him nausea. Its filmlike technique is scrappy, but its spirit is one of indignation and of disguised idealism.

A more detached attitude is noticeable in Nikolai Nikitin (born 1897)—a former Serapion Brother and admirer of Remizov. One of his best-known works, *The Crime of Kirik Rudenko*, is about factory life in a Soviet village. The workers are shown through some of those destructive passions which in the end prove stronger than any systems and theories. Other aspects of the workers' life are depicted by N. N. Lyashkov, whereas P. Nizovoy and L. Demidov deal mainly with the peasants in the light of the communist conscience. This conscience is at its best in such novels as Nikolay Ostrovsky's *How the Steel Was Tempered* and *Those Born by the Storm*. Ostrovsky, who is a former proletarian, depicts the new type of man—produced by the Soviet system—in the process of his growth. But here we touch already upon the realm of socialist realism proper.

CHAPTER XVII

Links with the Past and the Future

THE CHANGE in the social pattern achieved by Soviet Russia involved a change in the trend and spirit of literature. As far as the formal side was concerned, there remained sufficient contact—whether through Remizov and Bely or in a direct way—with the masters of the past. Amidst hectic experiments and some equally hectic claims for a proletarian class literature, the wish to preserve the organic continuity of national culture was not dead. A section of Soviet authors carried on at least certain traditions of the old realism at its best. This explains the revival of the psychological novel and of the interest in those deeper irrational elements of existence with which the intelligentsia realism had been preoccupied.

In her determination to outstrip Europe and even America in technical achievements, Soviet Russia first concentrated on mechanization at the expense of the inner man. In this respect the Soviet period offers a parallel with the efforts of Peter the Great. But once the danger of such a one-sided development became apparent, a reaction was bound to take place. Zamyatin ridiculed the very idea of a standardized society. Psychology plays a conspicuous part in the works of Pilnyak and even more in those of Leonov. The ethical and idealistic trend of such authors as Romanov, or the ardent communist Libedinsky, is hardly less significant. A number of Soviet writers—not in the least hostile to the socialist experiment—are seriously interested in those emotions and values which transcend any class or other barriers, simply because they are fundamental and therefore permanent.

Sergey T. Malashkin (born 1890), for example—known chiefly by his novel, *The Moon on the Right-hand Side* (1927), in which he attacks the erotic looseness of some younger communists—dwells, in a number of his works, on the complex inner problems of his generation. So does Ovady Savitch, whose *Imaginary Interlocutor* is a Dostoevskian novel, concerned with one's personal fate and death, amidst the everyday realities of Soviet Russia. The stress on the inner man is conspicuous in the works of Budantsev, Olyosha, and Kaverin.

After some stories and novels in the approved direction, Sergey Budantsev (born 1896) aroused much controversy by his *Tale of a Suffering Mind*. Its hero has nothing to do with Soviet Russia. He is an intellectual—a philosopher and scientist of the 'sixties, painfully searching for a deeper meaning of existence, in which quest he distrusts all ready-made formulae. Another outstanding and widely discussed novel is Olyosha's *Envy* (1927), later dramatized as *The Conspiracy of Feeling*. The title of the play version indicates the theme of the novel: personal emotions and inclinations versus imposed systems. Written in an impressionist style, *Envy* shows a truly Dostoevskian diffidence with regard to an overregulated, mechanized world. Olyosha's sympathy with Soviet Russia is proved, however, by his satirical tale, *Three Fat Men,* in which he ridicules the entire bourgeois-capitalist society.

A champion of individual freedom against ready-made rules or forms is also Venyamin Kaverin (born 1902). Originally one of the most gifted members of the Serapion Brothers, he vented his aversion to surrounding reality by a number of fantastic stories *à la* Hoffmann. Even his subsequent interest in the underworld, described in *The End of Khaza* (1925), has a romantic flavor. What concerned him particularly was, however, the inner reaction of the intellectuals to certain aspects of the October revolution, as we can gather from his early novel, *Nine Tenths of Fate* (1925). His *Scandalmonger, or Evenings on the Vasily Island* (1927) is a sprightly satire on the bourgeois *littérateurs* and artists. In 1931 he published a number of Five-Year-Plan stories under the general title, *The Prologue*. In the same year appeared his novel, *The Anonymous Artist*, in which he champions the right to one's personal fate and sponsors even the need for romanticism—that "wall-shattering weapon which still comes in handy for fighting against declining honor, hypocrisy, meanness, and boredom." A similar trend is noticeable in his longest and maturest work, *The Fulfilment of Wishes* (1934-1935). Its plot is based on the theft of a precious manuscript. The most valuable part is, however, the insight into the life of Soviet students, who are vexed by inner problems of their own. An experimenter in style and a connoisseur of literature, Kaverin is essentially a defender of spiritual independence, no matter how seductive the encroachment upon it may seem at times.

A few words should be said about two younger authors who belong to a similar category: Andrey Platonov and Leonid Solovyov. Fastidious and discreet in his method, Platonov is interested in the deeper aspects of the human ego, especially in the problem of suffering. One of his favorite and rather pathetic themes is that of orphan children. He seems to cultivate the sense of the tragic. Leonid Solovyov is known so far by his much-talked-of work, *High Pressure* (1938). This novel marks a return to essential human feelings: love, pride, jealousy. It is fresh and honest in its approach, even when it appears somewhat youthful. But the author himself is still young, which is all to his credit.

Another talented newcomer is Yury Gherman whose novel, *Our Acquaintances* (1937), is a tangle of emotions. Its chief character, Antonina, very immature at first, passes through two unhappy marriages and finds her own fulfillment in social activities. The principal value of the book consists in its description of everyday life in Soviet Russia, and the quiet objectivity with which this is done makes up for occasional lapses in style.

II

One could quote several other writers. But those mentioned are enough to prove that, in spite of the great cataclysm which has taken place in Russia, her literary continuity has not perished. The two salient aspects of the old intelligentsia literature—social idealism on the one hand, and interest in the human soul on the other—have both been preserved. The first has found an active application on a scale never dreamed of before. But the second, too, is affirming itself, thus keeping the continuity in this direction. Interesting attempts have been made to restore, through literature, even certain features of historical continuity. And this brings us to the unexpected revival of the historical novel in Soviet Russia.

It is a paradox that a period of the negation of old values often shows an increased interest in the past. This interest may be due to two apparently contradictory reasons. One is the desire to take a rest from the stress of the present by turning to the past. And the other is a tendency to reinterpret the past in the light of the present. In Soviet literature this second impulse prevails over the first. It is not only the dialectic method, so popular with young Russians, that fosters the historical sense. The latter is stimulated by the very changes which are taking place with incredible rapidity. These changes cannot be regarded as something detached or casual. Their pace and magnitude postulate some permanent element behind it all. The flux of external events must point to some deeper historical process, the single stages of which cannot be isolated or chopped up at will. Nor can it be confined to certain epochs at the expense of others. While permeating all of them, it shows not only the contrasts, but also the contacts and the analogies between them.

Hence the popularity of the historical novel in Soviet Russia is not something gratuitous. Nor does it show an escapist trend. The very method used seems to exclude such a propensity. What strikes one in these Soviet authors is first of all their fearlessness with regard to the material they deal with. Practically all have passed through the revolution and the civil war. And the merciless authenticity applied by them to the events of the civil war was naturally adopted also with regard to other historical periods. This is why the Soviet historical novel is unusually well documented. It is at the opposite end of the historical romance with its sentimental adulterations of the past.

Some of the narratives, dealing with the revolution and the civil war, can even now be regarded as historical novels—based on the personal experiences of their authors. Sholokhov's *Quiet Flows the Don* is an instance. And Alexey N. Tolstoy whose trilogy, *The Path of Suffering*, is a record of events witnessed by himself, has also written *Peter I*—one of the best historical novels produced by Soviet Russia. This work gives us an artistically reconstructed panorama of an entire epoch, carried out with great skill both as history and fiction. Its background is that of Russia in a crisis of transition, not unlike the present period. The wealth of characters and events is prodigious, even if the author's psychology is sometimes deficient. Peter himself is portrayed, of course, in a sympathetic light, almost as a distant precursor of Lenin. According to a Soviet critic, this grand novel is "an

approach to our present period from its far distant rear."
And in this process of exploration Alexey N. Tolstoy is all
the more lively because he himself is unable to see history
otherwise than in terms of agitated flux and movement.

Another prewar writer, Alexey Chapygin (born 1870),
wrote an exciting historical novel, *Stenka Razin* (1927), about
the exploits of the popular and almost legendary seven-
teenth-century robber: a kind of Russian Robin Hood. The
novel is full of atmosphere and local color, which the author
uses with such exactness as to make the background of the
novel seem unusually authentic. He, too, "approaches the
present period through its far distant rear" by showing
Stenka Razin as the leader of the first rising among the serfs.

Yermak, the Cossack conqueror of Siberia in the second
half of the seventeenth century, is another figure too tempt-
ing to be neglected by the Soviet authors. He is the hero
of Artyom Vesyoly's glowing and well-documented novel,
Gulyay Volga—a splendid title in Russian, but untranslatable.
(Its literal meaning is: "Volga, go on a spree.")

Of a different kind is such a work as *Tsushima* by A.
Novikov-Priboy (1877-1944). Its author is an ex-sailor who
has written some able stories about the sea and the marines.
This book, however, is primarily a well-told chronicle of
eyewitnesses, describing what they saw before and during
the *débâcle* of the Russian fleet in the Russo-Japanese War.
Which brings us to less distant times, discussed by the novelists Tynyanov, Vinogradov, Olga Forsh, and others.

III

Yury Tynyanov's principal novels, *Kukhlya, Vazir Mukhtar,*
and *Pushkin,* remind one of the *biographie romancée.* In
their cold detachment and documentation they are, however,
the reverse. The hero of *Kukhlya* (1925) is the Decembrist

Kuechelbecker—the title of the novel being a comic distortion of his surname. He was a minor poet, a schoolfellow of Pushkin, and altogether a quaint but lovable personality. The novel is a character study (or studies) in the first place, balanced by a careful rendering of that background which fomented the Decembrist conspiracy. The most pathetic pages are those about Kuechelbecker's exile in Siberia and his drift towards inevitable doom.

Vazir Mukhtar (1929) is a novel about the same generation and the dramatist Griboyedov—the author of *Woe from Wit*—is its central figure. We follow Griboyedov's fortunes, including his brilliant diplomatic career in Persia, where he was eventually murdered by the incited mob in Teheran. Less subtle in some respects than the previous novel, *Vazir Mukhtar* abounds in portraits drawn with a sure hand. The atmosphere of the period, too, is well rendered. But there is something static in Tynyanov's detachment and in his analysis of the epoch described, however dexterously he may use his fragmentary film technique. He seems to treat history as a rather cheerless setting for his characters. In his novel, *Pushkin,* which began to appear in 1937, he made an attempt to show both the hero and his background in a process of growth. But here he is almost too meticulous in his documentation, which makes the tempo of the novel very slow.

Anatoly Vinogradov's works are equally well documented, with the difference that he likes to underline the revolutionary side. The hero of his novel, *The Black Consul,* is Toussaint L'Ouverture, the rebellious leader of the Haiti Negroes. In his *Tale about the Turgenevs* Vinogradov returns to the realities of Russia at the beginning of the last century. This was the heyday of the Masonic movement with which the two Turgenev brothers were closely connected. Both of them play a conspicuous part also in his novel about Stendhal, *The Three Colors of Time.* We first see Stendhal in burning Moscow and in the chaotic retreat of Napoleon's army in 1812. Then we follow his adventures in France, and even more in Italy, where the author points out Stendhal's contact with Byron and the *carbonari*. The revolutionary *carbonari* movement is described at considerable length. The novel also touches upon the Decembrist plot in Russia. The breadth of Vinogradov's interest is further proved by the fact that the hero of one of his novels is Paganini.

Nearer to Tynyanov's genre are the novels by an elderly authoress, Olga Forsh (born 1875). Her debut goes back to 1908, but she found her proper genre only after the Revolution of 1917. Her favorite themes and characters are those connected with Russian thought, literature, and revolutionary activities from Radishchev onwards. Thus in one of her well-known novels, *The Contemporaries* (1932), she depicts the inner drama of Gogol and the painter, Alexander Ivanov, during their stay in Rome in the 'forties of the last century. In the background one feels the revolutionary "Young Italy" movement, but most of her psychology is centered on a typical superfluous man (Bagretsov) whose inner complications are in the tradition of Dostoevsky. Strongly Dostoevskian is also her best novel, *Clad in Stone*, dealing with the tragic fate of Beideman—a revolutionary of the 'sixties, who was thrown into the Petropavlovsk dungeons and there went hopelessly mad. One of the episodic characters in this novel is Dostoevsky himself—after his return from penal servitude in Siberia. Another is Karakozov who, in 1866, made an attempt on the Czar's life and was afterwards publicly executed. The technical device of this work is rather ingenious. Written in the form of reminiscences by a semi-mad aristocratic victim of the Revolution, the recorded happenings of the 'sixties are all the time punctuated by the irruption of the realities typical of Soviet Leningrad in 1923.

Olga Forsh's manner may strike one at times as being

somewhat sketchy and hurried, but she always has something to say, whether it has a bearing upon past or present. And when the past is a recent one, her work can be amusingly topical as is the case with her *Mad Ship*—a satirical skit on the Leningrad "Writers' House" in 1920, that is, during the worst period of famine, cold, and general disintegration of the old system. We are introduced to such literary figures as Gorky, Blok, Bely, Esenin, and Klyuyev (all under assumed names), but the main impression is one of incredible muddle and helplessness among the literary intellectuals. In *The Symbolists*, printed in *Zvezda* (*The Star*) in 1933, she treats the former symbolist movement in Russia as a negative phenomenon, typical of that decadent bourgeois mentality which preceded the First World War and all that followed.

These examples are enough to show how the historical novel and its kindred genre are helping to keep both the sense of literary and historical continuity in the consciousness of Soviet Russia. The link with the past has been or is being thus restored in the right direction. But there is another element which promises to strengthen this link with the passing of time: patriotism—as something different from nationalism.[1] When Stalin's slogan, "Socialism in one country," won a victory over Trotsky, patriotic pride in "our socialist fatherland" became a stimulus to further efforts during the first and second Five-Year Plans. It also cemented the country from within in view of the impending danger from both Germany and Japan—especially when the irresponsibility of various European statesmen clearly indicated what course the events would take. No wonder that patriotism penetrated into Soviet literature. There is much of it in

---

[1] A confusion of the two is misleading. Roughly, patriotism is the attachment to one's native land, whereas nationalism is the exaltation of one's own nation. The two may of course coincide, but they need not do so.

Alexey N. Tolstoy's *Peter I*. But if we want it in a more direct form, we shall find it in Pavlenko's novel, *In the East* (1937).

P. Pavlenko first made a name for himself with *The Barricades*, a novel about Paris during its Commune period in 1871. (Among the characters depicted is young Anatole France.) *In the East* is technically rather scrappy, deficient in psychology, yet the subject matter is of great topical interest in so far as it deals with the prospective clash between Soviet Russia and Japan. The novel affords many glimpses into the constructive Soviet activities in Siberia, and—what is more—blends unmistakably socialism and patriotism. This last feature was also one of the chief reasons why the book became a best seller.

IV

It is hardly necessary to mention further authors and novels. One thing is sure: with all its ups and downs, Soviet literature has broken new ground. Conscious of its social task and its responsibility before life as a whole, it strives to integrate all the creative elements of the present and the past for the sake of a better future. Thus we arrive at that socialist realism which was launched, in 1932, as *the* literary current of Soviet Russia.

What, then, is socialist realism? Its elements can be found not only in the best Soviet novels since 1922, but also in Gorky, as well as in several intelligentsia authors from Belinsky and Herzen onwards. Gorky himself calls it proletarian or socialist humanism. The latter presupposes a socialist society and that type of consciousness in which the individual and the community are no longer two hostile, but two complementary factors, helping each other's growth.

Our bourgeois realism is mainly one which criticizes life. As long as it reflects our modern society in its process of disintegration, it is almost bound to be devoid of faith, of any perspective for the future. It is skeptical and pessimistic by its very nature. Losing the last traces of social consciousness, the modern individual, too, is liable to become a self-centered pessimist, either indifferent or even profoundly hostile to the community. He is critical of the present mainly in order to take revenge for his own frustrated will and for his inner devastation. Socialist realism, however, postulates not only an integrated society, but also a creative scope for the individual and collective will, stimulated by a new faith in man and life. It can be as minute in its description and relentless in its criticism as any bourgeois analysis, but the spirit is different. To quote Gorky, "we are interested in accurate description of reality in so far as this is necessary for a deeper and clearer understanding of all that we must abolish and that we must build up."

Socialist realism thus integrates literature and life. Its aim is not only to reflect life, but to shape it, to imbue it with significance, to direct the creative present towards a more creative future. Such art can be profoundly tragic at times, but it cannot be pessimistic. And herein lies all the difference. Nor should we worry too much over purpose in art. For one thing, there is a great difference between affixed purposes and the inner direction (one is inclined to coin the word "directedness") in art and literature. Secondly, even purposes can be compatible with art as long as they are stated in terms of art, instead of being pasted upon it in the shape of pretentious labels, lectures, and sermons. An author is allowed to put forward any purpose, provided he makes it a part of the innermost life of the characters described, instead of using them as mere pegs for slogans and propaganda.

Soviet literature abounds in works belonging to both categories. But only when the two are fully differentiated can we expect a triumph of socialist realism. This would be all the more welcomed, since the bourgeois realism seems already to have exhausted most of its possibilities and is threatened by commercialized sensationalism on the one hand, and by commercialized subliterature on the other.

CHAPTER XVIII

The Second World War and After

It would be almost impossible to understand the character of Russian literature immediately before and during the Second World War without mentioning at least some of the facts typical of the havoc on the eve of the recent cataclysm. Whereas the carefully planned economic and social experiment in Soviet Russia proved a working proposition, there seemed to be no general directive in the world outside Russia capable of restraining the political gangsters on the one hand and the cynical indifference with its *après-nous-le-déluge* mentality on the other. The final bankruptcy of the League of Nations, and—together with it—of any collective security was itself one of the worst omens. Those who were able to read correctly the writing on the wall knew the hidden meaning of such happenings as the Manchukuo scandal in 1931, the Abyssinian campaign, the Spanish civil war, the *anschluss* of Austria, the notorious pilgrimage to Munich, and the rape of Czechoslovakia. They knew it, but all they could do was to state the complete cultural, political, and moral "decline of the West." Realistic from the outset, Soviet Russia was under no illusions as to what was taking place in a world which regarded it almost as its duty to be hostile towards everything she stood and worked for. Isolated, deliberately snubbed and slandered, she could not but think that the next conflict would be on a global scale and that, in any case, the brunt of it would have to be borne by her. Unwilling to be caught unprepared, she took the necessary steps in time to meet the situation both materially and morally.

This is not the moment to dwell on the reasons chiefly responsible for Hitler's decision to attack the two Western Powers first, that is, before turning against Russia. Yet this blunder helped Soviet Russia in so far as it gave her a certain breathing space during which she was able to complete her preparations in view of the coming blow. When the blow came, the world gasped not only at the savagery of the German hordes in Russia, but also at the magnificent exploits of the Soviet people whose heroism and well-nigh incredible endurance would have been impossible without the requisite moral stamina. This moral force was at least partly due to Soviet literature which, together with certain other factors, helped to train the will and the consciousness of the nation in the direction required.

A kind of gradual "transvaluation of values" was noticeable in Soviet literature from the beginning of the 'thirties onwards, and particularly after the acceptance of socialist realism as its general line. Since one of the principal tenets of such realism is a creative contact with life itself—a contact which at the same time provides the necessary directive in case of emergency, we need not be surprised if the Soviet authors did their best to counter the growing threat. For one thing, the former internationalism was gradually replaced by a more patriotic attitude, the novelty of which consisted in a complete absence of chauvinistic or any other form of nationalism. It was an allegiance to the soil as well as to the historical heritage, and not to the "race." The insistence on cultural and historical continuity was increased, but not in order to glorify the Russian nation at the expense of other national units inhabiting the vast Soviet territory. On the contrary, during the general "Balkanization" of Europe, the Soviets did their uttermost to consolidate the loyalty of all the national, racial, and linguistic groups within the Union. A cultural token of this broad supranational Soviet patriotism was the Association of Writers of the U.S.S.R. Founded in April, 1932, it not only replaced the former Russian groups and cliques by a compact literary body, but wisely included the authors of all the non-Russian nations in the Soviet Union on equal terms. More than ever before, the Soviet cause, whether in culture, in economics, or in politics, became their common cause, which they were ready to defend, together with the Russians, once danger began to loom on the horizon.

II

The impact of all this upon Soviet literature was obvious enough to explain some of its changes as well as its new orientation in general. The revolutionary momentum as such, for example, actually retreated before the patriotic one. Hence the sudden popularity of the patriotic novel (whether historical or otherwise) and the increased interest in such figures as Peter the Great, Alexander Nevsky, Dimitry Donskoy, Ivan the Terrible, Suvorov, Kutuzov, in the heroes of the Crimean campaign, and even in Brusilov—the one-time successful Czarist general during the First World War. History was now being taught from a less rigidly Marxian angle, and the role of Christianity in Russian civilization was no longer minimized. In addition to a changed view with regard to the significant figures of Russia's past, stress was laid (in the historical novel, for instance) on those events and periods in particular when the very existence of Russia had been at stake and saved by the effort of the people. Past events were interpreted in such a way as to make the people understand all the more the present crisis and at the same time realize that they themselves were now called upon to become the makers of history.

During the first part of Hitler's invasion there was hardly any time left for big-scale novels. Propaganda, pamphleteering, war poetry, reportage, snappy documentary war stories, and patriotic plays excluded, for a time, the long novel. Such well-known authors as Alexey Tolstoy and Ilya Erenburg (whose *Fall of Paris*—an example of high-class pamphleteering in the form of a novel—came out before Hitler's attack on Russia) were among the most spirited propagandists during the war. Soon the documentary war diaries began to appear in print. One of the earliest was Alexander Polyakov's brief but eloquent *With the Soviet Unit through the Nazi Line* (1941). Others had to wait until 1945, but their belated appearance by no means diminished either their documentary or their dramatic value. This applies above all to the Leningrad diary *Almost Three Years* by the poetess Vera Inber; to the *War Diaries* of the poet and dramatist Konstantin Simonov, and to those of P. Ignatov, dealing with the fighting in the Kuban area. Vasily Grossman's *With the Red Army in Poland and Belorussia* refers to a comparatively late and brief period: June and July, 1944.

As for the documentary or semidocumentary war story, it was represented, in addition to a number of newcomers, by the writings of Erenburg, Fadeyev, Kaverin, Panferov, Pavlenko, by the poets Konstantin Simonov and Nikolai Tikhonov, not to mention many others. It goes without saying that the material itself dealt with in many of these stories was still too tangible, too agitated to be entirely sublimated by art: it often remained nearer to reportage, the chief aim of which was to arouse in the reader all his indignation and spirit of resistance. The same holds good of quite a few war novels. Strangely enough, one of the earliest of these to appear in print was *The Rainbow* (1942) by the Polish authoress Wanda Wasilewska, who writes also in Russian. As if anxious to disburden her own impressions of the first German onslaught, the authoress piles up the atrocities committed by the enemy in an occupied Russian village: brutal extortion of corn, hostages, hangings, inhuman tortures of a guerilla woman who is thrown (together with her baby) into an ice hole, etc. The list is too long to be quoted, but this somewhat sensational treatment had its value as a moral stimulant, especially if its final note was one of hope and liberation, as invariably happened. Wasilewska's second war story, *Just Love,* which appeared three years later, is in a different vein, but its end is even more optimistic. It is a story about a wife who remains unconditionally loyal to her husband crippled in the war and finds in this her new happiness. "The good, the friendly apple tree," so the novel ends, "was rustling, growing, covering the motherland with its branches, in which glowed the stars of victory. The earth was overflowing with a supreme joy, with song, with a profound, austere, genuine happiness." [1]

Three of the shorter but in their own way powerful novels describing the earlier stages of the war should be singled out on account of their method and their spirit: *The People Is Immortal* (1943) by Vasily Grossman; *Taras's Family* (1943) by Boris Gorbatov; and *Days and Nights* (1944) by Konstantin Simonov. The strongest point of the first of these three novels is its vivid portraiture of the Soviet officers and soldiers on the Belorussian front (the Gomel sector) in 1941, when the *furor Teutonicus* was particularly ruthless. The ordeal of the population at the hands of the Germans is here depicted without any hankering after sensationalism. So is the specific new note of patriotism, evoked in both the civilians and the soldiers by the very brutality of the aggressor. As one of the soldiers naïvely puts it: "It is as if I've become a different person in this war: only now I

---

[1] Practically all the quotations are taken from the English editions of Soviet authors published by Hutchinson.

have seen Russia as she really is. Honestly, I mean it. You walk along and you get to feel so sorry for every river, every bit of woodland, that your heart aches. Life wasn't always easy for the people, but then the difficulty was their own, ours. Today I was walking in a glade and there a tree was rustling and trembling. It suddenly hurt me so much that I felt as if something was tearing at me. I thought, can it really be true that this little tree will go to the Germans?" This naïvely spontaneous and almost physical love for their native land—a love devoid of any "hurrah nationalism"— seems to unite all the individuals in that kind of heroic will and action which ceases to be personal and becomes an elemental vital matter of the entire people anxious to throw off the bondage. The story ends with a Russian bayonet attack, led by the commissar Bogaryov, in the German rear, and is accompanied by the following comment: "Bogaryov ran ahead and an unwonted emotion seized his entire being. He drew the men after him, but they, too, bound to him in a single, indivisible whole, seemed to be impelling him forward. He heard their heavy breathing behind him, and the rapid, heated beating of their hearts was transmitted to him. This was the people who had won their land in battle."

The moral effect of such literature at such a moment can well be imagined. Gorbatov's *Taras's Family* is another war novel of the same kind. The scene of action is a town occupied by the Germans on their road to Stalingrad in July, 1942. The central characters of the novel are the old worker Taras and his children. When one of his sons, Andrey, escapes from the German camp and secretly comes home, Taras treats him with contempt on having learned that he had surrendered to the enemy. During the general scarcity old Taras leaves his town and in search for food suddenly comes across his eldest son Stepan—an organizer of the guerilla activities behind the German front. Three months later, he returns with a sack of corn and the good news about the Russian success at Stalingrad and on the Don. His daughter, who is connected with the guerillas, is caught and hanged by the Germans shortly before they flee. In their panicky retreat they try to destroy the town, but an armed workers' rising, during which Taras is wounded, saves the situation. After the German rout, Andrey, who had meanwhile disappeared, returns a proud Soviet soldier once more, while Taras's third son, Nikifor, wounded in the defense of Stalingrad, comes home in the trail of the routed Germans. The fate of one single family is thus made symbolic, as it were, of the entire population smarting in the claws of the German Gestapo whose practices of the torture chamber were spun out over every sphere of life. "The torture chamber where they tortured the souls of children was the school. The torture chamber where the German doctors tried their poisons on wounded Russians was the hospital. The war-prisoners' camp was a torture chamber. The theater, the church, and the street were torture chambers." Yet here, too, the final note is one of hope, courage, and of the prospective renewal of life. It is expressed by the wounded Nikifor whose vitality remains undaunted even in the face of the devastation caused by the invader.

"Before him lay the land gravely wounded, as he himself had been. Everywhere were open wounds.

" 'Never mind!' said Nikifor. 'Never mind, brother, we're still alive and kicking! Ekh, how much work there is! How much work! What do crutches matter? Soon we'll throw them away! And then you just watch our chimneys smoke!'

"And he knew that it was in the nature of life that the wounds would heal. Yes, they would heal."

Somewhat different in character but equally bracing is Simonov's *Days and Nights*—a novel about Stalingrad during the worst and final period of the fighting for its streets and ruined houses. The central character, Captain Saburov, is an average young officer with a pathetically insignificant past, who gradually develops into a heroic figure in such an obvious manner that he himself is hardly conscious of it. He performs the most difficult tasks of courage and endurance with that simplicity and lack of any swaggering self-admiration which is typical of Tolstoy's soldiers in *War and Peace,* and indeed of the Russian soldiers in general. As in Grossman's *The People Is Immortal,* one can feel behind this unassuming hero the collective will of an entire nation fighting for its survival, for its future. Several scenes and episodes, based apparently on the personal experience of the author himself, are of great documentary value. Yet their grimness is somewhat redeemed by the intruding human feelings: Saburov's touchingly clumsy and reserved—but for this very reason all the deeper—love for a young nurse whose life he happened to save.

III

We are perhaps too near to the war itself to be able to assess the real value of the novels and narratives, reflecting the travail of a whole nation during the greatest crisis in its history. Still, it is highly interesting that during that crisis literature never ceased to play its part of a great spiritual and moral factor, unequaled by the war literature of any other belligerent nation. This is why the best known Soviet authors, such as Leonov, Sholokhov, Katayev, Panferov, Kaverin, Gherman, and others, regarded it almost as their duty to contribute what they could in order to keep up the heroic confidence and faith in the future.

A relatively short but beautifully written contribution is Leonid Leonov's *The Taking of Velikoshumsk* (1944). As in his previous works here, too, Leonov proves to be a good narrator and a good psychologist in one, even if he deals, this time, only with the men at war. The originality of this story consists in the contrast between the efficient up-to-date technique (exemplified by the tank and the battle of tanks) on the one hand, and the intensely human factors among the Soviet soldiers on the other—not the least of them being the coincidence of the commanding officer fighting for the liberation of the town in which he had spent his boyhood.

As for Sholokhov's forthcoming war novel, only one comparatively short episode, *They Fought for Their Country* (1944), is accessible so far outside the Soviet Union, but it is certainly worth reading. The whole of it is a picture of the Cossack soldiers crossing the Don during their retreat— a dangerous operation involving a number of wounded in the midst of great havoc, especially at the neighboring collective farm. As in *Quiet Flows the Don,* Sholokhov works with that broad sweep which he has inherited from Tolstoy. Another Soviet follower of Tolstoy, Alexander Fadeyev, gives us in his *Young Guard* (1945) a novel about the underground activities in the industrial Don area under the German occupation. It is written in the author's best vein. His descriptions, as well as his portraits of characters both Russian and German, especially of *komsomol* girls helping to sabotage the invader, are so well done that the author won the coveted Stalin prize.

Among the Stalin prize winners was also Valentin Katayev, known above all by his delightfully refreshing *The Lone White Sail.* In his war novel, *The Son of a Regiment* (1945), as in the mentioned work, the principal hero is a boy. Having been adopted by a regiment, the boy passes through many thrilling experiences to which he reacts in his own boyish fashion. Quite an important part is played by a boy also in the lively war novel, *The Two Captains* (1945), by Venyamin Kaverin. Its actual theme is the search for a lost polar expedition, helped by the enterprising boy adventurer who eventually becomes a captain. The title, on the other hand, refers to the contrast between the two captains—one still imbued with the old ideas and working for the glory of the old Russia, while the other is up-to-date and therefore much more in tune with the tasks of the epoch in which he lives.

About F. Panferov's novel, *The Struggle for Peace* (1945), opinion will probably be as divided as it was about his *Bruski*. The more so because, judging by the first volume, his new work threatens to become no less circumstantial and diluted than was his novel about the Volga peasants. More than half of the first volume—the only one published so far—deals with the description of the workers who were transferred (together with their factory) from threatened Moscow to the Urals. We are afforded a good insight into the difficulties of such a transfer, involving not only a new installation but the settling down of the personnel, especially of the engineers and the factory authorities, among the somewhat diffident local peasants. But while this is happening in the rear, the other half of the novel takes us to the war area itself, where the factory director's wife and baby son are caught by the rapidly advancing Germans. We follow the ordeals and trials of the two captives until they reach, together with a party of fugitive peasants, the partisans in the Bryansk forests. This first volume ends with the heartening news about the Russian victory at Stalingrad. There were, of course, a number of other novels about the wholesale transfer of factories in wartime. Their value is uneven, yet three of them can be mentioned as ranking above the average. *The Test*, by Arkady Perventsev, describes the removal of an entire aircraft factory during the early phase of the war, while the authoress Anna Karavayeva deals in her two novels, *The Stalin Foremen* (1943) and *The Lights* (1944), with the war industry in the Urals.

Nor were the sailors and the war at sea neglected by the Soviet authors. Apart from Leonid Sobolev (himself a navy officer) whose *The Soul of the Sea* (1943) and *The Path to Victory* (1945) are but collections of soberly told stories about the Soviet sailors, there were at least two recent novels (by M. Solovyov and A. Zonin) about them, as well as such excellently written longer tales as *By the Cold Sea* and *The Money Order* (1946) by Yury Gherman, the author of *Our Acquaintances*. The first of Gherman's narratives is about the Soviet officers and sailors stationed during the war almost in the arctic waters. Without any heroics it describes how the young Captain Ladynin and all his men sacrifice their lives in order to save an important convoy. The second story is more complex, with the prevalence of the human element over the military one, although the background is the same as in *By the Cold Sea*. This time the palm for brave exploits is given to a primitive Caucasian, but the emphasis is laid on such fundamental human qualities as friendship, love, family affection, and most of all on the love for children—any children, and especially those orphaned by the war. A rather pathetic adoption of such a child by a lonely naval officer forms the climax and the end of this story. In another narrative under the English title, *Be Happy*, Gherman portrays most sympathetically, in the form of a girl's diary, the British airmen stationed in the Russian North during the Second World War.

IV

The war novels, however varied or abundant, did not exhaust the literary production during those critical years. They were complemented and perhaps even surpassed by the historical novel—this time dealing with all the important periods of the Russian past and particularly with those when Russia had to struggle for her own survival. This alone is enough to explain the sudden popularity of the patriotic historical novel, to begin with V. Yan's trilogy, finished in 1945—*Ghenghis Khan, Batu Khan,* and *Alexander the Uneasy* (the nickname of Alexander Nevsky).

The first of these three novels describes the Mongol leader's conquest of Bokhara and Samarkand up to the battle on the river Kalka (1223) where the combined Russian and Kipchak or Polovets armies were beaten. The Mongol "conqueror of the world" is obviously treated as a predecessor and an Asiatic counterpart of Hitler, whose brutality he almost equaled. "When I put my foot upon a stubborn head, I love to see my enemy groan and plead for mercy, and watch the tears upon his wasting cheek." Such utterances on the part of Ghenghis Khan seem to point to Hitler as a worthy disciple of his Asiatic master who, after the battle on the Kalka, crushed the captive Russian princes beneath the boards on which the Mongol war leaders celebrated their victory. This, however, was only the prelude to the actual conquest of Russia, completed some time later by Ghenghis Khan's enterprising grandson Batu Khan, the hero of Yan's second novel.

The savagery with which Batu and his hordes sacked Ryazan, as well as a number of other Russian cities, before they were stopped by the spring floods from attacking Novgorod, is again treated as a thirteenth-century parallel of Hitler's invasion. Even the racial theory attributed by the author to Batu contains all the ingredients of Nazism. "The Mongols are the bravest, strongest, wisest people on earth, therefore they must rule the world! The Mongols alone are the chosen people, marked out by the sky; all other peoples must be our slaves and toil for us, if we allow them to live.

All who oppose us will be swept off the plains of the earth. They shall burn like the dung in our Mongol campfires." One could point to further analogies, notably the heroism of the Russian people even in the face of an almost hopeless calamity. No wonder the author prefaces the novel with the following lines: "This book tells of the unshakable courage of the Russian people fearlessly defending their native land against the invading hordes of merciless conquerors. Then, each man fought on his own, but they never yielded, dying on the threshold of their homes, defending their fields, their wives and children, their freedom and liberty." The implication is clear. Yet this does not diminish the objective validity of Yan's Tartar novels, written in a lucid and concise style. He not only shows a consummate knowledge of the period but seems to be familiar even with the languages and scriptures of the nations concerned.

Once Russia had been invaded and conquered by the Tartars, it was the gradual rebellion against their yoke that mattered most. This process reached its first climax in the battle on the Kulikovo Field (the district of Tula) in September, 1380, under the leadership of Dimitry, the Grand Prince of Moscow, and has been competently dealt with in *Dimitry Donskoy* (1942) by Sergey Borodin. The novel gives a broad and convincing picture of Russia in those days: from Moscow to the famous Troitsky Monastery and its prior, Sergey; and from the clandestine preparations against the Tartars to the first skirmishes and, later, to the final rout of Mamai's army, which, incidentally, was the first step towards the liberation of Russia in 1480. Written in an agitated but rich language, the novel is imbued with an optimism which was invaluable during the trials of 1942.

If we now turn to the pictures of a still later period of importance, we come across the unfinished trilogy about Ivan the Terrible and his time by V. Kostylyov. When, in

1941, its first volume—*Moscow on the March*—appeared, it caused a stir and the controversy aroused by it made the readers all the more anxious to see the next two volumes. For the interest in that indomitable "gatherer of the Russian lands" has undergone a complete revaluation. He is no longer looked upon as the prototype of a sadistic tyrant but as a great statesman and predecessor of Peter I. After all, it was not for nothing that Alexey Tolstoy wrote two plays about him, while Sergey Eisenstein recorded his life and work in one of the finest historical films. Kostylyov's interest is centered also on Minin and Pozharsky, the heroes of the subsequent troubled period which came to an end with the election of the first Romanov to the throne in 1613.

The era of Peter the Great was treated by Alexey Tolstoy in his novel *Peter I* brilliantly enough to discourage any literary competition on the same ground. So it is a pity that the third volume of this monumental work remained unfinished. The period and the background of Catherine II, on the other hand, had found a competent novelist in V. Shishkov, an old writer (born 1873) who was previously known mainly because of his Siberian stories. It was in his *Emelyan Pugachov* (1943) that Shishkov presented Soviet literature with one of its finest historical novels. Its hero is the same rebel as the one in Pushkin's *A Captain's Daughter,* but seen from a different angle. With all his love for freedom and justice, Pushkin was yet too much of a Russian nobleman to approve of any rebellion from below, and least of all of Pugachov's *jacquerie.* Shishkov, on the other hand, sees in that rebellion the emergence of a new social force which may have been suppressed at the time but certainly was not destroyed. The literary level of this novel is high, and the historical documentation is so well handled that one cannot but regret the author's untimely death which prevented him from finishing the second and final volume.

The critical era of 1812—the nearest parallel of Hitler's invasion of Russia from the West—had been so fully dealt with in Leo Tolstoy's *War and Peace* as to leave little room for any imaginative writing about that period. In spite of this, some of its aspects were tackled by a few Soviet authors, including Vsevolod Ivanov (in his *At Borodino*) and by S. Golubov in his historical novel *Bagration* (1945). In contrast to Tolstoy's leisurely plastic power, Golubov prefers a sketchy cinemalike technique, and the events he unrolls before us start with Napoleon's crossing of the Niemen and end with the battle at the Shevardino redoubt (near Borodino). Scenes, battles, and names familiar to the reader from *War and Peace*, with the additional description of the poet Zhukovsky's visit to the army, are, however, dominated by the personality of one of the ablest Russian generals—Prince Bagration, who was mortally wounded at Shevardino. All sorts of reverses, accompanied by those political and personal rivalries which resulted in the "Quaker," Barclay de Tolly, being replaced by Kutuzov, are presented with considerable skill but without that three-dimensional concreteness which is so typical of Tolstoy's masterpiece. Like most other novels of the war period, *Bagration* is full of warm patriotism.

The epoch between Catherine II and that of Napoleon's rival, Alexander I, looms large in *The Mikhailovsky Castle* (1946) by Olga Forsh. This work is not as absorbing or technically intriguing as her *Clad in Stone*, and its matter-of-fact language verges at times on baldness. On the other hand, it introduces to the reader the semimad Czar Paul I, as well as the social, military-political, and artistic atmosphere of that period. Incidentally, Paul's hatred for Suvorov, an account of whose exploits on the St. Gotthard Pass and at the Devil's Bridge is given in the novel, is plausibly motivated. So is the palace revolt organized by Count Pahlen (the military governor of St. Petersburg) which led to the liquidation of Paul I—with the tacit connivance of his son, the subsequent Czar Alexander I.

The three outstanding events between 1812 and 1941—the Crimean campaign, the Russo-Japanese War, and the First World War—have all been duly recorded in the recent Soviet fiction. The bulky but excellently written *Sebastopol Ordeal* (1941) by S. Sergeyev-Tsensky concentrates on the defense of Sebastopol in 1854 and 1855 on a surprisingly large canvas, with a panorama of Russia and Europe as the background. The portraits of the rulers, of military leaders, of soldiers, as well as the pictures of battle scenes are memorable, not to mention some of the wider implications of this truly ambitious work. The Russo-Japanese War, or rather one of its vital episodes (the capitulation of Port Arthur) is described in A. Stepanov's novel, *Port Arthur* (1944), with the conscientious and at times even pedantic scrupulousness of one who happened to be an eyewitness of those painful reverses in the Far East. And as for the First World War, it was again Sergeyev-Tsensky who tackled it in his two historical novels, *Brusilov's Break-through* (1943) and *The Guns Forward* (1944), both of which are further additions to his series of novels under the general title of *Transformation*.

Brusilov's Break-through deals with the Russian front during the first half of 1916, after the reluctant and inefficient General Ivanov had been replaced by Brusilov as Commander-in-Chief. The author has a lot to say about the intrigues and secret German sympathies at Court (already dominated by Rasputin), about the unimpressive personality of the Czar, as well as about the crosscurrents in the army command and the life on the front in general. The narrative ends with Brusilov's successful offensive in June, 1916: at the moment when Kaiser Wilhelm was convinced that the

Russian army was already done for and began to move large German contingents to Verdun. The second novel, which is much inferior to *Brusilov's Break-through*, limits itself to the events between June 28 and September 4, 1914, that is, between the assassination of the Austrian Archduke Franz Ferdinand in Sarajevo and the day when Great Britain declared war on Germany. Parallel with a rather mechanical (and not always reliable) account of the diplomatic and political happenings in Europe, there is a description of domestic humdrum existence in a Crimean town, but these two parts of the narrative fail to merge. One of the reasons for writing this novel was obviously the author's wish to demonstrate that the Germany of Kaiser Wilhelm was as aggressive and treacherous as that of Hitler, and this itself links the events of 1914 to those of 1939 and 1941.

v

It is hardly necessary to point out that during the duress of the war there was not much room for the dispassionate *biographie romancée* as devised by Tynyanov. The two novels about Pushkin—*Pushkin in the South* by Ivan Novikov and *The Death of a Poet* by Leonid Grossman—could have organized all the material they contain without any attempt at fiction. Otherwise the frankly "disinterested" narratives were often frowned on by the critics, as was the case with M. Zoshchenko's *When the Sun Rises* (printed in the numbers 6 and 7 of the periodical *October* for 1943). The noise aroused may not have been justified by the intrinsic value of the story, but the case itself was nevertheless highly significant of the period. Remote from the actualities of the war, *When the Sun Rises* is not a consecutive narrative but a series of inwardly connected fragments of self-analysis or even of psychic autotherapy turned into a work of art.

Zoshchenko calls it a book about how he freed himself from disappointments and, at the age of thirty, became a happy man. In this manner it purports to be a story of his own integration, but the critics reminded him soon enough of sterner duties than thinking of himself at the time of great national ordeals.

Among the disinterested, but in a less self-centered manner, were the wartime writings of P. Bazhov and Mikhail Prishvin. P. Bazhov (a former miner) achieved considerable success with his *Malachite Casket* (1942) which is difficult to place. For one thing, it is not a novel at all but a collection of *skaz* tales from the Urals and centered round the same mining area. Written in the language of the people, these stories are full of imaginative freshness, folklore, and the flavor of the genuine *spiritus loci*. When they appeared, they must have been welcomed by many not as an escape but rather as a relaxation amidst the travail of the war. The same can be said of Prishvin's perfect nature sketches, collected in his book, *The Forest Drop* (1943). One of his latest tales, *The Storehouse of the Sun* (1945), is about two orphaned children and their life in a swampy forest land.

Far away from the war is also Konstantin Fedin's novel, *First Joys* (1946). It may seem restrained and even tame if compared with his *Cities and Years*, but since it is only the first part of a trilogy dealing with Russian life between 1905 and the second war against the Germans, a definite verdict is hardly possible until the whole work has been published. This particular part depicts life in a bigger provincial center between 1905 and 1910—the year of Tolstoy's flight and death, some details of which are given. The love romance, with its early joys, between the two very young principal characters in the novel is frustrated, and we see how the heroine, married to a rich vulgarian, is beginning to adapt herself to a milieu in which she feels a stranger. This theme is however interwoven with what might be called a cross section of all the social layers (from the rich merchants to the down-and-outs) in a Russian provincial town, yet with the emphasis on two elements: the theater and the revolutionary youth of that period. There is also a charming portrait of a slum girl who is eventually adopted by the theatrical people with the prospect of a brighter future on the stage.

VI

Such, approximately, are the principal features of the Soviet novel during and immediately after the Second World War. No matter what literary genre one takes, one cannot but be aware of the fact that in Soviet Russia socialist realism has come to stay. This has a number of advantages and, at the same time, also certain limitations. Pure aestheticism is excluded. So are the escapist detective and other thrillers, which may be all for the best. On the other hand, the opposition to the narrative of an analytical subjective kind, such as Zoshchenko's *When the Sun Rises,* strikes one as narrow-minded to say the least. Even the enforced social and personal optimism in literature may often lead to false perspectives and valuations—quite regardless of the fact that creative freedom logically presupposes the right to be a pessimist if one has sufficient reasons for being one.

There is no doubt that the new intellectual emerging from the Soviet masses themselves is more realistic, efficient, and dynamic (even if he happens to be less interesting and subtle) than the highbrows of the prerevolutionary elite. Made all of a piece, as it were, he saves a great deal of his energy by adhering to a definite general line. But on the other hand, a conformity of this kind often becomes a weakness if one is precluded from ruthlessly questioning and criticizing its premises. This way lies that kind of well-meaning standardization which may raise the level of the average at the expense of what is exceptional and original. In Soviet literature the average level is, on the whole, rather high; yet so far it has not produced such exceptional geniuses as Pushkin, Tolstoy, and Dostoevsky, which does not mean, of course, that it is not likely to produce them in the future.

The blossoming out of the pre-Soviet culture in Russia took place after her victories in 1812. And why should not something similar happen even on a bigger scale after her victories over Hitler between 1941 and 1945, if she succeeds in creating the requisite conditions? Such conditions will however depend, to a large extent, also on the attitude of the rest of the world towards her great social and economic experiment. It is at this point that a more tolerant under-standing of Soviet Russia becomes essential for the sake of both Russia and the world. An important key to such an understanding is provided by her literature and particularly by the novel.

Conclusion

THERE IS hardly another nation in the life of which literature, and especially the novel, has played a more important part than it has among the Russians in the last hundred years. The vagaries and contradictions of Russian life during that period were almost incredible. But since they marked the stages of the nation's accelerated inner growth, they are faithfully reflected in the evolution of the Russian novel. It is a far cry from Karamzin to Dostoevsky, or from Aksakov to Leonov. Yet each marks some important phase in the life of the nation. The Russian novel reached the height of its perfection during the intelligentsia period, when the cleavage between the intellectuals and the people was acute and tragic. The revolution of 1917 made a change in the entire structure of society. Yet the importance of literature as a living social factor remained. It has even increased. So has the number of readers, now comprising the entire nation. In Soviet Russia there seems to be no essential gap between the author and his background, between literature and life. The two tend to converge and to stimulate each other's growth. As always, Russian literature tries to keep in contact with reality and the vital values of life. It is for this reason that a study of the Russian novel gives one not only a high literary pleasure, but also an introduction to the innermost spirit of Russia. A nation which has passed through such trials and experiences as the modern Russians, is bound to contribute something valuable to mankind as a whole. The Russian contribution has been rich and generous already. And there is no doubt that it will continue to be so in the future.

Index of Names

249